The Ethics of War and Peace

THE UNIVERSITY OF
WINCHESTER

THE ETHICS OF WAR AND PEACE

Cosmopolitan and Other Perspectives

NIGEL DOWER

polity

First published in 2009 by Polity Press

Polity Press
65 Bridge Street
Cambridge CB2 1UR, UK

Polity Press
350 Main Street
Malden, MA 02148, USA

ISBN-13: 978-0-7456-4167-6
ISBN-13: 978-0-7456-4168-3 (pb)

A catalogue record for this book is available from the British Library.

Typeset in 10.5 on 12 pt Times
by SNP Best-set Typesetter Ltd, Hong Kong
Printed and bound in Great Britain by MPG Books Group Ltd

The publisher has used its best endeavours to ensure that the URLs for external websites referred to in this book are correct and active at the time of going to press. However, the publisher has no responsibility for the websites and can make no guarantee that a site will remain live or that the content is or will remain appropriate.

Every effort has been made to trace all copyright holders, but if any have been inadvertently overlooked the publisher will be pleased to include any necessary credits in any subsequent reprint or edition.

For further information on Polity, visit our website: www.politybooks.com

CONTENTS

PREFACE

A word about how I came to write this book and my perspective in it may help the reader. While the content of a book cannot be judged by reference to the author's (auto)biography – an example of the genetic fallacy – this account may shed light on why I have focused on certain things. This book has two goals: its first and main goal, as should be the case with a textbook, is to indicate fairly and clearly the main arguments and positions taken up on the issues of war and peace; its second goal is to advocate a particular point of view about the ethics of war and peace. This may be summed up as 'cosmopolitan pacificism'. In most of my writings I have combined analysis with advocacy. I believe academics should be committed academics, not people who are academics and also committed people.

At the age of sixty-six I have been fortunate to have lived a wholly peaceful life. Although I have lived in countries such as the UK, the USA and Zimbabwe at times when these countries have been at war, where I have lived has been peaceful. I have never experienced war at first hand. I have never faced killing violence or had to respond to it. So you may feel that that disqualifies me from thinking about these issues. I hope not, since I have had occasion to reflect on war issues on many occasions.

My first memory of thinking about war was the Suez crisis in 1956, when my father was passionately opposed to the British response. In my teens I went to Quaker summer schools where, since conscription was still operating, the issue of conscientious objection was often discussed. I remember even then thinking there was something rather simplistic and unfair about the reported use of the 'Would you stop someone attacking your wife?' question as a way of undermining the objection to joining the military (an issue I take up later in the book). By the time I was seventeen I was deeply concerned about nuclear weapons and supported, though not very actively, the Campaign for Nuclear Disarmament (CND). I was as a postgraduate in the mid-1960s also opposed to the American involvement in Vietnam. In the 1970s I was mainly involved in organizations to do with world poverty, but these included the United Nations Association, and, through its literature and my attendance at its conferences, I became more engaged with peace and war issues. I found myself, though not at the time for reasons which I conceived of as pacifist, wholly opposed to the Falklands 'war', and I have been opposed ever since to all the UK's major military operations (the Gulf War of 1991, Kosovo in 1999, Afghanistan in 2001, Iraq in 2003). By 1981 I was teaching a special subject called 'Ethics and international relations', which in one form or another I taught most years until 2004, when I took early retirement, and which included material on many of the issues discussed in this book.

Where do I stand now on the pacifism issue? I feel it is less misleading to say that I am a pacifist than that I am not, but the matter is complex. I am more, in the language of Ceadel (1987), a pacificist and someone committed to what I call the way of peace, which is not just about personal lifestyle norms and attitudes (including the avoidance of violence, except perhaps *in extremis*), but about working for the conditions of peace in a variety of ways. I am clear that I could not myself join an army and train to kill (that is, it would be wrong for me to do so), though, as the world stands now, there is a limited role for armed forces, not least in UN-regulated roles, so it is not wrong for some people to join an army. (It will be apparent that I do not think the simple 'universalizability' test 'If it is wrong for A to do x it must wrong for everyone else similarly placed to do x' actually has much grip in these complex cases.) I also accept that an ordered society needs law-enforcement, which in the last resort requires the possibility of violence for its imposition (though we ought to encourage a culture that makes it really a last resort). I hope that in any personal conflict situation I would do all I could to tackle it nonviolently, but I recognize that, *in extremis*, I probably would use killing force against a direct attack on myself and my loved ones (and it may be that such action would be justified as the lesser of two evils). For reasons I will go into later, the common argument from personal self-defence to national defence is problematic.

While I can see a role for armed forces at some limited level – at least for the foreseeable future – I am deeply opposed to any country – certainly the UK – possessing nuclear weapons or any other weapons of mass destruction. And if the UK's position in the world partly depends on its wielding nuclear weapons, then we ought to accept a reduced status (but I do not think that a country such as Denmark is really any worse off for not being a nuclear power). It is painfully apparent to me anyway that the kind of life-conditions which I have enjoyed, along with the majority of UK citizens (I say the majority because there is an unacceptable inequality within our country too), is built on a legacy of past colonialism in which the colonial project was only possible because of the power of the gun, and is maintained by a continued economic will to make the world economy work to our own advantage and to the disadvantage of the poor of the world.

I do not lie awake at night fretting about these facts, nor do I recommend others to do so, but it is important that we who are privileged do what we can as citizens of the world to compensate for all this. My saying 'citizens of the world' is not a marginal claim. My whole account is cosmopolitan in an explicit way. My thesis is that we need to be in earnest about creating the conditions of peace not just for ourselves but for everyone else in the world, and that the desire for peace, which we all feel, needs to become a will for peace that transforms the whole way we think of ourselves, in particular, by escaping the undue levels of commitment to the nation-states to which we belong and which are the source of much of the conflict in the world.

I write this book as a philosopher trained in the analytic tradition in the 1960s. In the mid-1970s I found where my intellectual energy lay, which was in engaging in ethical thinking about global issues such as world poverty, development, the environment, international relations, human rights, and war and peace. (This kind of ethical engagement is sometimes called applied ethics, but the phrase is misleading in an oversimplifying and marginalizing way.) I have gained much over the last thirty years from the many classes I have taught on ethics and international relations and related issues. My approach is also significantly influenced by my Quaker background. I became a Quaker in 1980, but the influence of Quakerism goes back much further than that. It is important to make clear, as I have done in other books, that the kinds of arguments I am interested in here are genuinely accessible to anyone, of different faith and of none, who is willing to think about ethical issues in a calm and reflective way. There are no hidden religious premises or agendas – or at least none of which I am conscious. Of course each person will interpret their ethics and be motivated in what they do through different understandings of the world. In my case the Quaker idea of 'answering that of God in everyone' informs and energizes what I do. For each person a different account may be given. Indeed that is part of my wider view: that we can find many areas of ethical convergence with people whose personal worldviews may be different, and that, indeed, it is in this possibility that the prospects of greater peace in the world partly lie.

I am well aware of the book's inadequacies. Since the Polity Press in inviting me in 2006 to write this book wanted a textbook which would be accessible to a wide student audience, I have not taken, except occasionally, the philosophical analysis very far. For those wanting more advanced philosophical analysis there are a number of books available, such as Norman (1995), Paskins and Dockrill (1979), Rodin (2002) and the classic Walzer (1977), as well as many collections, such as Cohen et al. (1974), Coppieters and Fotion (2002), Evans (2005), Sorabji and Rodin (2006) and Wasserstrom (1970). I am also aware that the more I have read, the more I realize I have not read, and while I have, especially in the last two years, read more books than I have actively made explicit use of and they have influenced me indirectly in getting me 'ready' to write, I hope the critical engagement I have had with some of these texts has been sufficient to give an adequate and clear analysis of the field.

The book has been constructed in such a way that each chapter should be useable without prior acquaintance with others. This has involved a certain amount of repetition of key ideas, distinctions and arguments, for instance in chapters 4 and 5, where the criticisms of the just war approach from a pacifist point of view in chapter 4 become the arguments for pacifism in chapter 5 and vice versa. Chapter 1 is no doubt more substantial than some introductory chapters are, but it presents the key distinctions and the key elements of the approach of the book in such a way that it could be useful to students without their having to look at the more detailed developments later on. Each chapter concludes with questions for discussion.

The text was completed while I was teaching at Colorado State University, and I was able to 'test-drive' parts of it with my class on 'War, peace and the ethics of global responsibility'. One reason why I refer on a number of occasions to Iain Atack's book *The Ethics of Peace and War* (2005) is because I decided to use it as the main text on war/peace issues. His volume, like mine, adopts a cosmopolitan approach and, while at times I have been critical of some of his arguments discussed in the class, I believe it to be an important complementary approach to my own. I am most grateful to members of the class for their lively discussions of the ideas, and I am sure the book has benefited from these. I should also like to thank a number of people who took time to look at my drafts and offered useful advice and criticism: Jim Boyd, Gayle Dower, Hugh Dower, Mary Dower, Jim Martell, Salvor Nordal, Bill Shaw, Josh Shepherd, Wim Vandekerckhove, the Polity Press's commissioning editors Louise Knight and Emma Hutchinson and the referees for the book proposal and first draft. This book is dedicated to my mother, Jean, who understood and appreciated the idea when I started work on it but sadly now cannot appreciate its final production. But, as she understood it herself, 'she' lives on in the ideas she helped to create over a lifetime of discussing these and many other issues.

Nigel Dower
November 2008

1 THE ETHICS OF WAR AND PEACE: PRELIMINARY CONSIDERATIONS

1 Introduction

In 1989 the communist political orders collapsed in Eastern Europe, and for a short while many optimistically spoke of a 'peace dividend' through which the world would become more peaceful and the vast sums spent on armaments would get diverted to more socially useful purposes, such as increased aid to reduce world poverty. These hopes were short-lived. Various major wars took place, such as the Gulf War of 1991 to reverse Saddam Hussein's invasion of Kuwait, the NATO bombings of Kosovo in 1999 to stop Serbian atrocities against the Albanian Kosovans, the invasion of Afghanistan in 2001 to topple the Taliban regime because of its links with al-Qaeda, which had been responsible for the major attacks on the American mainland on '9/11', and then, in 2003, the invasion of Iraq to topple Saddam Hussein. Alongside these there have been numerous other conflicts, such as regional wars in the Congo, various wars within and between the countries in the former Yugoslavia, genocide in Rwanda and Burundi, the action of militias in places such as Darfur and border conflicts such as that between India and Pakistan over Kashmir. And there is the continuing conflict with terrorists in the so-called war against terror. Although some reduction of the arsenals of the nuclear weapons held by the major nuclear powers has taken place, nuclear weapons remain, and an increasing number of countries are acquiring them.

1.1 The relevance of ethics

The ethical challenges of war that confront us now may seem peculiarly modern, but in fact they arise out of a tradition of thinking about the ethics of war that goes back for many centuries. This has been called the just war tradition. As Norman notes, it has been 'the dominant intellectual tradition of thought about the morality of war' (Norman 1995: 117). As we will see when I analyse it fully, it provides a sophisticated account of the circumstances in which it is morally right to go to war, involving such principles as just cause, legitimate authority and last resort, and it also provides rules which ought to be followed in fighting wars – the most well known being the principle of non-combatant immunity, that is, that in wars soldiers may not directly attack non-combatants.

One of the issues to be faced in this book is whether modern developments in war have rendered the rules traditionally accepted no longer relevant. For instance, do nuclear weapons render the distinction between combatants and non-combatants irrelevant? Do responses to terrorists who clearly attack anyone need to be restrained by care not to attack those not involved? Does the totalization of war both in terms of the weapons developed and in terms of the democratic involvement of everyone – at least everyone adult and entitled to vote – render the traditional restraints in war irrelevant? Do the so-called new wars (as witnessed in the break-up of Yugoslavia) render the whole traditional ethical framework pointless?

1.2   The relevance of the traditional approach

I shall take seriously the traditional account and how it might be applied in my discussion. It may be that this continues to prove the best basis for thinking about the ethic of war or it may be that some other ethical framework would be better. But I take seriously the traditional approach for two reasons.

First, I believe it to be a feature of moral reasoning that moral principles are applicable in different times and places. Their being traditional does not make them belong to another era and therefore irrelevant. Local circumstances may lead to some variations in interpretation, but we need to accept a universal framework of thought – whether we sign up to the traditional arguments or develop our ethical analysis independent of that tradition.

Second, we must be very careful not to read off what actually *ought* to happen in modern warfare either from what *happens* in modern warfare or from what is *thought* by many ought to happen in modern warfare. For instance, if the nuclear powers threaten to destroy not merely non-combatants in the 'enemy' country but also people in other countries, non-human life and future generations, that is a fact, as is the fact that many in government, many military personnel and many citizens appear to be happy with this, but that does not make nuclear weapons ethical. Some people may think such a stance is ethical, but they need arguments for this; others, myself for example (as you will have guessed), need arguments against it (see chapter 7).

Since this is a textbook in which I try to present the various arguments fairly, it is important that the ethical justifications of war (such as that attempted in the just war tradition) are considered and applied to contemporary issues. If an ethical position is correct, then it can be applied to contemporary warfare. As it so happens, I am sceptical about the ethical justification of war. But that is not the current point.

1.3 The ethics of peace

This book is called 'the ethics of war and peace'. Many books even today on the ethics of war do not include – at least in the title – the word 'peace'. This is not because they do not have things to say about peace. Far from it. The importance generally of maintaining peace or, when war commences, returning to peace is widely acknowledged. Many would argue that a just war requires a commitment to a just peace that follows its cessation. But, on the whole, the ethics of peace takes second place. There are various reasons for this. Too often peace is conceived of in rather negative terms as the absence of war or the absence of violent conflict more generally. And, while it is important for us to have such an 'absence', it is not seen as a focus of much positive endeavour. Furthermore, discussion of peace often centres round a particular kind of commitment to peace, namely pacifism – that is, the position that says it is always wrong to fight in wars. Since this position usually gets dismissed rather quickly, much of the ethical interest in peace – as opposed to our universally self-interested (or prudential) interest in it – fades.

In this book I hope to provide a corrective to this bias against the ethical dynamics of peace, by arguing for a conception of peace as 'just durable peace' and for an obligation to promote peace. Commitment to peace is not merely about keeping it, but building, furthering or promoting it, and the dynamic behind these has at least to be partly ethical, particularly where the latter three are concerned. This general commitment I shall call, following the terminology used by writers such as Ceadel, pacificism, literally 'making' ('fic' from 'facere' in Latin) 'peace' ('paci' from 'pax') (Ceadel 1987: 101–34). This approach, which I shall link to what I will call the way of peace, is to be distinguished from pacifism as the principled commitment not to fight. Most pacifists (though not all) are pacificists, but pacificism is an approach that many thinkers with different views about the ethics of war can accept. It is no accident that the publisher agreed with my suggestion that I write the book on 'the ethics of war *and peace*' rather than 'the ethics of war'. I doubt if a hundred years ago anyone would have been asked to write with this emphasis on peace. What has changed, as the account below brings out, is that there is an increasing interest in the pacificist approach.

My strategy is to consider in the earlier chapters the various ethical issues which have been and continue to be raised about the ethics of war itself. I shall then move on in the second half to consider the ethical issues to do with peace. The rest of this chapter outlines the framework I will use for discussing the ethics of war, and concludes with a section 'further considerations' of one or two more theoretical issues to do with the nature of ethics, a survey of modern issues and an outline of the rest of the book.

2   What are war and peace?

At this point it will be useful to give some preliminary definitions of war and peace.

2.1   War

Hedley Bull, in his seminal work *The Anarchical Society*, characterized war briefly as 'organised violence carried out by political units against each other' (Bull 1977: 178). His fuller account is:

> Violence is not war unless it is carried out in the name of a political unit; what distinguishes killing in war from murder is its vicarious and official character, the symbolic responsibility of the unit whose agent the killer is. Equally, violence carried out in the name of a political unit is not war unless it is directed against another political unit. (Bull 1977: 184)

One feature of this definition worth noting is that war is characterized as a kind of violence. It is more honest to accept this, even if one thinks that some forms of violence are legitimate, than to restrict the idea of violence only to those uses of force which are illegitimate (see chapters 5 and 6 for further discussion of violence). Secondly, war is a form of *organized* violence. The organization is generally very elaborate, involving the formation of armies and other military units, generally trained and under chains of command. Indeed Paskins and Dockrill, aware of the definitional problems concerning war, note that the military dimension is important. This may seem self-evident, but we should note that the idea of the military as a group of people organized for certain purposes is not equivalent to war (see Paskins and Dockrill 1979: 105).

Third, the units using organized violence are political units. Generally speaking, in the last few hundred years since the development of the modern nation-state system, the key 'political unit' has been the nation-state. Wars were usually fought between such political units. International law, that is, the law made by the agreement of nation-states, developed a very precise and elaborate framework for armed conflicts between states, including a very formal definition of when war occurs with a declaration of war, and so on. As Bull noted, this formal definition never fully matched the material reality of war (Bull 1977: 185). One modern example was the Falklands/Malvinas war in 1982, when Britain sent a force to eject the Argentinians, who had taken over the islands. Neither side actually declared war, yet it was clearly war in the sense of highly organized violence with a political goal.

However, the political units which wage war with political objectives have always included units which have not been current nation-states, that is, the established governments of nation-states. In civil wars, wars of secession and wars of liberation – for example, liberation from colonialism (as in Africa in the 1960s), from occupation and from minority rule (as in South Africa) – at least some of the units fighting are not established governments. But they are pursuing political objectives and using organized violence to pursue their ends. Few now would deny that such units are fighting *wars*, though saying this does not imply that one thinks that what they do is right, if, for instance, one thought that they did not constitute legitimate authorities or have a just cause.

The current 'war against terror' is an interesting case in point. Clearly terrorists in bombing city centres are engaged in organized violence and have a broadly political objective, not so much in overthrowing any particular government as in challenging the political dominance of the West in the world in the name of Muslim values. The war *against* the terrorists clearly involves from time to time 'hot' war, as in military operations in Afghanistan or Pakistan. On the other hand, most of the 'war' is rather different, such as systematic intelligence work attempting to thwart future attempts and a wide range of security measures. This seems better called war only metaphorically.

Enough has been said to indicate both what the central idea of war is – killing violence organized in a military form by political units directed against other political units – and also what will be a continuing feature of discussions about war and peace, the issue of definitions and the many grey areas that surround them.

2.2   Peace

Commonly, a distinction is drawn between a negative conception and a positive conception. It should be made clear at the outset that the word 'negative' is not intended to have any connotations of negative assessment associated with it. It merely signals that peace can be defined as the 'absence' of something or other, whereas the 'positive' conception involves some actual characteristics. These characteristics are generally regarded in an evaluatively positive light, though logically they might not be.

In its bald form, the negative conception of peace is simply the 'absence of war'. If war is defined as it has been above, then peace is a relationship between different parties – usually nation-states or equivalent units – who are not currently fighting each other. In this sense Britain and Germany were still at peace the day before Britain declared war on Germany in 1939. On this view countries (or other units) are either at peace or at war. As Grotius noted, 'between war and peace there is no middle position' (Grotius 1625, quoted in Bull 1977: 185). Variants of this negative conception will include wider conceptions of war or other contrasts such as 'violence' more generally – the latter itself being open to many interpretations (see chapters 5 and 6).

On the other hand, many writers have advocated a positive conception of peace as, for instance, harmonious relationships or social relationships informed by justice and other moral values, as shalom (the idea of wholeness in social relations) or as the product of everyone achieving their own 'inner peace'.

As we shall see, while peace is generally regarded as good and worth promoting in either the positive or the negative sense, people may disagree as to which is the more important of the two in practical terms. Negative peace and positive peace are valuable but for different reasons. To be at peace in the basic sense of not being at war (or not being in a social situation in which there is endemic physical violence) is clearly immensely valuable as the precondition of ordered social existence and of people generally being able to achieve their well-being. Peace defined positively may seem like an even better state to achieve, but as something to be generally realized it may seem like an idealistic dream rather than a practical goal. It is not self-evident that we should, ethically, pursue or promote it as a matter of priority. Maybe, however, people will not generally achieve peace in the weaker sense unless at least *some* people commit themselves both to living peace in the richer sense and to promoting it. These issues will be considered more fully in the later chapters.

There are also conceptions of peace that fall somewhere between the two extremes. Before we leave this initial account of peace it is worth considering briefly the relevance of a middle position, which I shall call 'just durable peace'. The value of peace does not lie in its momentary character, but on its continuing for a time or its being sustained and, indeed, its being sustainable, that is, capable of being sustained. What enables it to be sustained is the fact that it is informed by justice or, to be more precise, perceptions by the various parties involved that their situation is sufficiently just to be acceptable. Once we ask the question 'What enables peace to be sustained?' we also need to consider a whole range of factors which are important, including international law, peace and global citizen-ship education and, some would say, 'living' peace and promoting peace in the wholly positive sense by at least some in society as catalysts of social change. As thinkers in the past such as Castel de Saint-Pierre and Kant saw it, the challenge is how we can create the conditions of 'perpetual peace' (Castel de Saint-Pierre [1713] 1927; Kant [1795] 1970). Whether we can achieve the conditions which would lead to perpetual peace is a matter for debate – to be considered later – but at least the attempt to make it sustainable seems both realistic and, indeed, imperative.

This initial discussion already brings out the point that, if peace is to be thought of as more than simply the absence of war, then we need to recognize that there are various relationships between groups which are to be seen neither as war nor as peace in any richer sense – and this is true whether we go for a perception of peace as something sustained by a variety of background conditions or in a more idealistic sense of harmony and wholeness. Unless I qualify it otherwise, when I talk of peace and its value I have in mind the idea of peace as a sustained relationship between countries or other groups. And it is precisely peace in this sense that typi-cally the pacificist defined earlier is keen to promote. If we take on board this idea of peace as worth promoting, then we can see that there are really two key questions in the ethics of war and peace: first, the classical one, 'When is it right to fight?' and second: 'What ought we to do to promote peace?' One of the purposes of this book is to invite readers to see this second question as being as important as the first, however we answer either.

3   Classifications in the ethics of war

3.1   The classical approach

In most textbooks on the ethics of war, the reader is generally presented with a simple division into three approaches: realism, just war approach/ tradition and pacifism. Put at its simplest, the realist holds that morality does not apply to war – considerations about when to fight and how to fight are based on calculations of power and national interest. The just war theorist holds that war is morally regulated; that is, that there are moral rules (many now encoded in international law) which apply both to decisions to go to war and to decisions about how to fight. (To say that war is morally regulated does not of course imply that countries always observe these rules or regulations.) The pacifist holds that it is never right to go to war and hence there is no right way to fight one.

Hugo Grotius (1583–1645), the Dutch jurisprudentialist whose thinking played a crucial role both in the development of the modern nation-state system and in the norms relating to war that have applied to the international order, put the matter in a crisp logical form: 'we need to find a middle way between those who think that in war everything is permitted and those who think that in war nothing is permitted' (Grotius [1625] 1925: proleg., §29). He saw that there were three logical options: either ethics does not apply to war at all (realism), or it rules out all war (pacifism) or there is a middle position according to which some but not all wars are morally permitted.

As the discussion proceeds we will come to see that this triple division, though logically neat, is misleadingly simple, but it remains a very important classificatory framework and I shall frequently use it. There are two points to make at this stage which illustrate how it may be over-simple.

First, there are, the reader may have observed, two issues over which a realist and a 'middle position' thinker might differ: on whether decisions to go to war are ethically regulated and on whether decisions about how to fight are ethically regulated. Since one could be a realist about one but not the other, one might have mixed positions, as noted by Coppieters and Fotion (2002: 4). Henry Kissinger, the noted American realist at the time of the Vietnam War, held that decisions about going to war should be based on national interests, but that the war should be fought according to certain rules. Conversely the American Unionist General Sherman in the American civil war held that the war on the Unionist side had a just cause, but it had to be fought ruthlessly (hence his statement 'war is hell').

Second, there is a wide range of positions in the middle. The middle ground contains not only the just war tradition, which itself embraced a lot of variation (as we will see), but a whole lot of other ethical positions according to which some wars are ethically permitted and others not, and some ways of fighting are ethically permitted and others not. On many occasions I refer to the middle position as including both just war thinking and other ethical positions; 'middle position' is too bland, so I will use the phrases 'war justification' or 'war justifier'. One could say that the just war theory covered all positions in the middle – that is, any position that 'justified' war – but the disadvantage of this is that many modern thinkers who adopt the middle position would not wish to be associated with the just war tradition.

3.2   Other approaches

Furthermore, there are other ways of classifying different positions. Coates, for instance, in a perceptive analysis identifies four main positions: realism, militarism, just war and pacifism (Coates 1997). Of note here is his intro- duction of a fourth category, namely militarism. This is recognized by a number of writers and is an important further approach. In essence it is the position that does not see war as a regrettable necessity, as both realists and war justifiers say, but as a positive good which strengthens community and expresses military virtues. (Mussolini's fascism is often quoted as an instance, but the approach is rather broader than this.)

Ceadel introduced a different classificatory scheme and identified five approaches: crusadism, militarism, defencism, pacifism and pacificism (Ceadel 1987: 4–5). What he says about militarism, pacifism and pacifi- cism is more or less what we have already indicated, but what he means by crusadism (fighting because one is promoting some value in the rest of the world) and defencism (fighting to defend one's country against aggression) somewhat crosses the earlier divisions, in that they could both be based on either 'just war'/war justification reasons or realist reasons.

My own view, which will become apparent as we proceed, is that we can combine elements of the above classifications and identify two sets of contrasts, first, the division I indicated, which is indeed the standard triple division – realism, just war/war justification and pacifism – and, second, the distinction between militarism and pacificism. For reasons given later, I see the dynamics of militarism and the dynamics of pacificism pulling in opposite directions, and what emerges is that some realists and war justifiers pull in the direction of militarism and some pull in the direction of pacificism. For instance, whereas some just war thinkers in the past have been enthusiastic about war in a just cause (consider the First World War at the beginning), someone such as Coates advocates a just war approach which is heavily committed to trying to create the conditions of peace, so that just wars are now rare and could become a thing of the past (Coates 1997: 117). In many ways the agenda of pacificism based on the ethical commitment to promote the conditions of peace is as important as – if not more important than – the ethical commitment to act peacefully (either as a firm commitment or, for some pacifists, as an absolute commitment).

4 Approaches to the ethics of international relations

The ethics of war cannot be discussed without also looking at the ethics of international relations. As it so happens, there is a second triple division often made in the area of international relations theory, and one which I have used elsewhere and will use again in this book (Dower 1998 or 2007). This is the division of approaches into realism, internationalism and cosmopolitanism. Again this triple division can be seen as simply and logically generated from answering two questions: first, Does ethics apply to international relations?, and second, if so, Are the ethical norms of international relations specific to the relations between states (and thus either independent of any global ethic relating all human beings as such to one another, or consistent with the absence of any such global ethic at all)? Or are the ethical norms of international relations derived from and ultimately justified in terms of a global ethic? If the answer is 'yes' to question 1, we have realism. If the answer is 'yes' to the first horn of question 2, we have internationalism. If the answer is 'yes' to the second horn of question 2, we have cosmopolitanism. Again this is a very useful division, but its simplicity can be misleading, given the complexity of views covered by these three labels.

In later chapters I will explain more fully what these positions are. Briefly, the position of the realist is that ethics is not applicable to international relations. This is claimed, for instance, because there is no common power to enforce rules, because there are no common values in the world, or because the world is so radically insecure that this justifies each country looking after its own interests above all else. The internationalist holds that a 'morality of states' has developed ever since the Peace of Westphalia of 1648 and the inception of the nation-state system, in which certain basic rules, such as respect for sovereignty, honouring treaties and agreements and including agreed rules of war, form the basis of the 'society of states'. There are various bases given for this morality, but what is characteristic of the approach is that it is not derived from any particular cosmopolitan theory or global ethic. The third position, cosmopolitanism, stresses both the moral equality of all human beings and the moral significance of all human beings as part of one ethical community with transboundary responsibilities across the community (even if most people do not feel the significance of this much). From a cosmopolitan point of view, the rules that should govern states ought to reflect these universal values, and the behaviour of states and the rules they actually observe can be criticized from this point of view if they do not.

What I want to draw attention to now, in order to dissuade the reader from making a very natural assumption, is the fact that the two sets of distinctions between realism vis-à-vis war, just war and pacifism and between realism vis-à-vis international relations, internationalism and cosmopolitanism are not parallel or the same. It is not the case, I repeat not the case, that realism in regard to war neatly goes with realism about international relations (though there are strong links). It is certainly and more obviously not the case that the just war approach neatly goes along with internationalism or that pacifism goes along with cosmopolitanism. A cosmopolitan might, for instance, believe that humanitarian intervention to stop human rights violations in another country was justified by cosmopolitan considerations. Some cosmopolitans take this line; others argue that cosmopolitan thinking commits us to pacifism. These relationships will be spelled out more fully as we proceed.

5   The three traditional approaches to the ethics of war

5.1   Realism

Realism in regard to war often goes hand in hand with realism about international relations. Suppose, for example, realism in regard to international relations was the view that there were no ethical relations between states and, likewise, partly as the background justification of this, that there were no ethical relations between human beings as such. Suppose too that realism with regard to war was the view that states could declare war as and when it suited their interests without regard to their having a just cause (though claiming to have a just cause may be part of the strategy) and that war could be fought in any way that achieved the advantage of the state fighting (though exercising some restraint in some circumstances for prudential reasons). On these suppositions the two views about war are simply corollaries of the two views about international relations.[1]

But this parallel might not be accepted. Someone could be a realist about the occasions of war, that is, that it is justifiable for a state to go to war to secure its advantage, but not be a realist in regard to international relations generally. That is, he or she might hold that states are indeed bound by conventions, established over time by the intercourse of states, generally to respect territorial borders and to honour agreements and established international law – essentially the programme of the internationalist – but, since this set of norms is established by custom and agreement rather than being based on moral truths established by reason, the political leader has reason sometimes to break the conventions. So what this is advocating is not a full-blooded realism for international relations but a rather weakly supported international morality combined with a realism in regard to the occasions of war.

Conversely, someone's general position could be non-realist both in regard to the general conduct of international relations, including decisions to go to war, and in regard to the particular relations between individuals who come into contact with each other in the world, for instance through economic transactions across the world or through travelling abroad. Nevertheless, when war occurs, the ordinary rules of morality are either overridden or suspended. They are overridden (or outweighed) because, once war has started, victory is paramount, and the distinction between soldiers and civilians is unimportant since everyone is part of the enemy and on the opposing side. They are suspended on a rather different view of morality if one thinks the norms of morality depend on convention, and it is precisely in warfare that the conventions lapse. It should be noted again, as we observed earlier, that, on either of these views, the overriding or suspension of moral norms need not be seen as 'all or nothing'. Atrocities can still be regarded as off-limits. Of course, in practice, in wars generally and particularly in wars informed by realist considerations, these limits are sometimes not observed, and atrocities occur.

5.2   Just war

Two branches of the just war tradition are presented:

1 *ius ad bellum*: the rightness/justice (*ius*) of waging war or going to war;
2 *ius in bello*: the rightness of the manner in which one conducts the war (whom you attack; what weapons are used, and so on).

A number of elements of *ius ad bellum* are usually identified, such as a war needing to be declared by a legitimate authority, that there is a just cause such as self-defence, that going to war is a last resort, and that there is a reasonable prospect of success and proportionality. These and other conditions will be examined later.

What are the issues raised by *ius in bello*? This relates to the manner in which war is waged. The principles of the reasonable prospect of success and proportionality also operate here with regard to particular operations. Perhaps the most significant element philosophically is the limitation on who may be a direct object of attack. It has generally been held that only combatants may be aimed at, and that it is wrong to aim to kill civilians or indeed soldiers once they have surrendered, become disarmed or become prisoners. This is known as the principle of discrimination or non-combatant immunity.

All we need to note here is that there is a wide variety of justifications that can be given for these just war positions and indeed any position in the middle that I have called war justification. These range over approaches such as utilitarianism, natural law, conventionalism, tradition, collective prudence, human rights, and so on. Many of the arguments have stemmed from the internationalist tradition I described briefly earlier, and a number of them come from cosmopolitan considerations.

5.3   Pacifism

The third main traditional approach is pacifism. As with all the key terms in this area there is considerable disagreement about the basic definition of pacifism which we will need to look into later. For the moment I shall simply offer what is certainly a common account, namely that, according to the pacifist, it is wrong to fight in wars. That is, it is anti-warism, as Teichman puts it (Teichman 1986: 1). It is presented usually as a general claim about what others should do, though sometimes as a purely personal commitment. It comes in two main forms, principled or deontological pacifism and contingent pacifism. The principled version claims that, apart from the general consequences of fighting, it is wrong to fight in wars *per se* irrespective of consequences (hence the ugly label 'deontological' which refers to the idea of obligation not based on consequences). This may be grounded on the particular character of fighting in wars (as opposed to killing in self-defence), or on the general rejection of all killing – at least of human beings. The contingent version claims that the consequences of not fighting in wars are generally better than the consequences of fighting in wars. Pacifism's motivation may be religious or it may be secular. Most pacifists are cosmopolitans at least by implication, but the connection is not straightforward. This is because pacifism as such is a stance about *not* fighting; it is not as such a commitment to *promote* peace. But insofar as pacifists are not merely interested in taking a stance about fighting but also in combating injustice and creating the conditions anywhere in which people do not have to fight, they are generally pacificists as well and, as such, cosmopolitans.

Often in books on the ethics of war, pacifism is discussed early on in order for it to put on one side as misguided or impractically idealistic, and then the discussion proceeds to the real issues. Since my intention is to invite the reader to see pacificism as an approach and pacifism as a commitment within it sympathetically as views that can be taken seriously in the real world, I look at them later, having identified various difficulties with the alternative approaches.

6 Cosmopolitan approaches

I advocate in this book a cosmopolitan perspective. In doing so I am not claiming that cosmopolitanism provides one single set of answers about the ethics of war and peace. As I indicated earlier in regard to humanitarian intervention, this is far from being the case. The ethical content of cosmopolitan values varies considerably, both in terms of its goals and in terms of the means thought to be appropriate. For fairly obvious reasons, to be elaborated later, cosmopolitanism does not overlap with realism about war, or at least with any robust realism that denies the reality or relevance of a global moral community, or questions a universal ethic altogether. But, as we shall see, a cosmopolitan position could just as easily support the just war approach as the pacifist approach.

Now it should be recognized that the cosmopolitan approach was often associated in the past with what we might now see as the imperialist project of disseminating the 'truth' – usually understood as religious truth – to other parts of the benighted world, through missionary activity and prose-lytizing, and this often involved armed conflict with those that resisted the 'civilizing' process. Nor is this only a thing of the past. The East–West conflict between the USSR and the West was in part a battle for hearts and minds in the rest of the world and often involved violence, for instance, in the so-called proxy wars in the Third World. The current conflict between terrorist networks such as al-Qaeda and liberal secular states/societies in the West can be seen in this light, as a conflict between alternative cosmopolitan visions for the world (though their positions may not be described as cosmopolitan as such). We tend to see the cosmopolitan projects of the past as being 'dogmatic'. But to some extent modern liberal cosmopolitanism can also be promoted in a dogmatic fashion, and certainly it is by some, but it is also possible to present it in a non-dogmatic fashion, as I indicate below. Part of any cosmopolitan's commitment is to want his or her views and policies to be adopted by others elsewhere all over the world who do not currently accept them, sometimes because of other rival cosmopolitan positions, but more usually because of other priorities incon-sistent with cosmopolitanism itself. So how, then, can we distinguish non-dogmatic cosmopolitanism?

What characterizes modern non-dogmatic cosmopolitanism is not the absence of agendas informed by ethical views, but two features, one to do with goals, the other to do with means. That is, first, there is the centrality and priority of certain core elements which are generally shared by all thinkers about the enabling conditions in which the equal worth of all human beings can be expressed. Such cosmopolitanism focuses on the evil of poverty and the need to empower the poor, a need for peace as generally necessary for development, the protection of basic rights and environmental security. Second, the way to secure these values and to advance one's more specific agendas is not by force, but by cooperation, dialogue, participation, democratic process, education and other forms of cooperative enterprise, and so on, and by respecting differences of culture alongside welcoming shared common values which may be supported from different worldviews – the latter elements relating as much to the way things are done as to what is aimed at.

Put another way, it includes views about what well-being consists in, such as freedom, meaningful work, stable personal relationships, economically viable activity, and so on; views about the appropriate ethical and social framework, such as peace, social justice, democratic culture, legally protected liberties, and so on; views about the appropriate institutional framework of governance, local, national and international; and views about the conditions necessary for economic well-being, for instance in material resources, technology and skills.

Non-dogmatic cosmopolitanism, however, does not as such provide a single answer to the questions about war and peace. What informs cosmopolitanism is taking seriously the answers to questions such as the following. Is the policy or action proposed such that it advances human well-being generally and is not discriminatory in favour of our nationals or at the expense of others who are not our nationals?, or: Is it fair/just from a global point of view?, or, at least: Can it be seen as advancing or protecting our own society's interests in a way that can be justified from a global point of view (as being a reasonable defence of our interests)? I put these questions disjunctively, since different cosmopolitans may prefer different key questions. But on any account, the answers to the questions will both check a tendency to go to war and endorse the promotion of the conditions of peace – now and into the future. That is, they include a commitment to pacificism. This checklist does not rule out going to war, but it surely reduces its likelihood. Later I shall be appealing to a range of cosmopolitan arguments which I think are fairly typical of most modern cosmopolitan thinkers – and I shall refer to this as non-dogmatic pacificist cosmopolitanism. Insofar as this book is advocating anything, it is this position.

From time to time it will be apparent that I also support a pacifist version of cosmopolitanism. This takes further the general emphasis noted above on the nonviolent ways of promoting cosmopolitan goals. I find illuminating and refer several times to the idea expressed in Gandhi's remark 'the means are the ends in the making' (see chapter 5, §3.2, for discussion). This commitment remains in the background. My main concern is that, if any of my readers sign up to some form of modern non-dogmatic pacificist cosmopolitanism, he or she will have reason to question the common assumptions made about war's justification, whether or not he or she is inclined to the pacifist version as well.

7   Two further considerations concerning the nature of ethical analysis

7.1   The moral regulation of war

Is the moral regulation of war possible? At one level the answer seems obviously yes, at another level the claim is disputable.

The moral regulation of war requires several conditions to apply:

(a) there are rules/norms (ethical/legal) which are applicable to war;
(b) the application of these leads to judgements that some wars/ways of fighting are permissible, maybe even obligatory, while others are not permitted;
(c) a belief in these judgements sometimes – if not often – actually forms the basis of the decision to wage/conduct war in a certain way. That is, if the politician, general or soldier had not believed this, then they would not have decided that way.

If (a)–(c) are the case, then war is morally regulated. Now the pacifist or realist may reject at least one of these claims. The realist may say that ethics is irrelevant to war and that the language of ethics, if invoked by war's agents, is based on a mistake, so the realist rejects (a) and (b). The pacifist may claim that, though (a)–(c) describe a certain sociological reality – that is, there are norms commonly accepted that are applied and acted on – they do not have any validity, since all wars and ways of fighting are to be ethically rejected; at most there are legal norms and applications, but these norms have no moral legitimacy.

At another level, these claims of the realist and pacifist do not affect the idea that war is morally regulated. It may be that war is beyond morality or that all war is morally wrong, but still it remains the case that many agents do accept certain rules, do believe in applying them and do act on their bases. War remains morally regulated by the moral beliefs of those who have these beliefs. If this key point is accepted, then the pacifist and just war theorist can discuss whether it is right to fight, while agreeing that whether one fights or not depends on the judgement one makes. Likewise someone deliberating with himself whether he should fight, for instance join an army, is deliberating with himself on the assumption that what he does depends on the outcome.

It is only if the realist also claims that, whenever war's agents claim to be acting on a moral basis, this is either a smokescreen for reasons of national interest or a form of self-delusion, that he might assert that war is not morally regulated, even in the latter case of those who think they are acting on the basis of moral norms. If it is the latter (self-delusion), then they may think they are guided by moral judgements, but in fact they are not (so (c) is rejected as well as (a) and (b)). Even if there is a moral reason, there is also another reason which in fact is sufficient to motivate the recourse to war without the moral reason, whether or not it is privately acknowledged. If it is the former (smokescreen), then there is a cover anyway for another motive that is not (fully) publicly acknowledged by the actors but (fully) explains the action.

In either form, this is a stronger interpretation which is neither necessary to the realist's main point, nor at all plausible. Unless one thinks that *all* ethical judgements are always supervenient upon other real motivations, that is, they are explanatorily redundant, then there is no reason to suppose that for war it is any different. We need to note that there is a common supposition that war is causally determined or inevitable, and determined by non-moral considerations, and thus ethics is irrelevant since ethics presupposes choice. However, the judgement of the necessity/inevitability of war does not preclude ethical assessment. War's inevitability is not like the inevitability of accidents. What people do depends on their decisions. The bases of these acts will include selfish motives but also beliefs about war's moral legitimacy. The inevitability of war does not entail the inevitability of any particular decision to go to war. People are still free agents even if one pessimistically believes that this freedom does not include for more than a few people the real option of not fighting at all.

Likewise, if pacifists claim that the justifications for war are always specious, for instance a cover for other motives or self-delusion, then they, like realists, see themselves as undermining the moral regulation of war. But this is implausible, and not necessary to the pacifist's main claim. The pacifist need not in any case claim that the reasoning of the just war theorist is like this – rather it is a case that reasonable people can differ. Indeed it is important to most pacifists that the ethical thinking of others is not dismissed. If it were, this would be like the demonization of the other and contrary to the pacifist approach.

Whether or not the moral regulation of war is to be welcomed by the pacifist as furthering pacifism's goals by limiting the occasions of war and the manner of its being waged, or rejected as making war more likely because it is rendered plausible, is a matter for debate (see chapter 5).

7.2 Different views about ethics

One of the reasons why thinkers take very different views about the ethics of war and peace is that very different views are taken about human nature, political theory and international relations and, I shall suggest, especially about the nature of morality. It may be thought that the last – different views about the nature of morality – self-evidently leads to different ethical views, but what I am suggesting here is that it is more complicated than that.

There are a number of dimensions to different views about ethics, all of which have a bearing on the issues.[2] It is not simply that different people will have different views about the *content* of ethics (for instance, utilitarianism, Kantianism or human rights thinking); they also have different views about a morality's primary focus, for instance on rules themselves, on particular acts, or on the motives and virtues which are displayed in behaviour. They may have different views about the basis of ethics, whether for instance there are universal ethical truths potentially knowable by all people, whether many if not all ethical values are relative to culture, or whether ethics is based on convention.

There may be different views on how far a social morality requires everyone to act on the same ethical principles, how far factors such as circumstance and individual moral conscience allow for some variation, and how far ethics has a social dimension, a political dimension or a global dimension. The latter two aspects relate, respectively, to the nature of political theory and how far it is dependent on basic ethical considerations or generates its own sets of values based on contract, communitarianism, contractarianism or democracy, and to the nature of international relations and how far the latter is constrained by ethical factors – and, if so, whether these are derived from some universal morality. Although the subsequent argument of the book will illustrate all these dimensions, let me just give a few examples of what I mean.

First, if the moral norms governing the conduct of war are thought be based on convention, then it may well be supposed that, in the absence of observation of the conventions by one side, then the other side is entitled to break the conventions as well. The direct targeting of cities in the Second World War through saturation bombing was no doubt seen as justified for many by the fact that the other side was doing it and the supposition, so easy to make by thinkers on each side through their respective subjective perceptions of what was going on, that somehow the other side had started it. On the other hand, if one thinks that the rules of war are based on moral principles which are to be observed irrespective of whether others observe them, then clearly one would take the view, as many in fact did, that it was wrong to engage in such direct attacks.

Second, a key issue in the ethics of war is over whether one adopts a consequentialist or non-consequentialist approach to ethics; for instance, whether at bottom what is right is determined only by the consequences – actual, foreseen or reasonably foreseeable – of that action, compared with the other alternatives which could have been undertaken, or whether what determines one's duty are quite different considerations in addition to general consequences. For instance, a deontologist (as many non-consequentialists are called) might argue that keeping a promise, such as a promise to the minister of another country, is a duty and ought to be kept, not because doing so will do more good that not doing so (though usually that will be the case), but because of the intrinsic character of the act, because one had entered an obligation by one's past act, and so on. Likewise a general may decide not to order the direct targeting of civilians because civilians have a right not to be directly attacked, even though some advantage may come from such an attack.

Deontologists need not be saying that there are never circumstances when it would be right to break a promise or violate someone's rights, since it might be right when there was a clash with another duty, but they would definitely rule out breaking a promise merely because more good would come from doing so. Consequentialists on the other hand are interested in the consequences of different actions, including the 'negative' action of refraining from acting. For example, they might argue that, since we can foresee the consequences of our omissions as well as our positive actions, we ought often to give aid to others, where more good comes from this than from omitting to give aid.[3] A famous example relevant to the ethics of war is given by Bernard Williams in his case of Jim, an American tourist travelling in rural South America, who comes across a situation in which Pedro is about to order his men to execute twenty Indians for cattle marauding. These Indians have not been proved guilty of the crime. Jim protests and Pedro gives him two alternatives: either Jim shoots one man himself and Pedro lets nineteen go free, or he does nothing and allows the executions of twenty to go ahead. Williams himself takes the view that Jim should preserve his moral integrity in not killing an innocent person, but argues that the consequentialist or utilitarian would conclude otherwise (Williams 1973: 98–9). The example is useful in showing up in a sharp form the difference between two styles of ethical thinking relevant to war issues.

Third, if one thinks that the moral code that governs the behaviour of people in one society (let alone the world as a whole) requires the universal application of these rules in a standard way, then in a society where it is generally accepted that it is both right and indeed the duty for its citizens to defend their society by fighting to protect it, it will be regarded as simply incorrect of a pacifist to say that it is not alright for him or her to fight to defend his country. If, however, a more complex account is given of how individual decisions may be legitimately reached, which for instance allows particular contexts such as vocational calling or particular deliverances of conscience to make a difference, then more flexible positions are possible. It is possible for the person who believes in the rightness of military defence to respect the position of the pacifist and even possibly to acknowledge that is right for him or her to take that stance. Conversely, it may be possible for the pacifist to accept that it is reasonable for others to have their conscientious decision to defend their community in the way they think correct, or at least acknowledge that such defence is not to be considered morally in the same way as militarist attitudes or particularly inhumane forms of fighting. This incidentally is not simply an admission that what is right depends on what people think is right – to be considered and rejected later, and actually very rarely held despite its subjectivist charm – but an acknowledgement that there is a multi-level range of possible responses which are capable of being integrated into a single moral worldview.

Fourth, there is an issue that belongs to the 'philosophy of action' concerning the role of intention in the moral character of an act. This issue has important implications for at least two areas of warfare. First, does the fact that, in a military operation, a commander may intend or aim at certain things, such as enemy military units, but not at civilians in the area, though he knows that quite a number will be killed as collateral damage, make any moral difference compared with an operation that simply aimed at the enemy, military and civilian alike? Some say that the different intentions make a big moral difference, others that they make no difference at all. Second, does the fact that in its defence policy a country threatens to do certain things or use certain weapons *if* the enemy does certain things, and does so precisely to prevent or reduce the likelihood of the enemy doing these things, such as attacking one's country, have the same moral character as actually doing those things or using those weapons? Or does the fact that there is the *further* intention of preventing certain things from happening and keeping the peace alter the moral character of the act? This issue has particular pertinence in regard to nuclear deterrence (see chapter 7).

8   Survey of war/peace issues in the modern era

In the remainder of this chapter I offer a brief survey of the most significant developments in regard to war and peace during what may be called the 'modern' period, which somewhat arbitrarily I shall regard as the twentieth and the beginning of the twenty-first century. At any rate, all the major issues concerning war and peace can be identified in this period. Then, using this survey, I indicate where in the remainder of the book the various issues are taken up more fully.[4]

8.1   Introduction

Whether one regards the modern period as the beginning of the twentieth century onwards or as having longer reach, back to the origins of the modern nation-state system in the Peace of Westphalia (1648), it is useful to see a contrast between various developments in the twentieth century in contrast to the paradigm of war and peace that had emerged by the end of the nineteenth century. This was a paradigm centred round the just war tradition and the assumption both that states themselves were *de facto* the key actors in global affairs and that they held the monopoly of legitimate violence. States were the legitimate authorities entitled to wage war; states could engage in war for just causes such as self-defence, but generally, because of the acceptance of political pluralism, wars to convert others or impose one's values on others were rejected. Strong emphasis was put on the rules of war as established in international law regarding non-combatant immunity and the proper treatment of soldiers; while the value of peace was recognized, peace was seen usually in somewhat limited 'negative' terms as the absence of war.

During the twentieth and on into the twenty-first century all these assumptions have been questioned by many thinkers in regard to modern wars. This does not mean that a new consensus emerged in regard to what wars could rightly be fought and how. Quite the contrary. In the outline which follows, divergent trends and ways of thinking emerge. What perhaps is most significant about thinking about war and peace in the modern era is precisely the loss of the consensus that had, at least in official circles, prevailed in the nineteenth century (though we should note that the norms that prevailed were often honoured in the breach).

In the next and main sub-section I outline some of the characteristic features of thinking about the ethics of war and peace in the twentieth century, often in contrast to the previous era (though sometimes going back to perspectives that prevailed earlier in the just war tradition). This is descriptive of certain major developments in what wars are fought and how, and of the efforts to pursue peace. This is needed to set the scene for the ethical responses. It is also descriptive-normative in the sense that it indicates the development of ethical thought about what is legitimate in war, and so on, and indicates the different ethical issues and perspectives that were and are taken. In the third sub-section I consider several different interpretations of what is happening overall in the modern world.

8.2   The twentieth century and beginning of the twenty-first century

(a) As is often remarked, the twentieth century witnessed the totalization of war. This involved several dimensions: (i) the development, thanks to technology, of more powerful weapons which, even if not aimed at non-combatants, tended to have widespread collateral consequences in terms of civilian deaths, harm and disruption; (ii) the increasing involvement of civilians, through wars being fought 'in their name', particularly within a country with a democratic mandate, and through extensive military conscription; and (iii), related to (ii), a tendency for civilians to become direct targets of attack.

(b) The development of international law and institutions was partly motivated by the desire to create the conditions of peace and to put limits on what could count as a just cause. Particularly since the setting up of the United Nations in 1945, the 'legalist paradigm', to use Walzer's well-known phrase, sought to emphasize that aggression is the key international sin and defence against it a just cause (Walzer 1977: 58). The development of international institutions such as the UN was seen as providing the basis for cooperation and negotiated resolution of conflicts, as a key element in the pursuit of peace. The UN Charter also set up the Security Council, which was meant in theory to be the only body that could authorize war, individual states retaining the right of defence only in emergency situations. In other respects the United Nations retained most of the features and rationale of the internationalist paradigm or 'Westphalian system' that had developed since 1648.

(c) Alongside this, and pulling in a different direction, was the widening of the just war criteria, especially those of legitimate authority and just cause. On the one hand, the challenge to states as the holders of the monopoly of legitimate violence has come from those who see freedom fighters, resistance movements, revolutionary movements, perhaps even terrorist groups fighting jihad, as having legitimacy, generally because they claim to have popular support and have political goals such as major changes in the political order. On the other hand, just cause has been widened from self-defence to take in opposition to unjust regimes/illegal governments (including liberation from colonialism) and to encompass humanitarian intervention, that is, not merely coming to the aid of another country (which may be an ally), but also aiding those within a country who are oppressed by their country's government. These developments, particularly humanitarian intervention and the UN endorsement in 2005 of the 'Responsibility to Protect' (R2P), have only recently re-emerged (they had been a feature of earlier just war thinking) in the face of the legalist paradigm. Non-state terrorism, while it has always been a feature of international relations, became much more widespread in the twentieth century, made dramatically prominent, at least to Americans, by the events on '9/11' in 2001.

The phenomenon of terrorism is important to the ethics of war both because it claims to provide a model – utterly unacceptable to the vast majority of people – of a legitimate body with a just cause, but also because it raises the challenge of how to respond to terrorism, both in terms of what measures are likely to be effective, and in terms of whether the normal restraints in war are to be loosened in fighting terrorists.

(d) The twentieth century saw the development of new types of weapons (not just larger and more sophisticated ones) such as nuclear weapons, chemical weapons and biological weapons. This raised a whole lot of ethical issues about the use of such weapons, generally because of the types of effect they have (radiation, poisoning the environment and the spread of disease) and the class of recipients of these effects, which include necessarily civilians on a wide scale as collateral damage, if not, as is more likely, as objects of direct attack. Attempts have been made to ban the latter two types of weapon – chemical and biological – in international law, though it would appear that many countries do in fact possess stocks of these. The status of nuclear weapons is controversial: some argue that, while they are not explicitly ruled out in international law, they are in effect contrary to international humanitarian law (and the Opinion of the World Court in 1996 is seen by many as supporting this view). Others hold that they are not – at least their use as a deterrent is not – and their use is a legitimate part of defence policy.

(e) Various other attempts to limit the barbarity of war have also been made, with limited success, for instance the attempt to ban the recruitment of child soldiers – itself largely a phenomenon of the twentieth century and not before. Another issue relates to a type of weapon which has been the centre of attention in modern warfare: landmines have been used extensively in many types of war and are widely condemned because of their far-reaching indiscriminate effects on civilians after conflicts have ended. The Ottawa Treaty of 1997 was a step in the right direction towards getting rid of these weapons. In recent years, especially with the 'war against terrorism', the question of what norms should govern the treatment of fighters who are not regarded in international law as soldiers has assumed a great urgency (as in the case of Guantánamo Bay).

(f) As noted earlier, in contrast to the official paradigms in the nineteenth century, the twentieth century saw a decided polarization of attitudes towards the ethics of war and peace. On the one hand, there was realism such as E. H. Carr's rejection of Woodrow Wilson's idealism which underpinned the League of Nations as making things worse (Carr 1939) and militarism as illustrated by Mussolini's fascist concept of war as ennobling, and, on the other hand, pacifism as the principled objection to fighting in war and pacificism as the earnest attempt to create or maintain the conditions of peace, inspired by past peace projects such as that of Kant's in his *Perpetual Peace*. In the middle there were various forms of the position that some wars are justified and others not, and some ways of fighting justified and others not. These may be presented as appealing to the just war in its received form, as modifying the tradition to take account of modern circumstances, or as an ethical position seen as independent of the just war tradition (seen as out of date). Clearly, from the first traditional just war point of view, much of what happens in the modern world is seriously wrong: there are violations of norms which still retain their validity even if they are often ignored (such as the principle of non-combatant immunity). The latter two positions – just war revised and independent ethical positions – make out the ethical arguments in different ways, but all are united in taking the ethical critique and control of war seriously.

(g) During the twentieth century there was a major shift in thinking about peace and security. The common assertion that peace was best understood negatively as the absence of war was often challenged by those for whom richer conceptions were important – ones that saw peace as opposed to a much wider range of phenomena (such as peace as the absence of violence) or viewed peace more positively as involving positive moral features (such as a commitment to justice and human rights). A very 'positive' concept would be that of peace as harmonious relations or shalom (Macquarrie 1973). On these views peace was seen a part of a much richer matrix of things: it was linked to the UN thesis of the indivisibility of human rights, and its interdependence with development for which it was both precondition and consequence was often claimed.

Likewise the twentieth century saw a broader conception of security. Although national security continued to be considered as a central goal of foreign policy and to be achieved by strong defences, nevertheless alternative modes of thinking became widespread. On the one hand, there was interest in 'common security' as advocated by the Palme Commission (ICDSI 1982); on the other hand, there was a broadening of the concept of security as 'human security', to include such things as economic, health and environmental security, as promoted by the United Nations Development Programme (UNDP 1994). The effect of this broadening, especially if coupled with a cosmopolitan perspective – itself a perspective that became widespread in the second half of the twentieth century – was to set a different agenda that questions the predominance of national security conceived of in military terms.

Both pacifism and pacificism are approaches which have gained support (see, for instance, Ceadel 1987). Pacificism is an approach focused on the conditions of peace, opposing the militarist glorification of war, and taking issue with the view that human nature dooms us to perpetual war, since we can check these tendencies if only we find the right forms of education and institutions, and so on. Pacifism as an individual stance of not fighting in war – and usually presented as a universal claim about others too – underwent much development in the twentieth century. It was largely a religiously inspired stance historically, but other kinds of argument have come to be offered. During this period attitudes towards people who wished to be conscientious objectors also changed, with many countries coming to recognize a right in law. There was the work of the former UN Human Rights Commission to get a universal right to conscientious refusal/ objection recognized. New forms of pacifism developed. This was partly because of contingent arguments concerning the cost of war in terms of the resources thus spent not being available for such things as poverty-reduction, and concerning the cycle of violence begetting violence, partly because of general arguments against the nature of war itself, as indiscriminate or inherently violating human rights, and partly because of the growing recognition that, in respect to particular wars, an individual can appeal to the argument, implicitly if not explicitly cosmopolitan, that their state is conducting an unjust war (this position being very apparent in the opposition to the Vietnam War).

(h) Some of the thinking in the twentieth century, particularly in the latter half, was cosmopolitan, that is, thinking that emphasized the idea of global ethics and of global responsibility and welcomed our self-identification as 'citizens of the world'. This had effects on the way people think about war and peace. This led on the one hand to arguments for interventions such as military humanitarian action (as in Kosovo), and on the other hand to arguments for promoting the conditions of peace for everyone through human rights protection, development, and so on.

(i) One feature of the twentieth century was the emergence of numerous 'new wars': wars that were often asymmetrical wars, wars that occurred within borders (such as civil wars, wars of secession, or 'proxy' wars fought in poorer countries), or wars between states and non-state actors such as terrorists. These raised many issues to do with just cause, legitimate authority, how to fight, and so on.

(j) Despite the UN paradigm on non-aggression, many wars were fought and continue to be fought (and are regarded by many as legitimately so) as wars of 'good' versus 'evil', and this partly explains why these have often involved a relaxation of *ius in bello* restraints – such as wars against Nazism or communism, against illegal regimes or regimes flouting international law (Iraq), or against militant Islam/al-Qaeda. The aim of such wars may be limited to checking or containing 'evil', but, more ambitiously, may be extended to effect regime change, so as to eliminate the 'evil' and replace it with a regime that is 'good' or in accordance with one's values. A manifestation of this is the idea of war crimes, as illustrated in the Nuremberg trials of leading Nazis. At another level the setting up of the International Criminal Court at the end of the twentieth century appeared at the end of a long process of establishing international legal instruments that can try individual soldiers for war crimes and crimes against humanity.

8.3   Interpretations

Given the above picture of war and peace in the twentieth and twenty-first centuries, which shows an almost bewildering range of developments and perspectives, what interpretations can be given ethically to these? One general approach is to retain the belief that war can be morally regulated. Either one takes a fairly traditional approach to justifying war, and thus resists the extension of legitimate authority beyond states (or the UN Security Council acting on states' behalf), resists widening the range of just causes, and remains firmly committed to principles such as non-combatant immunity (thus unreservedly condemning saturation bombing and the atom bombing of Hiroshima); or one takes a modified just war approach or an independent ethical position and argues for new lines to be drawn, such as extending legitimate authority, accepting just causes such as humanitarian intervention, and seeing non-combatant immunity as something that can be waived where military necessity dictates. Either way one still retains the central view that war can be ethically regulated: many wars are unjustified, and many things done in war – unnecessary killing of civilians, mistreatment of captured soldiers, other war crimes – are simply to be rejected.

On another reading the phenomena of the twentieth century show – or show more starkly – that the whole ethical framework attempted by the just war tradition as well as the latter-day ethical stances that also try to provide a principled ethical basis for war are flawed. What is shown is that war cannot really be ethically regulated (even though it may be regulated in the sense that people who believe it is ethically regulated are influenced by their beliefs, as discussed in §7.1 above) and that the extent to which such ethical regulation is attempted merely perpetuates it as 'not so bad'. This comes from several perspectives in some ways opposed to one another. On the one hand, there is a realist perspective which says either that war lies outside the domain of ethics altogether (war is a breakdown of moral relations) or that defending national interests prudently (as opposed to pursuing moral ideals or following universal principles) actually is more likely to lead to peace and international order; and there are the militarist attitudes that glorify war. On the other hand, there is the pacifist perspective that all war is wrong (so it cannot be morally regulated) and the pacificist perspective that the important thing is to build peace.

Both the realist who is interested in international order and the pacificist can agree that certain general goals – such as peace – are desirable, and that our overall commitment is to do what is necessary to generate these conditions. Indeed, if realists are seriously interested in international order and peace (and are optimistic about making progress), then they may be pacificists of a sort. But for most pacificists, even such a realist has radically inappropriate views about the means to do so. For the realist there is a focus on the national interests: strong defence, decisive stances where necessary, effective threats, and so on. For most pacificists the focus is on building cooperation: redefining defence (common security), the culture of dialogue and negotiation, nonviolence as a means, acceptance that violence begets violence and that the means are (factually) the ends in the making, cosmopolitan obligations to all human beings, and so on.

9   The plan for the rest of the book

In chapter 2 we look first at realism, both as a general approach to international relations and as a specific approach to war, and then at militarism, and consider various criticisms that can be made of both. In chapter 3 we survey two other ways of viewing international relations, the internationalist tradition and cosmopolitanism, since a fuller understanding of these two approaches will help us understand the more specific issues of war and peace that follow. In chapter 4 we look at the justification of war, especially in the just war tradition, and offer a range of objections to this approach. Chapter 5 examines the philosophy of nonviolence and pacifism and considers some of the arguments for and against the general approach. In chapter 6 we investigate the idea of peace and the rather different approach called pacificism as indicated earlier and defend the latter against possible objections. Then in chapter 7 we pick up on a number of issues arising in the modern world that were identified in the preceding summary but have not been given more than passing treatment earlier on – namely nuclear weapons, contemporary wars, terrorism, humanitarian intervention and security in relation to human security. Finally a brief concluding chapter summarizes the main goals of the book, illustrates these with some of the main ways religion informs war and peace, and then outlines the practical implications of the non-dogmatic pacificist cosmopolitanism I have commended in this book.

Questions

1 Why does the author stress that we should discuss the ethics of peace and not just the ethics of war?
2 Is Grotius's view, that we need to find a middle position between those who think that in war everything is permitted and those who think that in war nothing is permitted, useful in thinking about the ethical issues?
3 Can war be morally regulated?
4 What are the most significant features of modern warfare from an ethical point of view?

2 REALISM AND MILITARISM

1 The realist view of war

At the heart of the realist view of war is the notion that what nation-states ought to do in their foreign policy is to pursue their national interests (see, for example, Morgenthau 1954; Niebuhr 1932; Butterfield 1953; Waltz 2001). If going to war will best achieve this, then a country ought to go to war – even if it be a war of aggression to weaken another country, a war to acquire resources, a war to check the spread of alien values which threaten a global order that suits one's interests, or whatever. If the prosecution of the war requires one to do things which are contrary to the so-called rules of war, then military necessity dictates this and this is what a country ought to do. Realists also tend to make a corresponding factual claim, which is that, on the whole, this is what happens in the world, however much the just war theorist might argue against it. My main concern here is with the normative claim.

Realism is sometimes presented as the thesis that ethics does not apply to war – either to its being waged or to the manner in which it is waged. This as a rough approximation is right, though many qualifications are involved. To be sure, leaders who make decisions to go to war are not devoid of *choice*; they are not victims in a remorseless process (though the idea of the inevitability of war sometimes misleadingly suggests this). But their choices are to be informed by considerations of national interests (which is generally the case). Indeed, it may be on some accounts that the leader has a *moral* duty to be so informed. What is denied – and this denial is meant to imply that ethics does not apply to war – is the applicability of universal moral rules that are meant to *limit* the pursuit of interests (as moral rules are generally accepted by most thinkers, including most realists, as doing in the case of an individual's interests). What is also denied is the pursuit of moral ideals that go beyond concern for national interests.

Realism, that is, is in a sense a response to two ethical tendencies: first, the principled application of rules, which is precisely what the rules of the just war tradition are, in regard both to going to war (*ius ad bellum*) and to the means of fighting it (*ius in bello*); and, second, what is called idealism or moralism, the pursuit of ethical goals, such as spreading Christianity or furthering democracy or stopping communism. These are among the 'just causes' that some just war thinkers of a 'crusader' mentality might regard as important bases for war. It is called 'realist' precisely because it is a rejection of idealism in favour of a more sober view of how the real world works and of what is needed if the world is to achieve such limited order and peace as is within its capacity. One well-known realist who was concerned with the latter was E. H. Carr, who criticized foreign policy and the misguided idealism of the League of Nations after the First World War, and took the view, with which many realists agree, that, if countries stuck to looking after their own national interests (including going to war if necessary), then on the whole greater peace and order would prevail in the world (Carr 1939).

Realists cannot deny that, as often as not, foreign policy – including decisions about going to war – is couched in moral terms. Politicians and others use the language of just cause or last resort, commit themselves to moral goals and moral rules in warfare, and sometimes endorse the idea of an 'ethical foreign policy'. Sometimes indeed, for a realist, the 'use' of moral language may be an effective means of promoting national interests, namely as being a smokescreen for other motives privately recognized but not publicly announced.

It is not, however, essential to realism to deny that sometimes moral motives can influence politicians and others into taking action in war or indeed other aspects of foreign policy. Only if realists were committed to a strong empirical thesis that ethics *never* actually plays any role in decisions about war, and about international relations generally, would they have to interpret the phenomenon of moral language being used in foreign policy as a form of self-delusion where other considerations are really operating – or at least as being explanatorily redundant in the face of other considerations which, while these moral considerations are acknowledged, are really explanatorily sufficient on their own.

All these interpretations are in fact often given, but if it is the case, as it seems reasonable to believe, that sometimes politicians believe in an ethical position and act on that basis (and this seems to be the correct explanatory analysis), then the realist can still stick to his or her *normative* claim – that, though it is possible to be guided by ethical principles, what leaders ought to be doing is pursuing the national interest.

At the heart, then, of realist thinking is a view about the irrelevance of ethics as the application of universal moral rules to war. But that is all it is. It is not, for instance, the same as militarism. The realist does not – or at least need not – glory in war or see it as essentially expressive of being fully human. War is a necessity, a means to vital goals. On the whole realists, unless they are also informed by militarist ideals, are keen to avoid war if at all possible. They regard the condition of peace as highly desirable, certainly for their own country, and indeed everywhere – but it is a condition that must be upset if national interests require it. Furthermore, the view that the conduct of war requires any action necessary to 'compel the enemy to do our will' (to use the idea of Clausewitz, whose thinking informs much realist analysis) is a doctrine about military necessity (Clausewitz 1832: 1). Soldiers should do what needs to be done. Gratuitous killing for no military advantage would not be seen as appropriate. The killing of soldiers once caught would not be acceptable unless the situation required it (for instance, if there was the need to retreat quickly); the bombing of civilians would not be accepted unless it was seen as necessary. Furthermore, crimes against humanity, such as raping women, are usually ruled out as being actually beyond the activity of war, and, though they happen to be done by soldiers in uniform, they are wrong by ordinary standards of morality. Only if realists were also inspired by militarist motives or took a completely relativist view that ethics really did not apply at all to those outside their own society – and neither of these further assumptions is essential to the realist position – might they regard such actions as all right.

I have presented the realist view in a plausible form, not because I agree with it, but because it needs to be taken seriously. While most people would shy away from being completely realist in regard to international relations generally, many do feel the force of the realist analysis of war.

2   Sources of the realist approach

2.1   General arguments in international relations

One of the sources of realism about war comes from a more general realist view of international relations (see Dower 1998: ch. 3 or Dower 2007: ch. 2 for a more detailed account). This is the view that in international relations ethics is irrelevant to foreign policy, which is always shaped – or at least should be shaped – by national interests. Clearly if this view is correct, then, since going to war and prosecuting a war are both actions that are implementations of foreign policy, all these actions are outside the sphere of ethical assessment.

The latter form of realism about international relations is sometimes also called international scepticism, anarchism and Hobbesianism. The latter two labels reflect one of the most powerful arguments put forward by realists, which found its eloquent expression in the writings of the seventeenth-century political theorist Thomas Hobbes. His view was that obligations have force only if they are enforceable. Within a political community the basic rules are enforceable by the sovereign or 'common power', which can ensure that they are generally observed: indeed for Hobbes the security thus achieved for citizens is the basis of a political deal (which he understands hypothetically) whereby they contract with each other to submit to this common power. But, Hobbes notes, international relations is quite unlike this. There is no common power, only a number of independent sovereign bodies each jealous of their independence. So, in the absence of an 'arche', that is, a ruler at the global level (hence the label anarchism), morality does not apply to international relations. (See Hobbes [1651] 1991: ch. xiii.)

Another kind of argument for international scepticism is that there is no universal morality or global ethic. Different countries have different moral codes or cultures. In the absence of an agreed international ethic, states stand in a moral vacuum in relation to each other. This is an application of the general thesis of ethical relativism, namely that morality is relative to particular cultures (see, for instance, Wong 1984; Brandt 1967; for a classical statement, see Benedict 1935).

Another argument, related to this but different, is the communitarian argument that the world is made up of many different communities (for an account of communitarianism, see for instance Taylor 1989; Sandel 1982). Within each there are significant obligations of members towards one another, but there are no obligations to human beings outside one's society, or, at least, there are only much weaker ones which have application only when they do not clash with the former. There is no global community – talk of it is really only talk of an idea yet to be realized.

The above three arguments are based on the idea that, for various reasons, there is no ethical framework at a global level, or, if there is, it is a very weak one. The following arguments for realism depend more on stressing the special nature of the state which in various ways overrides any moral obligations we might accept in principle vis-à-vis any other human beings.

First, the international system is made up of separate political communities called nation-states. The system's effectiveness depends upon each state's having primary responsibility for its own well-being and interests. The logic of the state system is to prioritize the pursuit of national interest, and for the realist this priority means quite simply that states are always entitled to consider their own interests first. Thus although the idea of ethical norms governing war, and indeed other aspects of foreign policy, might be accepted, they are always overridden, and rightly so in regard to foreign policy. A state might indeed act ethically according to the agreed international norms, but this would be either merely consistent with its interests (including an interest in being thought well of by other states) or something done where interests are not affected either way (such as contributing emergency aid for a distant disaster).

Two other arguments supporting realism in international relations quite generally are in a sense particular specifications of the argument just given. The first stresses the duty of governments to their nationals. Whether one sees political community in communitarian terms or contractarian terms,[1] or as based on a democratic mandate, the duty of leaders is first and foremost to further the interests of their nationals (see Dower 1998: ch. 4 or Dower 2007: ch. 3). If war is needed to do this, then the leader must engage in war. Second, given that states exist in a fragile and insecure world, the need for state leaders to protect and advance their country's interests as best they can is reinforced. (This argument has the counterfactual implication that, were the world to become much less fragile, the duty of governments might be less focused on the nation's interests.)

We should note that someone who was a realist in international relations quite generally may still not go the whole hog in applying this to war. It is clear that a realist in international relations will necessarily see a decision about going to war as being shaped by national interests; indeed, that is one of the most significant applications of the realist doctrine of international relations. On the other hand, a realist such as Henry Kissinger, as we noted in the last chapter, may still regard the rules concerning how to fight a war as important to follow. This could be because these conventions are so well established that breaking them has costs greater than the realist wishes to bear (including the cost that all breaches are likely to be reciprocated); but it could also be based on the thought that, though international relations is guided by considerations of interests, actual fighting involves individuals in face-to-face relations, and a realist may feel that there are some universal standards about person-to-person relations which, though irrelevant to the formation of foreign policy, have application at this level.

2.2   Special arguments to do with war

The realist view of war does not have to depend on the more general view of international relations. It is possible to hold that, in normal peacetime, countries have duties towards other countries in a society of states. International law is to be observed, international institutions are to be used to pursue common goals, cooperation generally is to be encouraged, and indeed a duty to maintain or promote peace is to be accepted. Nevertheless, states may, when it suits them, withdraw from the moral conventions of international society and engage in war for reasons not sanctioned by those conventions. They may choose to withdraw from the conventions about limiting the occasions of war or withdraw from the conventions relating to the way war is prosecuted, or both.

The conventions relating to peaceful coexistence and *ius ad bellum* may be seen as overridden if vital national interests dictate, so in effect one withdraws from the conventions and also from the protection of the conventions. Normal international relations are resumed after the war is over. Nevertheless, even if this is the case, one may still wish to stick to the conventions regarding *ius in bello*, either, as I said above, because these conventions are seen as more important or because of some commitment to a basic ethic relating to person-to-person interactions.

Conversely, even if one thinks that war should not be embarked on without the conditions of just cause, and so on, being satisfied, nevertheless, once war has commenced, normal moral relations either lapse vis-à-vis one's adversaries or are overridden by the goal of winning. That is, depending on how one understands the nature of moral rules, one will see the rules of war as lapsing because the convention has been undermined, or, if one thinks that the rules still apply – they cannot just lapse because they are objectively valid anyway – one has to see them as being overridden by another duty to protect or advance one's nation's interests.

3   Militarism

Often in discussions about the ethics of war militarism is not identified as a separate position. It is often, from a just war point of view, associated with realism, insofar as it similarly takes the view that there are no constraints in war. Alternatively, from a pacifist point of view, militarism is seen to be an aspect of the just war approach since, whatever the restraints of action and motive that the just war theory is meant to impose, wars fought as just wars often have a militarist character. We will, I think, be able to account for this ambiguity and indeed see that, as I indicated schematically in chapter 1, militarism is not so much an alternative to realism and just war thinking as a feature of the thinking of *some but not others* of those who support realist or just war/war justification positions. It needs stressing that the militarist/pacificist distinction *cuts across* the realist/just war/pacifism classification: it is a serious mistake to think of realism as either being or entailing militarism.

In recent years there has been a trend to identify it as a separate approach, for instance by writers such as Ceadel, Coates, and Coppieters and Fotion. According to Ceadel, militarism can be associated with the rise of fascism, and in particular with the approach adopted by the Italian dictator Mussolini. The following quotation gives the flavour of the position. Mussolini rejects pacifism:

> Where the future and development of humanity are concerned generally speaking, and leaving aside any considerations to do with current policy, fascism believes, above all, that perpetual peace is neither possible nor useful. It rejects Pacifism, which is a cover for fleeing in the face of struggle and cowardice in the face of sacrifice. War alone lifts all human energies to a state of maximum tension, stamping the hallmark of nobility on those people who have the courage to confront it. All other ideals are but secondary, and never bring man face to face with his own self, where he is forced to choose between life and death. (Quoted in and translated by Coppieters and Fotion 2002: 7, from Mussolini 1936: 28–9)

Coppieters and Fotion, in their introduction, claim that there are two main differences between militarism and realism: militarists are more prone to go to war; and for militarists ethics is indeed relevant to war (Coppieters and Fotion 2002: 7). Militarists are more prone to go to war because they see, as the quotation from Mussolini brings out, war as a positive activity, one that expresses human virtues. Furthermore militarists do regard ethics as relevant to war; namely that going to war is a positive moral good! In terms of the initial triple distinction we discussed in chapter 1 (realism, just war, pacifism), militarism can be seen to be like realism in saying that everything is permitted, but like just war thinking because it regards fighting as a moral issue and not forbidden and unlike realism, which sees ethics as irrelevant.

Coppieters and Fotion put the militarist position thus:

> Militarists are also aware of war's horrors but are convinced, in contrast to realists, that these horrors are much more than compensated for by the gains of war. For militarists, war transforms individuals into what they were not, and perhaps could not be, before. It makes Men out of men. It gives those

who participate in war a sense of identity and accomplishment. It also develops their character. The rigors of war teach those who participate in it such virtues as discipline, self-confidence, perseverance, loyalty, responsibility and courage. So, along with the costs of war, there are also important gains for the individual who lives in the militarist society.

But there are gains for the nation as well. War turns the nation from a collection of individuals or members of this or that group into a single Community. It unites the people by giving them a common purpose. They develop a sense of 'we'. . . . (Coppieters and Fotion 2002: 5)

Coates's discussion is more extensive (Coates 1997: ch. 3). The following points emerge from this. For Coates militarism includes:

(a) a crusading mentality: the enemy is the other/different, and either they or the values they stand for have to be crushed, with a preference for unconditional surrender rather than compromise or negotiated peace agreements;
(b) the celebration of war as a virtue, in the sense that soldiers are fulfilled in ways that others are not and whole communities are strengthened by the conduct of war;
(c) the absence of restraints in war: what motivates it – and does so reasonably – is hatred and blood-lust;
(d) war as an importantly expressive activity, not a mere instrumentality which has to be entered into or prosecuted in certain ways – with regret by a just war thinker, or as a matter of necessity by the realist;
(e) war as a natural way of coping with human differences, to be seen as first rather than last resort, as the just war thinker or realist both prefer for different reasons.

I shall return to further analysis when I criticize this position, but would make two points at this stage. Coates's analysis largely fits Coppieters and Fotion's account except for condition (a), the presence of a crusading mentality. This is somewhat controversial, both because Ceadel sees the crusading approach as a distinct category and, as I remarked earlier, because the crusading objective may well be among the objectives that many people, thinking of war's justification, would regard as a possible just cause. In any case, someone who has such a crusading objective may not accept the further characteristics of the militarist approach. It is also worth noting that the militarist approach arose in part out of the chivalric tradition, in which the life of knights was indeed seen as expressive of human virtue, but that conception did not necessarily go along with the other potentially more negative features of the account.

4   Critique of realism

I will now examine in turn the various arguments we considered earlier for realism. First I consider the general arguments for realism in international relations. (See Dower 1998 or 2007 for further exploration.)

4.1   Hobbesianism and enforceability

The famous Hobbesian argument depends in part on a particular view of obligation, namely that I am not obliged to do something unless some 'body' can coerce me into doing it (and can punish me if I deviate). It is not clear that moral obligation does depend on this condition: morality, it has been said, is obedience to the unenforceable, which for many people are the dictates of conscience. Most of us accept many obligations which are not backed by the sanctions of enforceable and enforced law or indeed the sanction of social pressure. It is not clear that states' leaders need be in any different position. Hobbes is right that in international relations there is a lack of an 'arche' which can enforce rules, and because of this there is a degree of uncertainty about how states will behave that is not so much a feature of domestic society. Perhaps uncertainty and hence lack of security create a basis for nations being concerned with their own interests, but that is a separate argument I come on to later.

We do not have a world government which might provide the 'arche' that Hobbes was looking for, but we do have many features in international relations which make the international scene less disanalogous to the domestic scene than Hobbes supposed and, to be fair to Hobbes, than would have been the case in his day. But latter-day Hobbesians do not acknowledge these developments sufficiently. We do have now an extensively developed body of international law, much of it relating to war. It is true that it cannot be enforced in the same way as domestic law, though there has been for over a hundred years an International Court at The Hague where cases about international disputes are occasionally heard, and recently, in 1999, a second court, the International Criminal Court (ICC), was set up, which has a different function of making it possible for individuals to be taken to court for war crimes. And we now have an elaborate international organization, namely the United Nations, which coordinates activities across a broad range, adherence to which is embedded in widely accepted norms.

It is hard to deny that an extensive body of norms exists as expressed in international law, including the conduct of war. The lack of world government does not undermine this fact at all. Since international law is backed by a high degree of moral consensus that the laws express certain very general moral principles, it seems clear that international relations is subject to ethical assessment. Now this point does not depend on each person thinking about the issue having to accept the ethical consensus underlying international law. If one's ethical views are that international law and the ethical norms it expresses are incomplete, inadequate or even wrong in certain respects, this does not invalidate the claim that international relations is assessable by ethical norms that are not enforceable. One's view is not that there should be no law and no international ethic, but that there should be an improved law based on a better understood ethic.

4.2   Relativism

A similar move can be made in relation to another common argument against ethics in international relations, namely that we need to accept the thesis of ethical relativism. Since there are no agreed moral norms across the world, there is no basis for an ethic of international relations between different countries with different moral traditions. This argument is wrong on several counts.

First, even if it were true that there were deep differences between cultures, it would not show that there could not be an ethical basis for international relations. Such an argument could simply be based on considerations of what it would be reasonable for countries with different traditions to agree on, just as within a diverse society we can agree on certain common values essential to living together in a society – what Rawls called the 'overlapping consensus' (Rawls 1993). In any case, apart from what it would be reasonable to have, in fact certain norms have come to be agreed in the society of states anyway, whatever variation there is in the ethics internal to each society.

But, second, the relativist rather exaggerates the claims of difference. There are certain core values in all societies, and all that is needed for an ethical basis for international relations is agreement about these values, whilst accepting differences in regard to other values – which is also what happens within culturally diverse societies anyway. Indeed it is precisely because there is almost universal consensus about what is valuable in life, and how war destroys what is of value, that there is an agreed basis for various rules which limit the occasion and expression of war. By such core values I mean both the core elements of what makes a life go well – health, freedom from hunger, sufficient means to exercise real choices, friendship and participation in community – and basic moral rules to do with not attacking others, telling the truth, keeping promises and respecting property.

Third, as noted at the end of chapter 1, the ethical point of view involves making claims about the similar behaviour of others, whether or not they accept these judgements themselves. This 'universalizing' feature is certainly accepted as being the case within societies, and there is no reason in principle why it cannot be extended globally. One of the initial (but misleading) attractions of relativism is its critique of cultural imperialism – that is, imposing the values and norms of one society on another society. But to reject a universal ethic on this basis is to throw out the baby with the bathwater. To be sure, a reasonable global ethic is one that includes respect for diversity (of practice and of worldview), but it can also make proposals for universal norms and values which 'are-to-be-accepted' if they are not already widely accepted across the world – based on what the thinker regards as reasonable for others to accept.

Fourth, in any case, a relativist promoting the value of respect for diversity faces a dilemma. Either this is a proposed universal value for all to accept, so it is not a relativist principle at all, or it is just one local value that might not be accepted in another local culture (see Dower 1998: ch. 3, or Dower 2007: ch. 2, for more extensive treatment; and Borchert and Stewart 1986).

4.3   Communitarianism

A similar response can be given to the communitarian argument, though this approach raises a number of very serious issues, especially in regard to war. The communitarian argument is that the extent and strength of our obligations to others is a function of the kind of community to which we belong. Although we all belong to a number of different communities (our town, our church, the voluntary associations we join), the political community is the most significant one and shapes our primary loyalties. If we accept at all that there is wider community of humankind, it is a very weak one compared with our political community. On this view, our obligations to people in other parts of the world are significantly less in principle. Thus in deciding on a war the effects on other people can be discounted. If we are to fight enemy soldiers, the value of their lives can be discounted. On this view, we can indeed accept in principle that the life of an enemy soldier has as much value to him and to his community as the value of one of our soldiers has to himself and our community. But, from our point of view, it is of no or little significance. He belongs to another community.

Now there are three rather different ways of responding to this challenge. The first is to take on the communitarian on their own terms: the wider community of mankind is far more significant than this argument acknowledges. It is an error to privilege one's own political community as having some special status. This kind of argument has some kind of pull nowadays, especially at the beginning of the twenty-first century, when the processes of globalization have indeed created a whole new set of identities and have challenged the supremacy of national citizenship identity. But still it is a somewhat precarious argument, since there can be endless arguments about the relative strengths of different communities. Apart from the development of global community, there is and has been for a very long time another significant community, namely the community of nation-states, which in its own way creates a framework of obligations, not least about the occasions of war and the manner of fighting wars. The realist can deny that such a community really exists or, if it does exist, that it has any real significance. But many features in the world suggest otherwise: well-established international bodies hold frequent meetings, make many agreements and develop international law, and this looks like genuine community – and one cannot have a community without some shared values.

Second, one can argue that, in warfare, the direct contact soldiers have when fighting with each other challenges the separateness of communities. It is one thing for a country's foreign policy to be oriented towards its national interests, quite another for a soldier to privilege his own status and downgrade the status of the men he is fighting. The acknowledgement of our common humanity should lead to an acknowledgement that enemy soldiers (or civilians) have the same status as our own soldiers (or citizens). At least some kind of global ethic, that is, a universal ethic that recognizes the equal status of human beings, has to be acknowledged. In saying this I am not overlooking the painful fact that in war soldiers (or civilians supporting them) tend to demonize those whom they are fighting, and in extreme cases come to regard the enemy as sub-human and so on (as was the case in the Bosnian conflict in the mid-1990s). That there is a tendency – sometimes quite extreme – to distort and limit our understanding of the enemy is one of the problematic features of war. But here I am addressing the argument to the realist who is willing to take a relatively detached look (as I am attempting) at what is to be said when *humans* come into contact with each other in warfare.

Third, the communitarian perspective needs to be taken on fully by challenging its basis. What we need to recognize (and I shall be arguing for this throughout the book!) is not merely that there may be universal values – for instance, that all human beings need security, do not want to be killed, and so on – but that acknowledging this leads to a cosmopolitan perspective. I shall be explaining this idea more fully in the next chapter, but for now I want to indicate a feature of the cosmopolitan perspective:

this is the idea of transboundary responsibility. In principle, the cosmopolitan says, we have responsibilities towards everyone. Now in practice, for most people much of the time, what they are reasonably concerned with is a very limited group of people with whom they interact, whether it is in their own town, state or country. The cosmopolitan is not denying this fact. What he or she is saying is that sometimes our concerns should extend either to particular people in other parts of the world or to what happens more generally in other parts of the world or in the world as a whole.

The key point is that, if I am in a position where I affect the interests of other human beings in significant ways, then I need to take their interests seriously. There are, related to our concern here, two such cases: when a leader is contemplating going to war, and when a soldier is engaged in killing others. (There is a range of cases but these illustrate the point.) If one is a leader contemplating war, one cannot say, 'Well, the effects on others do not count as much because they are not our own people' – at least one cannot say this and adopt a cosmopolitan perspective, though it could be said from a communitarian perspective. If one is a soldier engaging in killing, one cannot say, 'Well, they are the enemy, their being killed does not matter'. Taking seriously the significance of the effects of the acts of soldiers does not in itself show that it should not be done. Some cosmopolitans who are pacifists take this line, but it is not implied by the point I am making.

In saying that the cosmopolitan maintains that, in principle, we have obligations towards everyone, I am aware that this will seem like an extravagant claim. Is it not obvious that we all have particular allegiances to some others (family, friends, and so on) whom we care very much more about, and likewise all have allegiances to particular communities (our town, our country) which we also care about more? Is cosmopolitanism denying these special attachments? The answer is that it is not, and the full story would take us too far from the present concerns. In a nutshell, the point is this: having particular allegiances and relationships are part of human nature, and it is from these that humans achieve a significant part of their well-being. Cosmopolitanism is committed to sustaining and creating the conditions of human well-being, so such allegiances are to be welcomed. What becomes problematic is when, in the light of these allegiances, we privilege some people at the expense of others in areas where we should not do so. How to draw the lines between the areas of legitimate partiality and the need for fairness and equal treatment is one of the challenges. The idea of a human rights framework setting limits to partiality is important here, and it has particular importance in relation to decisions made by people in public office and in situations where our

actions most dramatically impact on the rights of others, which is precisely the case in war.

The difference between communitarian thinking, which privileges the status of certain groups of human beings, and cosmopolitanism, which does not – or does not to the same degree and in the same way – is one of the most significant fault-lines in ethics, and the way we handle it makes some difference to how we handle the ethics of war (see, for instance, Cohen 1996; Dower and Williams 2002).

4.4 The role of the state, the duty of government and the democratic argument

As the world is now, nation-states are the dominant reality. The role of government is to exercise control throughout the territory over which the state has sovereignty. It is generally assumed that the duty of government is to look after the interests of its nationals (and others residing within a country). This is often seen as a kind of contract of government: in return for obedience to the laws, citizens get security, freedom and the conditions of material well-being. In a democracy it is expected that governments carry out what they are elected to do.

Do any of these arguments have the realist conclusion that government need only be concerned with promoting the national interests in foreign policy? This is far from evident. That the role of government is to further the interests of citizens, or even that there is a kind of 'deal' with citizens to do so, is one thing, that they have an *overriding* duty to do so is quite another. Consider a parallel, namely parenthood. Whether parenthood is a natural duty or rather a socially constituted family role, it is certainly a practical arrangement that serves the interests of children. The role and duty to further the interests of their children does not entail that parents can do anything they like in so doing. It certainly does not entail that they should not accept duties to other particular people or to society as a whole, and it certainly does not sanction activities such as stealing from others in order to provide one's children with what they need or want. The duties of this special relationship may be central, but they are consistent with other positive obligations and general moral limits on how one may exercise one's duty. Likewise with states. Given that we have states (there might be other ways of securing human stability, freedom and prosperity, but this is the current reality), their governments have special duties towards their nationals, but this should be seen as circumscribed by other duties towards other states and towards the international community (such as duties of humanitarian assistance in disasters) and duties of restraint. It is precisely in the area of war that these duties of restraint are significant.

What exactly these should be is a matter for debate: that they exist at all seems overwhelmingly plausible, *pace* the realist.

A similar way of dealing with the democratic argument is available, though this issue is rather complex. Suppose in a democracy the overwhelming will of the people is for war based on realist considerations or, for that matter, for militarist adventures. Does it follow that governments ought to pursue realist foreign policies and engage in wars without regard for moral restraints, or to engage in militarist adventures? This hardly seems to follow. The point to be made is analogous to one that J. S. Mill recognized long ago that, unless there are limits placed on what may be democratically authorized, there can be a 'tyranny of the majority' – the majority deciding that a minority may not live the way they want to or, worse, the majority wanting minorities to be subject to attack or to be persecuted (Mill [1859] 1962: introduction). What may be decided by democratic mandate in internal matters is often understood in terms of certain basic rights that may not be violated even by democratic decision (and sometimes these rights are expressly included in a bill of rights which constitutionally limits what may be decided democratically).

Exactly the same line of argument appears to make sense when we look at what may be done in foreign policy. If there are basic rights which all human beings enjoy, then a democracy cannot decide to pursue a policy which violates them. The just war approach can be understood as doing exactly this, providing a set of rules grounded in the rights of all that should limit how wars are fought and thus what may be democratically authorized. Exactly what those rules should be is a matter for debate. We do not currently have the equivalent of a bill of rights internationally linked to a global constitution. Perhaps international law including international human rights law is half-way there and may one day become cosmopolitan law as a part of a global polity. But it leaves much to interpretation, as things stand.

Commonly it is held that the targeting of non-combatants is morally off-limits, so that, in theory, a democracy cannot legitimately authorize it. Given that in the Second World War both Germany and Britain did directly target cities, we may have to conclude that either what was done was not legitimate, even if favoured democratically, or the lines need to be drawn in another place. Another area of controversy is nuclear weapons. If people in a country such as Britain are overwhelmingly in favour of having nuclear weapons, does that make the policy right and a legitimate form of defence? That is, it may be a necessary condition of policy being right, but is it a sufficient condition? Surely not. That depends on what one thinks of the ethics of nuclear deterrence. Some would say, yes, having nuclear weapons is fine, since conditionally to intend massive destruction is morally satisfactory even if carrying it out would not be; others would say that such a deterrence posture already violates the basic rights of millions of people and cannot be acceptable, even if it is democratically mandated.

Furthermore the democratic argument can lead to a different outcome even on realist grounds. If in a democracy the vast majority wish wars only to be fought if they meet certain ethical standards, then the foreign policy of that country ought not to follow the realist logic. In one sense it *is* the realist logic, since the 'interests' of the country are partly constituted by the 'moral' interests expressed by its electorate (cf. Morgenthau 1954: 10), but the conclusion is rather different from that which realists advocate. Likewise, if a country's electorate regarded or came to regard nuclear weapons as immoral, then a government would have a duty not to introduce or to discontinue them respectively.[2]

4.5   Security in a fragile world

This argument for the realist starts with an assumption which is as follows: in the world there is a real possibility or risk that other states may either attack one's country or, by the threat of attack, coerce it into situations contrary to its interests. They may do this either because they have expansionist ambitions or because they wish to project their different values. In order to reduce or eliminate this risk, one needs to develop a strong armed force, first to deter other countries from attacking or coercing one, second to deal with an attack if it occurs, and third to protect one's interests by attacking or threatening to attack other countries. Of course, if each country adopts the same reasoning, the argument from security becomes a self-perpetuating cycle of escalation.

The argument from security does not, however, lead to the realist conclusion that there cannot be any moral restraints in warfare. First, the argument for deterrence and defence, namely that a country needs to have a defence system which it is prepared to use, does not as such lead to the realist conclusion. All it leads to is the kind of argument, familiar enough, that in an insecure world we need to have military defence. That position is consistent with the ethical regulation of war and, indeed, is exactly what just war theory postulates. Having a defence force which one is prepared to use for the purposes of self-defence – something which, if anything does, counts as a just cause – and to use according to the rules of war is an ethically based argument.

Only if one thought that the only effective way of defending oneself was to be prepared – and to be publicly explicit about this – to attack when it suited one, and to use any methods necessary, would there be a realist account of defence. This variation of the motto 'attack is the best form of defence' really relies on cowing the enemy: other countries stay in line not because they know they will be repulsed if they attack, but through fear of what another powerful country might do. Now it may be sadly the case that in the real world the exercise of power by dominant countries works to some extent like this, but it certainly is not necessary to the idea of defence that one has both to threaten and to engage in war in a realist fashion. Defence and actual military operations premised on ethical criteria of just cause, non-combatant immunity, and so on, would appear to be all that is required. Whether even that is really necessary or – a separate question – ethically appropriate is another matter, to be taken up in later chapters. All I wish to show here is that trying to reduce insecurity based on the possibility of attack from other countries is not something that requires a realist response.

The realist may also want a country to be in a position to attack and to threaten to attack for whatever reasons as an aspect of foreign policy and advancing one's interests. But this is not something that is a *conclusion* drawn from being in an insecure world. It may be, though I doubt it, that this is the best way to advance one's interests in a world that is insecure because of the possibility of other countries attacking, and so on, but this is to assert the realist first premise, not to have it confirmed by insecurity. The general argument that one country can pursue its interests in any way that is effective has already been criticized: it gets no support from the fact that the world is insecure because of what other countries may do for realist reasons.

It may be thought that there is some kind of argument from reciprocity: in a world of realists one can act as a realist. But we should note that this does not get very far. First, it already concedes an ethical dimension: 'If you do x, it is all right for me to do x'. Second, it is in any case a dubious argument: it may be that attacking civilians is regarded as 'OK' because the other side is doing so, but the same is not going to go through for other kinds of action – if, for instance, enemy soldiers rape women and destroy historic monuments. It all depends on what is thought to be 'OK' in the circumstances, and that is an ethical argument after all. Third, it simply is not the case that the world is made up of states wholly pitted against each other for realist reasons: 99 per cent of international relations are in fact conducted on the basis of ethical norms, with the 1 per cent of actions undertaken out of naked self-interest, either as an unacceptable exception or as a justified defensible departure from the norms – but this does not support the realist denial of the applicability of norms in international relations.

4.6   War as the big exception

What can we make of the move that the decision to go to war is a decision to withdraw from the conventions of international society, namely that international relations are usually governed by moral norms, but the decision to go to war dispenses with this? The first difficulty with this is that it assumes a very limited notion of moral norms. The norms of international society can be seen either as based on conventions that arise from agreements and custom over time or as based on some theory about the nature and role of states. The latter can include the claim, for instance, that states have certain rights, or some wider ethical theory such as natural law (as in Aquinas or Grotius), or a cosmopolitan account which sees the state system as serving wider human values.

If the norms are seen as based on the second kind of reasoning – as I shall argue that they should be – then the moral norms governing states, including those to do with going to war, are not the kinds of norms one can decide to withdraw from. They apply, whether one likes it or not.

If the former approach is adopted, that the norms are based on conventional agreement, then there is the further question: Are those conventions to be seen as genuine moral norms such that a state cannot simply decide not to be bound by them? Or are the norms to be seen as based simply on prudence – each state signing up for the benefit of cooperation – in which case a state could decide to withdraw from the norms and the benefits of them too. Some conventions which we call 'moral' certainly seem to be of the latter kind, but they are barely 'moral' conventions, and it is questionable whether the norms of international relations really are as superficial as that.

In any case, what is striking is that a decision to have recourse to war is not really seen as a departure from the conventions of international society. A state that goes to war against another state still expects to be part of the international society in its dealings with all other states, and still expects the norms regulating other parts of international transactions – for instance to do with trade, telecommunications, and so on – to remain applicable. If a state really cast itself outside international society by withdrawing from all the conventions, that would be another matter – but it is not a real case (though a country such as North Korea has some of these features).

The situation with regard to the conduct of war is rather more complex. If one takes it that the norms about fighting wars are merely moral conventions, then the same points can be made: the conventions may be little more than considerations of prudence, to be dispensed with as appropriate, particularly if the other side does the same. If, on the other hand, the norms of war are seen as grounded in some basic moral principles, for instance about human rights that lead to the ban on attacking the innocent, and so on, then the option of withdrawing from the norms is not open. This seems right, as I shall argue later.

But the real challenge here is that, once it has started, there is a certain logic to war which militates against the idea of principled moral restraints. War just is, someone might say following Clausewitz, the compelling of the will of another country or group and requires the most effective means to do so. The fact is that war is dominated by the logic of the end, which is in conflict with the logic of the means. By this I mean that the prosecution of war *qua* war is dominated by an end or goal, that is, victory, and requires what is most effective to that end. By contrast, if the ethical conduct of war is shaped by the ethics of the means, then that suggests that there are certain ways of fighting which are acceptable and others which are not. The means has an independent moral character. It is not merely what is effective. The trouble is that the two clash.

The realist may be wrong to suppose that ethics is not applicable to the conduct of war, but he or she is right that the ethical impulse is always liable to be compromised by the logic of war. This is partly why the pacifist, in agreeing about this, regards the ethical conduct of war as problematic, and it is a question that the just war theorist has to weigh heavily: if wars are unlikely to be consistently conducted according to just war criteria, ought they to be embarked on at all?

5 Critique of Militarism

5.1 Crusading and lack of constraints

Referring back to the earlier discussion, I shall critique together (a) the crusading mentality and (b) the no restraints in war thesis.

Some wars have certainly been of a crusading nature – the attempt to destroy others because of their different values/beliefs or to undermine their values and beliefs by conversion or imposition of values after conquest. Hence in the late medieval period we have the 'crusades' so called, when Christians and Muslims pitted themselves against each other over several centuries of intermittent warfare in the Middle East. Militarism tends to see war always in these terms, and certainly recommends that it be so regarded. There are generally two consequences of this: the desire for absolute victory and acceptance of extreme measures. If after all 'right' is on one's side in a fight against evil, anything goes. This reflects in an extreme fashion a more general observation sometimes made, that the more one fights a war in the spirit of 'right against wrong' – as opposed to, say, fighting over issues of power and competing interests – the greater is the tendency and temptation to regard the means taken as merely justified by the end and not to exercise restraint in how one fights. This, however, is not a point about logic, since it is perfectly possible – and much just war thinking stresses it – that, however much one may think one's own side is on the side of 'right' (justice, Truth or whatever), one should observe moral restraints on how one fights for those ends (see Bull 1966 for an interesting discussion of this tension).

Two questions arise about seeing wars as crusades: Should all wars be thought of in this way? Should any wars be thought of in this way? Many wars are justified as fought for self-defence or in the defence of others, for instance other countries (allies such as Poland in the Second World War) or other people within other countries (humanitarian intervention) – for details, see chapter 4. These 'justifications' (often seen as part of what the just war theorist wants to claim) seem more reasonable. (Whether, all things considered, they do really make going to war right is another matter considered later.) They are also more likely to involve conditional surrender and negotiated peace, that is, termination of a war sooner rather than later, with less loss of life, greater chance of an acceptable (and sustainable) peace afterwards, and so on, even if one's victory is not so total by so doing, and a greater willingness to restrain the means of war.

What about wars that really are about opposing evil, such as currently the war against terror, or trying to convert others to such values as human rights or democracy, for example the ongoing war in Iraq, which is partly aimed at imposing democracy there? Are any such wars justified? Even if opposing evil is justified, does that mean destroying the other or demonizing/dehumanizing them as such – as opposed to merely checking or disabling them? Can we really impose our values elsewhere? Perhaps we can seek to convert others, but not by force. There are really two issues here. First, are such 'just causes' really just causes? Arguably these are not just causes for military intervention, as I shall argue in chapter 4, though other ways of trying to influence others may be acceptable. Second, even if one thinks that on some occasions such a just cause is an acceptable basis for war, it does not follow that the rest of the militarist approach applies. For instance, supposing such goals are permissible (either for a realist or for a just war thinker), does it follow that absolute victory is desirable or that any means goes? Absolute victory is costly and makes durable peace more difficult, and extreme means violate the ethics of the means (as we observed in regard to realism).

We may note that my criticisms are a mixture of arguments which could be addressed to some realists and to some just war thinkers. This is not surprising since, as recorded earlier, militarism is not so much an alternative to realism and just war thinking as an approach which characterizes what many but not all theorists in these two groups may believe. This same point will also be illustrated when we look at the remaining militarist arguments.

5.2   Military virtues and the life of community

The next two arguments, (c) that war is an expressive activity and (d) that war brings out military virtues and creates real community, may be taken together, since they seek to render war as something desirable.

There are various elements to military virtue, such as discipline, bravery, self-sacrifice and pushing oneself in extremis. But there are downsides: blind obedience, soldiers trained to be desensitized to the humanity of the enemy, and the general consequence of the exercise of these virtues being that terrible things are done to other human beings, military or civilian. If men become Men, are there not other ways in which men can become Men, or rather humans become Humans, which do not have these negative consequences? We might, for instance, think of service to others in difficult, dangerous or challenging situations, such as fire-fighting or grappling with the natural environment (without trying to destroy it). William James had something of this idea in his famous pamphlet 'The moral equivalent of war' (James [1910] 1970: 4–14). Likewise, strenuous sport, either competitive or simply challenging (such as rock climbing), exhibits virtues similar to those shown in war.

Let us concede for the sake of argument – what many would be reluctant to concede – that in army life and in combat some soldiers exhibit virtues. It is one thing to say that *if* there is war, then some humans find fulfilment in the virtues involved in fighting war; it is quite another to say that these virtues are *necessary* to human fulfilment (even to the fulfilment of these men in different circumstances). There is a parallel issue to do with community. Maybe a community finds a larger sense of community in war, but that does not make it preferable (given the consequences) to other forms of community bonding, nor does it imply that solidarities have to be formed at the expense or exclusion of others.

Is war an expressive activity? Yes, it can be, but that does not make it *essentially* expressive in the sense that without such manifestation humans are not fulfilled in their expressive activities. Service to others and working for peace/justice are also expressive, without the same negative consequences.

5.3   The human condition and the inevitability of war

Let us now turn to (e), the claim that war is a natural way of coping with human differences (as part of the human condition) and related claims.

If war is part of the human condition, does it follow that we need not avoid it, that we can arm aggressively to court it, and so on? If war is inevitable, it does not follow that its frequent outbreak is inevitable, or that we cannot at least reduce its incidence by treating it as a last resort, not arming to the teeth, and so on. Only if one thought that it was easily justifiable and/or a desirable thing would one have no reason to reduce its incidence.

But is war part of the human condition? Could we abolish war as we abolished slavery? Perhaps the institution of war, like the institution of slavery, could be abolished, but just as slavery continues to occur in other forms (see van den Anker 2004), no doubt various forms of war-like activity would continue. But, still, the resort to war and war-like activity could progressively become reduced over time if we devised a whole range of measures for doing so – and this is the agenda of pacificism. When we come to examine pacificism more closely (in chapter 6), we will see that in many ways its character can be brought out by seeing it as a series of assertions of the opposite points to those made by militarists.

What in sum is wrong with militarism is that its analysis of human nature and the human predicament is wrong and its system of values is wrong. Whether or not we can ever abolish war, we can at least work for the conditions in which its incidence is reduced: this is both possible and desirable. While it is no doubt true that there are forms of success and achievement associated with military 'virtue' (what it is that makes a *good* soldier), particularly in a society where such activity is accorded high recognition, the position that wars are a good thing fails to acknowledge its essentially negative features, not least the fact that, for any engagements in which there are acts of military virtue, significant losses will occur to both sides. War is necessarily a win–lose activity. Peace is generally a win–win state of affairs. There are plenty of other activities that can be undertaken that bring fulfilment even for a soldier in peacetime, and their being undertaken does not mean that someone else is dead and therefore no longer able to lead a fulfilling life.

As I remarked in chapter 1, militarism is not strictly an alternative on a par with realism and war justification. Many realists and war justifiers tend to have militarist attitudes, but there again many do not and tend more to the pacificist approach, and there are various positions in between too.

Questions

1 Should the pursuit of a state's interests be restrained in any way by ethical considerations?
2 In warfare, should normal moral rules be seen as suspended or overridden, or neither?
3 How is militarism different from realism?
4 Are there military virtues? If so, should they be cultivated, or should substitutes for them be found?

3 INTERNATIONALISM AND COSMOPOLITANISM

This chapter examines two approaches to international relations – internationalism and cosmopolitanism – and then locates various approaches to the ethics of war within them. Later chapters will look at the two main approaches to the ethics of war in their own right – the just war approach/ war justification position and pacifism – referring back at times to the international relations approaches. This chapter is largely descriptive. My defence of a certain form of cosmopolitanism is given elsewhere.[1]

1 Internationalism

1.1 Historical origins of internationalism

In 1648 the Peace of Westphalia concluded the so-called Thirty Years' War, which had raged on and off throughout Europe for many years. It is usually remembered because it was this peace treaty that formalized what is called the international system or nation-state system (see, for example, Miller 1990: ch. 2). The central principle in the new system was that Europe should be divided up into discrete geographical areas over which secular powers should exercise absolute control and authority. This way of understanding the division of control has broadly remained until the present day (though various forces seen as aspects of globalization have challenged it in the late twentieth and early twenty-first centuries). It started out as a European international 'society of states', but has now enlarged to cover the whole world. The process of European colonialism, in which each dominant European power took control of other areas of the world as parts of its 'imperium', spread the form of the European state apparatus. With the processes of decolonization now virtually complete, the world is understood as being made up of autonomous nation-states – over 190 of them as measured by current membership of the United Nations.

It is worth stressing an implication of the above. The world has been organized into the system of autonomous states for only a small period of its known human history. In earlier eras and in different parts of the world there have been considerable differences in how societies have been ordered – who has control over what, how relations between different groups have been understood. During the period of Greek history we call classical, Greece was divided into many different city-states, but then became absorbed as a whole into the Macedonian Empire. Rome at a later stage established an empire covering the whole of the Mediterranean area and beyond. From the fourth century AD onwards, after the collapse of the Roman Empire, Europe broke up into many different areas of rule, some large, some small. But by now the Christian Church was well established, and these new centres of rule were informed by the power and influence of the Roman and Orthodox churches. One of the continuing sources of conflict was over the respective power and influence of the religious authorities, such as those under the headship of the pope, and the separate principalities and kingdoms. Italy, for instance, in Machiavelli's day (sixteenth century) was dominated by strife between different principalities, not least the papacy itself, which controlled significant areas of Italy.

One of the important gains achieved by the Peace of Westphalia was the clearer division between the domain in which the Church exercised authority – spiritual matters – and that in which secular powers exercised authority – earthly matters. The rationale behind this was that, if a system could be established in which rulers had undisputed authority to rule over their subjects in a given geographical area and in which other rulers accepted this and respected their sovereignty, then the chances of peace and order were greatly improved.

Although a number of other justifications for it can be given (and will be discussed below), in its origins the nation-state system was grounded in the 'natural law' thinking of the Christian Church, which in the centuries before the Peace of Westphalia, so far as Western Europe was concerned, had meant the Roman Catholic Church. The natural law approach, which represented a complex tradition rather than a single doctrine, had nevertheless a central tenet. Thomas Aquinas, who is seen as the most profound and systematic exponent of this kind of theology, called the natural law the 'eternal law' as the latter pertained to the *nature* of a human being, and regarded it as discoverable by the exercise of natural *reason* (Aquinas [*c.*1270] 1953: I–II, qu. 94). The first precept of practical reason is that we should 'seek the good and shun evil', and this is understood in terms of the values of three levels of human life: existence as such, our animal nature and our rational nature, and so, correspondingly, we should accept the moral rules not to kill, to further life and seek life in society, and to seek knowledge of God and pursue generally the life of reason (see ibid.: I–II, qu. 91 art. 3; see also Finnis 1990 and, for application to international relations, Midgley 1975).

This conception is a universalist conception of human well-being, and the rules of morality deriving from it apply to our relations to *all* human beings. Fundamentally we all belong to the *civitas maxima*, the 'greatest city' of all human beings. So it is in a sense a cosmopolitan conception, as we will discuss later in the chapter. Nevertheless, Aquinas and others recognized that, because of our human weakness and proneness to sin and wrongdoing, we need to live in organized societies. The order within such societies can only be maintained by coercion, which involves having *rulers* with the power to enforce moral rules through the sanctions of punishments.

Aquinas was concerned with the need to justify the use of violence and coercion where it was needed in contrast to the general use of violence. Strictly speaking, from his point of view the use of force (including killing force) was not violence if it was legitimate: violence is the illegitimate use of force.[2] Rulers had the authority to use killing force and to go to war to defend what they ruled, but others, such as private citizens, pirates, and so on, did not. Such use of force maintained social order. For Aquinas the authority which made killing force which would otherwise be violence into legitimate force and the exercise of law (civil law as the expression of the natural law) was given essentially by God, that is, it was a divinely instituted arrangement whereby rulers ruled particular groups of people for the common good.

Other forms of justification for rule have been given by other thinkers. These include such factors as tradition, consent, democratic mandate, and so on, and these will be considered later in this chapter. What they all seek to provide is a justification for the power of rulers or states and their use or threat of killing force, either against their own citizens (if they step out of line) or against others in war, which would otherwise be sheer power and violence.

It is against this background that we can understand the thinking which led to the international system formally instituted at the time of the Peace of Westphalia. Although there was an appeal to the universal natural law and the idea of a *civitas maxima* in the background, the practical task was to establish principles of legitimate rule, and especially to establish respect for the *de facto* division of power in Europe at the time.

Hugo Grotius was a Dutch jurisprudentialist whose *On the Law of War and Peace* in 1625 made a large impact on the thinking about international relations and the regulation of war at the time and since (Grotius [1625] 1925). He accepted in the main the natural law framework, but made much of the fact that, in an uncertain and hostile world, the right of individuals to preserve themselves and promote their interests was central. This applied equally to nation-states, which had by then become the dominant reality in Europe. But, unlike Hobbes, Grotius also affirmed the other central ethical principle that we ought not to cause unnecessary or wanton injury to others. So, on the basis of these two principles, we can formulate a relationship between states in which states are primarily concerned with their own survival and advancement but are also obliged to respect the like aspirations of other states. We should also note that this kind of morality is not a very extensive one, and its limited scope has been a feature of the 'morality of states' or internationalist tradition.

Before leaving Grotius, we should note his observation – the so-called impious hypothesis – about the laws derived from the natural law that, while they were (of course) the commands of God (as applied to human nature), they would be valid even if there were no God to command them (Grotius [1625] 1925; see also Tuck 1989: 20–3; and Jeffrey 2006), and that, whatever Grotius's personal theological views, there is an implied secularization of the ethical basis of morality in this remark. Later thinking within the internationalist tradition, and indeed in cosmopolitanism too, lost the original theological anchorage and provided various secular bases for a commitment to some kind of global ethic which is universal in the way the natural law theory postulates a universal moral order. A number of these will be considered later in the chapter. Others in the internationalist tradition also lost sight of the key cosmopolitan idea that the natural law applied to one's relations with all human beings, that is, that the ultimate justification of the moral rules governing states resides in the impacts these have on human beings as such, but rather saw the international norms as based on custom and conventional agreement. For example, insofar as the rules of war (*ius ad bellum* and *ius in bello*) are associated with the internationalist tradition, there are different bases for these which are discernible, some grounded in universal morality, others in the conventions of states.

1.2   The main elements of the morality of states

In *The Anarchical Society*, Bull identifies four values or goals of the international society. These are, in descending order of importance (Bull 1977: 15–21):

(a) the preservation of the system or society of states itself. States together make up a 'society' of states, and as with any society there is an inherent tendency towards self-maintenance. Furthermore there need to be rules of conduct for the representatives of states which enable international relations to be conducted as smoothly as possible, such as the complex but important rules to do with the treatment of diplomats – ambassadors, messengers, peace negotiators, and so on – and the whole system of international protocol.

(b) the maintenance of the independence and external sovereignty of individual states. It is an essential goal of the international society to maintain the independence and external sovereignty of individual states. In practice this is the most prominent feature of the morality of states, since it concerns the key duty to respect one another's sovereignty, and therefore not to attack or threaten to attack other countries, to intervene in the internal affairs of other countries, and so on. This right is regarded as crucial but not absolute, since it does not follow that there are no occasions at all in which interference or intervention may not be justified for the sake of goal (a). For instance, it may be based on reasons of 'common security', which in UN terminology picks first upon goal (a), or on reasons to do with rectifying injustice, which links to the idea of the just war, or on reasons of maintaining a balance of power or spheres of influence.

(c) the maintenance and pursuit of peace. It is only in conditions of peace and order that the central goals of social life can be pursued, and so peace is regarded as an overall goal. But peace is not seen, as perhaps some idealists might see it, as an overriding goal, something to be aimed at above all else or understood in idealistic terms. There may be circumstances, such as the need, under (a), to maintain international order or, under (b), to defend one's state or to rectify injustice, in which peace may be deliberately and justifiably abandoned. However, the development of the 'just war' tradition was an attempt to put limits on violence, by seeking to clarify just what were the limited circumstances in which the decision to go to war was justified and also by putting restrictions on who may legitimately wage war, namely nation-states themselves as 'legitimate authorities'. Historically, since the development of the nation-state system, the just war approach belongs to the internationalist tradition, though, as we shall see later on, it can be supported by some cosmopolitans as well. How far an internationalist is keen to set limits to violence and pursue peace depends on various factors, for instance, how easy or difficult it is to establish a just cause. It may seem paradoxical, but by seeking to limit legitimacy to states themselves and claiming that states have the 'monopoly of the legitimacy of violence', to use a phrase of Weber's (Weber [1919] 2000), the goal was to limit violence in the world.

(d) the common goals of social life. Bull identifies three main goals of society as the security of the person against violence, the honouring of promises and agreements, and the stability of possessions, and this is reflected in the rights and corresponding duties concerning respect for life, promises and property. Bull takes it that these goals, because they are common to all societies, also form the basis for the way states interact with one another. That is, insofar as the international community has an interest in social values for the morality of states, it is interested in those on which there is universal agreement. In practice this does not mean that states have a duty or right actively to promote these values in other societies. This is far from being the case, since the whole thrust of the approach was to protect the internal affairs of states from external interference. Rather, these values inform the morality of states with respect to those areas where interactions between states take place. The most obvious areas are war and commerce.

While war is intrinsically destructive of life, the rules of war (*ius in bello*) can be seen as an attempt to limit the violence of war and its destructiveness by placing restrictions on who may be direct objects of attack and in what ways one may legitimately fight. Likewise, if international trade and commerce are to flourish, then there needs to be some general principle of honouring agreements (even outside a mechanism to enforce compliance which Hobbes thought necessary). Similarly international law develops alongside particular agreements and treaties between states. This would not be possible unless there was a general expectation that these agreements would be kept. This principle concerning the general honouring of agreements is often still referred to as *pacta sunt servanda* ('pacts are to be kept').

Bull's identification of the common goals of social life as a basis for part of international morality raises a further question. Are these the only common social goals? What about the value of liberty or the norm of truthfulness, or the norms of mutual caring expressed in benevolence or social justice? These are not as well reflected in international norms, partly because there is less agreement both about them and about their importance for international relations. Certainly the norm of truthfulness has only been partially observed in international conduct, since deception and lack of transparency have often been the norm in actual behaviour. And there has been a conspicuous absence of any norm of benevolence and social justice in international relations. Indeed, what is striking about this international morality is what is not included as much as what is. The point is important because the dispute with cosmopolitanism arises partly because certain things are missing.

One thing that is missing is any reference to a duty actively to promote the global common good, except insofar as the maintenance of the society of states and international order is itself a crucial common good, or to a duty to promote the good of other individual states or the well-being of individuals who may be suffering within other states. Generally the right of states to pursue their own interests is the central principle, and provided that what they do does not actively damage or undermine the interests of other states, which would be seen as a form of interference, they legitimately have no interest in such positive global goals – unless they have entered into specific bilateral or multilateral agreements (that is, pacts) to come to other states' aid.

Beitz characterized this general feature of the morality of states as the 'international analogue of nineteenth century liberalism' (Beitz 1979: 66). Traditional liberalism (like modern libertarian thinking) put stress on the value of liberty, economic and otherwise, of consent as the basis of transactions and of non-interference, but did not assert a general obligation of positive caring for those who were less fortunate (even if the latter's misfortunes were a result of the way the economic system operated).

Another thing which is missing from the tradition is a certain approach to the status of the individual within the system, which also puts it in conflict with cosmopolitan thinking. Individual human beings were from a legal point of view regarded as objects, not subjects, of international law. The implication of this was that, in terms of the 'laws of nations' or, following Bentham, 'inter-national' law, states were the only legal 'persons' involved; individuals had no rights under international law and could not take legal action against states, and they affected states only insofar as states took them into consideration in their dealings with one another.

The development of human rights thinking, particularly in the second half of the twentieth century, has challenged these presumptions. Apart from the more technical issue to do with international law (which is changing, partly because of human rights thinking), it is in this area concerning the relationship of the individual to the state in the international context that many cosmopolitans have reason to take issue with the traditional morality of states approach. For instance, human rights thinking, informed by cosmopolitan assumptions, has both an ethical and a legal expression, and leads to the idea of both ethical and legal justification for intervention in other countries in defence of human rights, possibly involving humanitarian military intervention. Not all cosmopolitans would support the latter, but the point is that individual human beings have for many theorists a new status in thinking legally and ethically about international relations (see chapter 7, §4).

In summary, then, we can identify the following key ethical elements of the 'morality of states' approach:

(a) States have a duty to support the society of states.
(b) States have a duty to respect the sovereignty, autonomy and independence of other states.
(c) States have a duty not to interfere with or intervene in the internal affairs of other states.
(d) States alone have the right to engage in organized violence.
(e) States have a general duty to promote peace, but have a right to wage war if they have a just cause.
(f) States have a duty to observe restrictions in the conduct of war.
(g) States have a duty to keep agreements, including international laws to which they are signatories.
(h) States have a duty not to harm other states, but have no duty in general to promote a global common good, the good of other states or the good of individuals living in other states.
(i) Individual human beings are objects, not subjects, of international law and do not have rights against any states except perhaps their own.

Thus, in summary, the underlying rationale of the internationalist approach is the preservation of the international order of states. Both 'order' and 'states' are important. It is a basic order in which states themselves, and other organizations such as business companies and individuals, conduct themselves according to rules which maintain by and large peace and stability. But states themselves are the primary actors and intend to maintain that. States reserve the right to engage in military activity, either on their own or in concert with others, to defend themselves if their sovereignty is challenged, and for various other reasons – different reasons having been accepted at different times (see also Nardin 1983).

For instance, it was regarded as legitimate to acquire foreign territories as part of colonial expansion, in order to pacify a world according to the understanding of the colonizer, but also as an exercise of national interests seen as a legitimate reason for military operations. Towards the end of the twentieth century humanitarian intervention, as in Kosovo in 1999, was seen as another reason for military engagement. On the other hand, the right of states to defend themselves, which had been central to international relations, came to be modified by the middle of the twentieth century. Ever since the setting up of the United Nations in 1945, the UN Security Council has technically, according to the Charter, taken over the right to wage war on another state, with individual states retaining only the right of self-defence in emergency situations. Rules about when it is legitimate to fight wars, and also about how to fight then, have evolved over the centuries and have come to be accepted in the international society of states and generally encoded in international laws such as The Hague Conventions (1899, 1907) and the Geneva Conventions (1949).

2 Cosmopolitanism

2.1 The setting

Cosmopolitanism is the claim that all human beings are in some sense 'citizens of the world' (see, for instance, Heater 2002; Dower 2003). The idea of being a world citizen goes back to the classical world of the Stoics (though actually the idea first surfaced among the less influential Cynics). Many of the Stoics, such as Epictetus, Pliny, Seneca and Cicero, asserted in one way or another that we were 'cosmo-politeis', which literally translated means 'citizens of the universe'. As MacIntyre put it: 'There is one divine universe, one rational human nature, and therefore one appropriate attitude to all men. The Stoic is a citizen of the *cosmos* not of the *polis*' (MacIntyre 1967: 107). What they were concerned with, then, was not primarily asserting membership of a society or political community in this world, but about a certain religious or metaphysical conception of our relationship to the universe and the divine order.

The affirmation of our common humanity was, however, a significant part of the conception. The Stoics were distancing themselves from a view that one's being a citizen in the ordinary sense was a central fact of one's identity. Membership of this or that political community – a city-state, a larger state or even the Roman Empire – was a contingent fact of one's birth at a particular time and place. This was in contrast to a common Greek understanding as expressed in Aristotle's famous claim that 'man is a political animal' – a being, that is, who realizes his nature or essence by living and participating in a particular political community, namely for Aristotle the Greek city-state (Aristotle [*c*.350 BC] 1988: 1252 b30-1253 a3).

One might have been born into quite a different society – that is accidental – but one's being human is a more basic and essential fact. This perception of themselves did not generally lead the Stoics to give up allegiances to their communities or to the Roman Empire, and generally it did not lead to an otherworldly lack of interest in the social issues of the well-being of people. (The issue is discussed by Nussbaum and her critics in Cohen 1996.) Indeed, one of the interesting metaphors which they employed was that of a series of concentric rings in which there are different levels of identity, meaning and loyalty – such as family, state, world, universe.

2.2 Four dimensions to cosmopolitanism

Four areas of issues can be identified within cosmopolitanism.

That which first comes to mind in thinking about cosmopolitanism is the general area of global ethics – identifying, defending and applying a kind of global ethic, or world ethics as I called it (Dower 1998, 2007). This subdivides into two areas.

First, there is global ethics as applied to individuals conceived of as 'citizens of the world'. This is about the basic universal values and moral rules that ought to inform human conduct *in* any part of the world, and about transnational obligations *towards* people in other parts of the world. The latter include our responsibility for addressing world poverty, promoting peace or helping to save the environment. For instance, cosmopolitans either have certain views about the rules that ought to govern fighting, that is rules governing the actions of individual humans in relation to other human beings – and these may or may not coincide with the received wisdom on *ius in bello* – or reject warfare altogether in the light of their global ethic. Likewise, cosmopolitans have views – sometimes differing views – about the nature and extent of the commitment of individuals to promote the conditions of (sustainable) peace, not merely for their own society but for people generally in the world.

Second, there is global ethics – sometimes called international ethics – as applied to nation-states and international relations, but also to other corporate bodies such as business companies, as the global dimension to business ethics. Here cosmopolitans, given their basic ethics, assess the behaviour of states as meeting or more or less falling short of their values, especially in the area of war and peace. If a cosmopolitan is a pacifist he or she will criticize states for their war preparations and military activities, and also argue for a strong commitment – stronger than is usually shown – for promoting the conditions of peace. A cosmopolitan who is a war justifier is nevertheless likely to criticize states for their military preparations, postures and activities insofar as these are not justified by his or her cosmopolitan ethic, and argue in addition for a strong commitment to promoting the conditions of peace. That is, cosmopolitans, at least of the non-dogmatic kind I commended in chapter 1, are generally pacificists, because they all share a strong ethical commitment to promote or further peace anywhere (see §§2.3 and 2.4 below for further elaboration of non-dogmatic cosmopolitanism).

A quotation from Charles Beitz, a modern cosmopolitan, illustrates both levels. He reinforces the implications of asserting the thesis in his work when he says:

> It is cosmopolitan in the sense that it is concerned with the moral relations of members of a universal community in which state boundaries have a merely derivative significance. There are no reasons of basic principle for exempting the internal affairs of states from external moral scrutiny, and it is possible that members of some states might have obligations of justice with respect to persons elsewhere. (Beitz 1979: 181–2)

We now come to the area of cosmopolitan thought which is concerned with the social, political or institutional expressions of cosmopolitanism (what 'polites' and 'polis' capture in the idea). This too subdivides into two further main areas of enquiry.

The third area is concerned with the social and political expression of global citizenship – in, for instance, social organizations and networks, non-governmental organizations (NGOs) and global civil society; in political engagement in international contexts, for instance in international NGOs, but more commonly in globally oriented engagement in politics in one's own country; in legal expression such as human rights instruments; and in the development of shared 'global ethics' such as *The Earth Charter* (Earth Council 2000) or the *Declaration toward a Global Ethic* (Parliament of World Religions 1993). The relevance to war and peace is this. The greater involvement of people as global citizens in political and social movements, the less likely it is that nation-states adopt the 'national interest' policies that lead to war. The greater the extent to which people around the world work together with shared ethical codes which respect the diversity of worldviews that may support them, the less likely the resort to war is favoured.

Finally, there is the area that focuses on the character of global governance and the kinds of global institutions which are needed to realize the cosmopolitan vision, such as the United Nations or future modifications of or alternatives to the UN. This is important to the cosmopolitan in regard to war and peace because it is only if we can develop the right kinds of global governance that we can create the institutions through which a more sustainable peace can be achieved. Cosmopolitan proposals for various forms of global governance may range from fairly modest proposals for improving the way the international system works through to proposals for world government – with various positions in the middle such as the proper institutional recognition of the roles of global civil society and proposals for cosmopolitan democracy (see, for example, Archibugi and Held 1995 or McGrew 2000).

Chris Brown characterizes cosmopolitanism in a way that illustrates these differing approaches:

> In the first place, cosmopolitanism has no necessary connection with the desire for world government. The Stoics lived under a 'world' government; that was precisely the problem – how to make sense of life in a context in which the coming of Empire had eliminated the previous focal points of existence. Cosmopolitanism is compatible with the rejection of politics, or with a pragmatic acceptance of existing political structures such as the states of eighteenth-century Europe. What is crucial to a cosmopolitan attitude is the refusal to regard existing political structures as the source of ultimate value. (Brown 1992: 24)

These four areas can be indicated diagrammatically, as in table 3.1.

2.3   What kind of a global ethic is a cosmopolitan ethic?

This idea of a cosmopolitan ethic is of course an example of a global ethic, but it would be a mistake to regard the two phrases as meaning the same thing.

First, a global ethic need not, though usually it does, include any claim about transboundary obligations, whereas a cosmopolitan ethic stresses this. A global ethic *qua* global ethic is simply one that stresses that certain values are either, descriptively, universally or at least widely accepted all

Table 3.1   Four areas of cosmopolitanism

	Ethical	*Institutional*
Individual	Global citizenship as a commitment to a global ethic or possession of a universal moral status	Global citizenship as embedded in global civil society, cosmopolitan democracy, globally oriented citizenship, international human rights law, etc.
State	Ethics of international relations from a global ethics point of view, hence generally a critique of international relations	Proposals for (new forms of) global governance, a new global political order, a neo/post-Westphalian order, stronger international institutions, cosmopolitan law, world government

over the world or, normatively, universal in applicability and so should be regarded as universal (see Kim 1999; Parekh 2005). Such a global ethic might be concerned with, for instance, universal norms which are applicable to *how wars are to be fought*. As such it would not be cosmopolitan, especially if the reasons for going to war were centred on national interests or the rights of states. Coates provides an example of the acceptance of just war theory as being universalist but not cosmopolitan (Coates 1997: 7). For a global ethic to be cosmopolitan it would need to be concerned not merely with how one behaves in relation to war (concerning decisions about how or in what circumstances one fights or whether to fight at all), but with *promoting* certain core values. If one's cosmopolitanism is non-dogmatic and pacificist, this includes promoting peace and, whether or not a cosmopolitan supports occasional military action, generally opposing war as an instrument of policy, because it usually undermines the global common good.

Second, while anyone calling him- or herself a global citizen or a member of a global community would subscribe to a global ethic, the converse does not hold. Someone accepting a global ethic may nevertheless have reservations about the more complex claims of global citizenship, membership of a global community and cosmopolitanism. At the very least the 'citizenship' bit of cosmopolitanism implies a claim about the current status of human beings: namely that all human beings belong to one moral community where declaring that we all belong to a moral community says more than 'I have moral obligations towards all human beings as such'. An internationalist might accept a global, that is, universal, ethic as applicable to war, but not see him- or herself as a cosmopolitan.

This idea of community is important for two reasons: first, a claim is made about common values which apply to everyone in the community, and, second, a claim is made that members of the community have obligations towards one another across the membership of the community. Someone who makes a claim that he or she is a global citizen is usually making a twofold claim: (a) that he or she has a certain identity, accepts transboundary responsibility and, as an active 'engaged' global citizen, expresses this in various ways; and (b) that all human beings as such have a certain moral status as global citizens, even if they are not 'active' global citizens and do not even acknowledge that status.

Within the broad field of cosmopolitan thought there are also varieties of cosmopolitan ethics themselves – that is, different views about the content of a cosmopolitan ethic, its scope and its justification, and indeed different views also about the critique of international relations, and about its institutional expression in things such as global civil society or world government. For example, the cosmopolitanism based on religious dogmatism bent on promoting its specific worldview everywhere is at odds with a cosmopolitanism that promotes liberalism, democracy and respect for human rights,[3] and this again may be at odds with a cosmopolitanism that wants to combine as much respect as possible for diversity of cultural practice with a firm international commitment to create the conditions for the good life, however that is to be defined.

As noted above, a cosmopolitan ethic is capable of many interpretations and diverse justifications. It may be based on religious premises, for instance, about the implications of the religious idea of the brotherhood of humankind, or philosophical theories about, for instance, human rights. Kantianism and utilitarianism are both examples of global ethics which propose universal values and transboundary obligations, as indeed does Beitz's application of Rawls's theory to the world as a theory of global social justice (Beitz 1979: part III). (See §5 at the end of this chapter for an account of some of these.)

2.4   The relationship between a global ethic and its supporting worldview

One important difference implied in the above between dogmatic and non-dogmatic cosmopolitanism is between a cosmopolitan global ethic that includes a particular worldview such as a religious worldview as part of what is to be promoted, and a cosmopolitan global ethic which consists in a number of general norms and values but which does not include any particular worldview. In other words, the latter is presented as a global ethic which could be supported by people with different worldviews, including many with religious worldviews. For each cosmopolitan their worldview supports or rationalizes the ethic they accept, but they recognize that others will support the same ethic for their own different reasons. As Kim notes,

> Charles Taylor attempts to throw new light on the relationship between diversity and universality by making a distinction between the fact of cross-cultural consensus on certain norms and values and the divergent ways of their justification. Background justification may differ from society to society, whilst factual agreement on the norms themselves would be left unaffected by the differences of underlying belief. (Kim 1999: 30)

Likewise Parekh argues for a global ethic to which we can give both our *assent* – given our own particular but differing intellectual stories – and our *consent* as a product of cross-cultural dialogue (Parekh 2005: 26). In a sense a global ethic can be seen as a set of norms/values (GE) supportable from many points of view, or as a set of norms/values *plus* supporting story/worldview (GE+). Any cosmopolitan thinker has a global ethic in this full sense (GE+): the question is whether his interest is in seeking convergence over a GE or persuading others to accept his GE+.

Cosmopolitanism has often been inspired by a religious or political truth the promotion of which is felt to be important, if necessary by war and conquest, for instance holy war or jihad. In other words, the global ethic included the theological story which is to be imposed on a world that does not accept that story. If conquest is necessary to create political order in the world through empires, then conquest can to some extent be justified in terms of this cosmopolitan vision. This approach is still common in the modern world – witness right-wing Christian fundamentalism and a common assumption in Islam, both of which may, but neither of which need, involve advocating the use of violence in the spreading of the message. An extreme example is the agenda of Islamic terrorists which may be partly inspired by the desire to create a world ordered under Islamic principles, as is the agenda of some Western thinkers who want to impose Western liberal democratic values on others elsewhere by force.

What is characteristic of much modern cosmopolitan thinking, however, is the non-dogmatic approach, which not only advocates respecting diversity and generally using nonviolent means, but stresses the importance of a global ethic, not a global ethic +. My main concern from now on when discussing cosmopolitanism is with the non-dogmatic approach and its implications for thinking about war and peace (unless the context makes it clear that I am referring to other kinds of cosmopolitanism).

It is not that modern cosmopolitanism is not motivated by a desire to create a world inspired by certain basic values and structured with appropriate institutions to express them. It is merely that, in the modern world, trying to do so by conquest is often seen as not appropriate. This is partly because the vision that most modern cosmopolitans have in mind is not one based on specific moral or religious principles not currently accepted or available to people in other parts of the world, but one based on certain primary goods and principles of social order which are both reasonable for anyone to accept and, it is believed by a holder of the view, likely to become acceptable through a process of consultation and dialogue, and so on. It is partly that the values of consultation, participation, dialogue and democratic engagement are among the core values that the cosmopolitan wants to promote anyway. It needs to be stressed that 'vision' here does not equal 'worldview'. It may be that the vision of traditional cosmopolitans was precisely to create a world in which their worldview was accepted. This is not the goal of non-dogmatic cosmopolitans. They have a worldview – religious or secular – which may be their inspiration, but their vision is of a world of converging values informed by a variety of world-views.[4] Indeed many of the strongest advocates of peace and a cosmopolitan responsibility to promote it are people of religious conviction, whether from a Christian, Buddhist or other approach (see chapter 8, §2 for further remarks on the contribution of religion to thinking about war and peace).

3   Cosmopolitanism and internationalism: some contrasts

3.1   General contrast between cosmopolitanism and internationalism

We can see first that the general *goal* of the cosmopolitan is rather different to that of the internationalist. The cosmopolitan has a set of values and norms which he or she thinks should be universally adopted and seeks ways to promote these. Typically modern cosmopolitans are concerned with finding the appropriate ways of promoting the conditions of the good life and a reasonable social order for all people anywhere, supporting international institutions to the extent that they do this, and proposing and working for institutions of global governance that will do so more effectively.

If we turn to the means which the cosmopolitan either accepts or advocates, we will find significant differences. Differences of view over the means can be over what is regarded as effective in promoting one's goals and over what kinds of means are ethically acceptable in themselves. Whether and to what extent cosmopolitans will endorse the use of force depends on a number of factors, some to do with their more specific goals and values aimed at, some to do with the kinds of means that they recommend, both in terms of effectiveness and in terms of their inherent moral character. Such differences would not have been apparent so much in the past since, as I noted in the last section, traditional cosmopolitans embarking on holy wars would justify the resort to violence as much as would internationalists, though their reasoning might be different. But in the modern era it can be said that, generally, whether a non-dogmatic cosmopolitan accepts the use of force occasionally or not at all, his or her general approach to war and peace in regard to what is right to do and what is effective tends to be rather different from that of the internationalist.

Non-dogmatic cosmopolitans on the whole believe that the appropriate means for achieving positive change in the world according to their vision is to promote change internationally by peaceful means, by working on international institutions in such ways as to make them more effective, to limit the kinds of contexts in which states might be tempted to act militarily for their advantage, and to tackle the root causes of tension in the world, such as addressing as significantly as possible the challenges of world poverty and environment insecurity.

This does not exclude the possibility that such a cosmopolitan could recognize that there may be circumstances in which military action is necessary, both where particular political communities are threatened by other political communities and where human rights violations occur within some territorial boundary. Even those cosmopolitans who accept these two kinds of case do so with circumspection, and with an insistence that such action is authorized by the UN Security Council, rather than action taken by a state or group of states acting independently.

It is worth noting here a kind of paradox. Since 1945 basically the right to wage war has been transferred to the United Nations Security Council. Officially this is still a position within the internationalist tradition, that is, a position which has come about because states themselves have authorized this body to act on their behalf. Nevertheless there is a sense in which, if the Security Council genuinely acts on behalf of humanity rather than reflecting power struggles, it reflects a cosmopolitan approach. I shall have more to say later on about how we should conceptualize the United Nations, both in terms of what we have now and in terms of future possibilities (see also chapter 7, §4.3 and chapter 8, §3).

It is, then, perfectly possible for a modern cosmopolitan (of the non-dogmatic kind) to accept the need for military activity, but it is equally the case that many cosmopolitans in the modern world would be reluctant to endorse the use of military force for these reasons.

The dilemmas facing a cosmopolitan can be brought out with the following question: Is the idea of a 'cosmopolitan military' an oxymoron? That is, can we make sense of the idea of a military force that, instead of being a force of a particular country pursuing the goal of that country's government, is cosmopolitan in either structure or purpose, or is the very idea of a cosmopolitan approach inconsistent with such a force?

The answer, given certain pacifist conceptions of cosmopolitanism such as Soran Reader's (see chapter 5, §3.2) and how it applies to the world, is yes, the idea of a military based on cosmopolitan values is absurd. A cosmopolitan could not support armies and hence wars fought by armies. But on other conceptions of cosmopolitanism and readings of the world, the idea of a military either pursuing cosmopolitan goals or constituted by a cosmopolitan authority does make sense.

If operations were carried out by a country (such as Tanzania in its invasion of Uganda in 1979) or an alliance (such as NATO in Kosovo in

1999) *and* the operations were wholly devoted to cosmopolitan goals such as humanitarian intervention, then such a force might be called a cosmopolitan military in virtue of its goal. If the UN – not formally a cosmopolitan authority but the nearest we have to one – organized or authorized such a force, then such a force would arguably be one in virtue of its authority. In a way a UN peacekeeping force already has some of the form of this, insofar as the troops contributed by member countries in assuming the blue helmets take on (or at least should take on) a new set of allegiances. If in a future world there were a world state, then action against recalcitrant states, areas or groups, if it involved the systematic organized and hierarchically controlled use of killing force, would be a cosmopolitan military, though our being able to conceptualize it as in effect global 'policing' may turn out to be a significant move. Whether our form of cosmopolitanism allows us to support such a future force or the various current examples that approximate to a cosmopolitan military is another matter.[5]

There are two further questions that could be asked here: First, does the internationalist justify more occasions for war and a wider range of ways of fighting war than does the cosmopolitan? Second, does the internationalist tradition provide a more effective basis for limiting warfare, or does the kind of non-dogmatic cosmopolitanism I am advocating have a better prospect of limiting warfare? These are not the same questions, though similar. The first is about the nature of the justification; the second is about the effect of a certain kind of approach.

3.2   Would cosmopolitanism limit war?

To take the second question first: the internationalist tradition is a tradition with certain well-established sets of understandings which provides a certain stability to the way things go in international relations. Cosmopolitanism does not have the advantages of such a tradition. I do not mean that there is not a tradition of cosmopolitan thinking, but it has hardly been mainstream and, because it has not been mainstream, it comes in a variety of forms. This very variety may, it could be argued, have an unsettling effect on how diplomatic decisions are made, and the fact that cosmopolitanism adopts a critical stance, however diplomatically expressed, vis-à-vis the primacy of the nation-state itself contributes potentially to disorder. To draw on an idea that Hedley Bull once used, cosmopolitans are often more keen on ideas of justice in the world at the expense of order in the world, and this, it may be thought, while highly principled, is a prescription for instability and thus, ironically, the occasion for more military conflict in the world (Bull 1977: ch. 4).

On the other hand, non-dogmatic cosmopolitanism may be thought of as providing a different way of looking at the world in which the principles of peace and justice go together and in which the typical occasions for war are regarded as problematic. It is one in which any decision to resort to war, if justified at all, is taken with great care and reluctance, and with greater willingness than is often currently shown, seriously to use the international organization we already have, namely the United Nations, and its organs such as the Security Council, for genuinely global goals.

3.3   Would cosmopolitanism justify fewer wars than internationalism?

Going back to the first question, it seems fairly clear that historically both internationalists and cosmopolitans were more inclined to accept various reasons for going to war than nowadays. Indeed in the early years of the Westphalian system in many ways there was a cosmopolitan basis for the internationalist order, and reasons of justice as a basis for war had a foundation in a universal global ethic, generally understood in the natural law tradition. Insofar as a war might be based on a firm commitment to a principle of objective justice (such that one was clear that one side was in the right and the other side in the wrong), there might be reason to treat the enemy more harshly as being evil or the infidel in terms of the restraints on how to fight the war. Later, especially in the nineteenth century, there came to be accepted the principle of political pluralism according to which it was difficult, if not impossible, to ascertain whether one side had justice on its side and the other side did not, since both sides claimed it, and this led to greater emphasis being put on the rules of war concerning how to fight. This kind of approach is less attractive to a cosmopolitan (and cosmopolitan thinking was very much in abeyance or sidelined at the time). The principle of pluralism, however, did not stop wars; it merely meant that, if wars were waged, both sides could claim they had some degree of justice on their side.

If we look at the modern situation, it would appear that the internationalist approach has become somewhat tamed by the modern 'legalist paradigm', to use Walzer's phrase, which restricts just cause to defence against aggression (Walzer 1977: 58). Cosmopolitan thinking tends to go in different directions. On the whole a non-dogmatic cosmopolitan focuses primarily on building the institutions of peace, the conditions of development and the principle of respect for diversity of cultures, and will, as I said above, support only a limited number of military activities, if any. But this does not mean that there are not some thinkers who are cosmopolitan and still have more specific agendas and are willing to use military means to achieve them. It was not all that long ago that the Cold War dominated international thinking, and to some extent it was a rivalry premised on alternative global visions of how the world should be ordered, which sometimes expressed themselves in various proxy wars in different parts of the Third World.

So there is no simple answer as to whether cosmopolitanism justifies certain kinds of wars or not. Some cosmopolitans will take this approach, but, because of their concern about the equal status of all human beings, they will be the first to stress the importance of various restraints in warfare. Whether cosmopolitans doing this wish to call themselves advocates of the just war approach or not is another matter. For some modern thinkers, including some cosmopolitans, the whole idea of the just war is too closely associated with the internationalist tradition in which it was developed. But there is nothing in the logic of just war criteria to make it available only to someone in the internationalist tradition. What is important, however, is the possibility that some cosmopolitans may defend certain kinds of military intervention and argue for various restraints in warfare. On the other hand, many cosmopolitans prefer to adopt the pacifist approach. Rather more cosmopolitans – certainly almost anyone signing up to the non-dogmatic approach – will adopt a pacificist approach, since that, as a commitment to promoting the conditions of peace, is something which both just war theorists/war justifiers and pacifists can agree on (see chapter 6).

4 Further considerations: justifications of internationalism

How is the morality of states justified? One approach, which we considered briefly at the beginning of the chapter, assumes that there is a universal moral framework. For instance, it is given by natural law: a world divided up into discrete areas of political control where those in power act within them represents the most realistic way in which those universal values can be achieved. This approach underlay Grotius's thinking and that of earlier theorists such as Vitoria and Suarez (Vitoria [1532] 1991; Suarez [1597] 1866).

Many thinkers since have adopted a rather different approach to the justification of the norms in the international arena. For them the moral rules governing international relations are to be seen as something agreed, emerging out of state relations themselves. This agreed basis is seen as self-justifying, either because there is no wider universal moral framework, or because, if there is one, it is one about which there is so little agreement that it is not a sound basis for a morality of states. Various accounts may be given of the agreed basis, such as the idea of convention, custom and tradition, the idea of an inter-state contract, and the idea of states having mutually accepted rights within the society of states.

4.1   Universal ethical framework

A natural law account can be used to support a morality of states approach so long as certain assumptions are made. These are that the only effective way in which violence can be contained within reasonable limits in the world is to have political rule over discrete areas of control with minimal interference from others. But the question can be raised whether, in the modern world, this system and these rules are the most appropriate ones for advancing the universal goals associated with the natural law. If not, then the natural law approach would not support the morality of states in its traditional form and might even question the society of states approach more generally.

Whether or not one still supports the natural law approach – some do, especially among Catholic and Muslim thinkers – it is worth noting that the universal ethics approach remains an important source of support for the morality of states. It is not restricted to natural law thinkers, but is an approach of any cosmopolitan whose values and/or reading of the world lead them to endorse the morality of states as the best way to realize those universal values. Most cosmopolitans, however, are not so conservative and generally propose more demanding norms for international relations – even new forms of global governance that challenge or modify the way the nation-state system works.

Kant's theory is interesting in this regard because, although he is ethically a cosmopolitan (see §5.2), in one sense he supported the nation-state system – not as it was with the rules it had, but with a better set of rules, which he called 'articles of peace'. Kant's cosmopolitanism allowed him to support the existence of the nation-state as a necessary institutional structure, particularly in a republican form (Kant [1795] 1970), for both containing human impulses to unsociable behaviour and giving expression to our nature as autonomous agents choosing to live under a political regime.

Michael Walzer, in the course of his influential work on the ethics of war, spells out a modern variety of the morality of states which he calls the 'legalist paradigm', and provides a justification for it which is in many ways reminiscent of Kant (Walzer 1977: esp. 51–63). Although he does not call himself – and is not – a cosmopolitan, Walzer nevertheless invokes an idea of universal rights, and it is the crucial role that a political community has in protecting these rights which provides the basis for defending the legalist paradigm. In particular it is because any act of aggression attacks the political community in which people's rights to liberty are invested that the rules defending state autonomy and sovereignty must be held to firmly.

4.2 The morality of states as a product of state interaction

I now turn to how the justification of the morality of states can be given, if we reject a firm grounding in a cosmopolitan/universal ethic conception. If we take it that the nation-state is the embodiment of community, the expression of nationhood, or the product of a contract, its primary drive will be to maintain, defend and assert itself, but cooperation with likeminded states is generally the best way forward. Though hard-nosed realists will also accept the latter but read such cooperation as being based merely on prudence, most theories would see in this situation the development of a genuine morality of states in which respect for one another's aspirations is built in. The justification for this lies in one of a number of considerations.

Perhaps first and foremost one can simply point to the role of custom and convention in developing a community of states with shared values and traditions. Among writers who have adopted this approach are, historically, David Hume and, in recent times, Hedley Bull (Hume [1742] 1978: bk III, pt III, esp. ch. XI; Bull 1977). Likewise, Nardin argues for a society of states as a *practical* (rather than a *purposive*) association, and Thompson for a 'society of communities' (Nardin 1983: ch. 1; Thompson 1992: ch. 9). Both make the point that a society may not be quite the same as a fullblown community. Nevertheless the *general* communitarian conception (as a contrast to cosmopolitan-style thinking) acts both as the source and as the model for the morality of states. The fact that states represent separate communities seeking their own advancement leads them to cooperate, and the morality of that cooperation is itself similar to the communitarian one (see also chapter 2).

Two other forms of justification might be offered. There is an approach, associated historically with Vattel (Vattel [1755] 1853), but also apparent in Hegel's account of international law (Hegel [1821] 1942), which stresses the analogue with the person in a strong form: just as natural persons have rights (inherent in their nature) so too do artificial persons, and states have rights inherent in their constitution as members of a society defined precisely in terms of international law.[6] The nature of the state system simply generates these rights, which are international in nature.

Finally, there is the contract approach of John Rawls, which is concerned not so much with the justification of government as with principles of justice. Rawls applies his method for determining principles of justice *within* a society to the society of states and argues that representatives of states meeting together to decide on principles of justice to apply to international relations would choose 'the familiar principles' of the morality of states (Rawls 1971: §58; cf. his later treatment in Rawls 1999 and a very different application of his method globally in Beitz 1979; see also Dower 1998 or 2007).

5   Further considerations: justifications of cosmopolitanism

There are many varieties of cosmopolitanism, both in respect of content (what values or duties are recommended) and in respect of intellectual sources (different types of religious worldview, different philosophical theories). Not all theories are necessarily radical or revolutionary, as we have already noted. Chris Brown considers three versions: Kantianism, utilitarianism and Marxism (Brown 1992: ch. 2). We can add other approaches, such as human rights, natural law and contract theory, as well as explicitly religious approaches and ones that stem from environmental considerations. What is striking about the first two that Brown mentions is that they represent two main approaches to ethics generally, namely what is called non-consequentialism, or deontology, and consequentialism (or sometimes teleology). I indicated this key distinction in chapter 1 (§7.2), since it plays quite an important role in discussions of war and peace. Here I outline three of a number of approaches: utilitarianism, Kantianism, and human rights. (For a fuller discussion of these and other views, see Dower 1998: ch. 5 or Dower 2007: ch. 4.)

5.1   Consequentialism/utilitarianism

Utilitarianism is the best known of the consequentialist theories. In its classical form, in Bentham and Mill, it was understood in terms of the maximization of happiness, itself understood hedonistically as pleasure. There are many variations, and later theories understand the good to be promoted in other ways. But at heart the theory is about the promotion of the best balance of good over bad. One of the most attractive features of utilitarianism is its global reach. 'Everybody to count for one, nobody for more than one' (Bentham, quoted in Mill [1861] 1962: ch. 5). The theory is that all human beings are in principle relevant, and equally so, for ethical decision-making. What is crucial is whether one's action may affect the well-being of any other human beings (or, more generally, sentient beings), however distant in space or time. Membership of one's community or state is not the determining factor. Utility is no respecter of borders.

Bentham himself was very interested in this dimension, and his advocacy of international law was premised on his view that its strengthening would lead to greater human felicity. A good example of this approach is Peter Singer's application of utilitarian reasoning to the alleviation of world poverty (Singer 1972, 2002). Several modern writers adopt a utilitarian approach to the justification of the rules of war (Brandt 1972; Hare 1972b; see chapter 4, §3.1), and several adopt the utilitarian approach explicitly as a foundation of international ethics (for instance, Elfstrom 1990; Hare and Joynt 1982). The work of Hare and Joynt was an early example of the modern return to interest in normative issues in international relations, and is interesting for a strategy they adopt which is of wider significance. Having characterized the ethical point of view, in contrast to the prudential point of view, as that in which one considers everyone's interests, the authors then recognize that although, if we are thinking critically, we need to justify everything – actions, policies, rules, moral training – in terms of consequences, nevertheless in practice it is important that people act according to rules or the dictates of conscience without calculating consequences. This is because having well-established rules and habits of conscience generally leads to the best results. So at the 'intuitive' level we appeal to rules without thinking of consequences (Hare and Joynt 1982: ch. 1). The utilitarian is certainly entitled to argue for rules, institutions and habits of thought which he justifies on consequential grounds, but whether our judgements of what is right are to be understood in this way is precisely what deontologists dispute.

5.2   Kantianism

The label 'Kantian' is often used as a way of describing a general approach inspired by the writing of the eighteenth-century German philosopher Immanuel Kant. The fundamental feature of this approach is the idea of all human beings standing in an ethical relationship to one another on the basis of their being fellow rational beings or 'persons'. As rational beings we are required to act on certain principles (not based on consequences) in relation to fellow human beings.[7]

Kant saw moral duties as demands of our 'practical reason'. They are 'categorical' demands or 'imperatives'. Categorical imperatives are contrasted with 'hypothetical' imperatives because, whereas the latter are based on desire, namely on what reason requires us to do to get what we *want* (on the 'hypothesis' of desire), the former are demands of duty, or simply what we are rationally required to do whether we want to do it or not. Kant formulated the basic categorical imperative in several ways, including:

- Formula of universal law (universalizability): act on that maxim which you can will to be universal law.
- Formula of ends: so act that you always treat humanity, whether in yourself or in other persons, as an end and not merely as a means. (Kant [1785] 1949: 88, 96)

Consider the case of a lying promise, and more generally coercive and deceitful behaviour. First, to act on the maxim of making a lying promise to get out of some difficulty is to act on a maxim which cannot be *universalized* (since communication would be unintelligible) and is therefore contrary to practical reason and wrong. Second, to make a lying promise to someone is to fail to *treat him as a rational pursuer of ends* (because to respect him would be to give him a true and not a false picture of the world), but rather to treat him merely as a means to one's own ends. The point here is that any human being *qua* rational agent is the object of respect/concern, and what is universalized is behaviour by any rational being. The framework is clearly global. Kant's vision was one of a global ethical order, or what he called a 'kingdom of ends'.

In *Perpetual Peace*, Kant develops a threefold analysis of *recht* (right) – republican, international and cosmopolitan *recht* (Kant [1795] 1970). He conceives of republican states as based on consent/contract and thus as the positive expression of a citizen's liberty or autonomy. Because of their 'unsocial sociability', men also need to live in political communities with laws enforcing areas of the moral law. These political communities will not succeed in their purpose unless states are free of the threat of external attack. Therefore perpetual peace needs to be established. For perpetual peace to occur certain articles of peace need to be accepted. Kant thus recommends a moral framework for international relations going beyond what was established or acted on, but he simply accepts – at least for the foreseeable future – the nation-state system. What he calls cosmopolitan *recht* concerns the duty of hospitality to foreigners, that is, as citizens of the world we owe certain things towards any human being. This is a surprisingly modest requirement, but perhaps understandable given the state of the world in Kant's day. What is important is the potential for more significant duties we may all have as citizens of the world, and also that, for Kant, the justification of international *recht* was firmly grounded in its contribution towards the well-being of all. (See Bohman and Lutz-Bachmann 1997 for discussion of Kant's *Perpetual Peace*.)

In the international relations literature Kant has often been associated with the label 'revolutionary', though his own actual recommendations are hardly revolutionary, nor does the Kantian approach require one to be revolutionary. (The label has stuck partly because of his support for the French Revolution.) Kant's views were certainly progressive and challenged any realist interpretations of international relations. Other writers in the Kantian tradition, such as Onora O'Neill, see Kant's theory giving rise to a more radical critique of state practices, and as underpinning a more radical demand for social justice (O'Neill 1986: chs 7 & 8). She makes much of the principles of non-deception and non-coercion, which apply as much to the actions of corporate agents such as nation-states or business companies, and also of what she calls the principle of material justice – that we are required to come to the aid of those whose material needs undermine the development of their rational autonomy.

5.3 Human rights

If all human beings have certain rights in virtue of their human nature (and rights are not all socially constituted), then this universal framework provides a firm basis for cosmopolitan obligation to respect and further them. There are various theories which ground these rights (notably but not only natural law/rights theories). We should note a distinction here, of wider significance and related to the discussion of a global ethic earlier in this chapter (§2.4), between human rights as (part of) a 'source' story or worldview about the nature of global ethics and as something established by consensus (of many people throughout the world) and supported by diverse ethical theories.

A human right is a right (i) attributed to a human being as a human being; (ii) asserted to exist on the basis of a moral theory or moral reasoning. Feinberg states: 'I shall define "human rights" to be generically moral rights of a fundamentally important kind held equally by all human beings unconditionally and unalterably' (Feinberg 1973: 85). Thus a human right is contrasted to a legal or conventional right which exists in virtue of the laws and conventions of a particular society. People have conventional rights as members of a legal community, not as human beings. Even an international declaration such as the United Nations' *Universal Declaration of Human Rights* (UN 1948) neither establishes the existence of human rights nor limits what are, ethically, human rights. For instance, a right to conscientious refusal may be a human right before it is encoded in international law.

A human right exists in virtue of a universal moral theory which postulates the whole world as one moral sphere or community. As Vincent
says: 'it is at the level at which what is appealed to is not any kind of
positive law, but what ought by some rational calculation to prevail' that
the justification of human rights is looked for (Vincent 1986: 11). Among
the approaches are theories such as the natural rights tradition, global
contract theory, and a rational construction of morality theory such as
Gewirth's (Gewirth 1978). A theory of human rights is therefore opposed
to any form of ethical relativism which denies universally applicable
values.

What kind of cosmopolitan theory we get from the assertion of human
rights depends upon a number of factors, but most notably, at the level
of theory, what rights are asserted and the nature and extent of the
correlative duties. Traditionally a distinction has been drawn between
negative rights (liberty rights; rights of action) and positive rights (socio-
economic rights; rights of recipience). Broadly negative rights are rights
to be free from certain kinds of interference or harm, and positive rights
are rights to receive some benefit if one has not got it. The duties corresponding to these are duties to refrain from certain kinds of action
(restricting someone's liberty, stealing or attacking other persons) and
duties to engage in certain kinds of positive action (help or intervention)
respectively.

Do all these kinds of right exist? That was a matter of great contention
as part of the battleground in East–West ideological confrontation until
the end of the 1980s, the West championing liberty rights and denying or
downplaying socio-economic rights of recipience, and the Eastern communist bloc stressing the socio-economic rights and the collective duties
of the state to provide these, but downgrading liberty rights. But there was
also a more theoretical issue at stake over what conditions are necessary
for the asserting of a right. Must a right be realizable to be a right? Liberty
rights can in principle be universally achieved simply by everyone refraining from actions invading these rights, whereas socio-economic rights of
recipience cannot be realized for all because of lack of resources. But if
rights are not absolute (that is, they can be overridden by various other
considerations, including appeal to other rights), the assertion of socio-
economic rights of recipiency is not undermined by the impossibility of
universal fulfilment. Even if there is a dispute about the above two kinds
of rights, it is important to recognize that the right to security (not being
attacked in one's person or property, and so on) is neither a liberty right
nor a subsistence right, and, as Luard noted, is a right universally recognized in all societies which no government of any political persuasion has
any business undermining (Luard 1981: 19).

For many the distinction between positive and negative rights is over-drawn. For instance, liberty rights need active defence as well as actions of restraint, and subsistence rights are rights not to have one's well-being undermined as well as to receive assistance. We should note the right to liberty and the right to socio-economic well-being in the light of the three-fold correlation of duties put forward by Henry Shue in his influential study of rights. All basic human rights have three correlative duties: duties to *avoid* depriving, duties to *protect* from standard threats to deprivation and duties to *aid* the deprived (Shue 1996: 52). If we see the framework in this way, it is clear that both individuals and society/the state have duties in connection with virtually all human rights. The state in particular has a role in protecting people from standard threats to their rights.

But the usual point of human rights thinking is not merely to assert a range of rights and correlative duties, but also assert that those duties are in principle global in character (though strictly the *universality* of human rights does not entail this: see chapter 3, §2.3, and chapter 7, §4.2). The duties extend in principle to all other human beings. As Shue puts it, basic rights to subsistence, security and liberty are 'everyone's minimum reason-able demands upon the rest of humanity' (Shue 1996: 19).[8] If all human beings have obligations to one another, then governments ought in their foreign as well as their domestic policies to further the realization of human rights. If universal human rights are accepted, how far can their impact be denied or resisted by international actors? As Bull notes, 'the framework of international order is inhospitable also to the demands of human justice' (Bull 1977: 83; by 'human justice' he means appeal to human rights).

There are two respects in which this has powerful implications. First, there are direct obligations to further the realization of human rights in other countries, for example through aid/better trade, protecting a global common good such as the environment, and promoting the conditions of peace as the basis of personal security. Here the obligation arises partly because other countries actually want one to do this. Second, there are obligations to take action to prevent/discourage other countries from vio-lating human rights within their own borders. This idea comes up against the ideas of national autonomy and UN Charter Article 2.7, and raises particular problems with regard to intervention generally, but especially by military means (see chapter 7, §4).

Questions

1 What are the main intellectual motives for supporting a morality of states?

2 What is the difference between ethical and institutional cosmopolitanism?
3 How do the approaches of cosmopolitanism and internationalism differ in respect to war and peace?
4 Which, if any, of the three approaches to a cosmopolitan ethic – Kantianism, utilitarianism or human rights theory – seems acceptable to you? If none are, what approach to the ethical relations between people across the world do you adopt?

4 THE JUSTIFICATION OF WAR

1 Just war and tradition

1.1 The ethical status of the just war tradition

The just war approach can be cast narrowly in the role of a particular evolving tradition or broadly in the role of a middle 'catch-all' position between realism and pacifism (though many modern supporters of this would not wish so to identify their position), that some wars and some ways of fighting are regarded as morally justified and some not (cf. the Grotius quotation in chapter 1, §3.1).

A large body of international law and norms, for example the Geneva and Hague conventions, has grown up over many years establishing both the rules of war on how it is to be fought, and the circumstances in which it would be legitimate for states to declare war, and these are developments initially out of the just war tradition but with many additional arguments drawn later from various ethical and legal sources.

In the former narrow sense the just war approach is a body of well-established criteria or norms summarized as *ius ad bellum* and *ius in bello* backed by a range of theoretical positions – drawn partly from Catholic theology and natural law, partly later from other religious and secular sources, partly from the theory of international relations, partly from the conventions of statecraft, and so on. For any thinker interested in such justifications, it can hardly be authoritative. Rather it may provide norms and ideas which each person, thinking from first principles, comes to accept.

In the latter broad sense – as shorthand for any war justifier's position in between realism and pacifism – it is an approach which includes of course many different accounts, and it is up to each thinker to make his or her own case for adopting some middle position or other. I shall turn to these other accounts later, but first focus on the just war tradition.

While the just war tradition has evolved with different stories and different kinds of justification offered at different times, still, insofar as there are common elements (such as just cause, proportionality, and non-combatant immunity), the appeal to the just war approach as a tradition can be attractive, either because it appears to reflect a large measure of agreement over a long period about what is reasonable in warfare (so it is an implicit global ethic by emerging consensus) or because it is at least an element of the European common tradition which gets its validity from the fact that it has been widely shared.

The appeal to the just war tradition as providing some kind of authority to the moral rules it presents has limited value. It may have some force as a way of replying to realist claims that deny the relevance of ethical principles. But to anyone who does think that ethics applies to warfare, what has been agreed in the past is neither here nor there. What matters is the ethical basis for war. It may be that the just war tradition is right on certain things, but, if so, its being a tradition does not make it right, and modern just war thinkers are interested in the various *arguments* that are advanced in the tradition.

1.2 The main traditional thesis: *ius ad bellum* and *ius in bello*

This tradition combines a balanced mixture of consequentialist and non-consequentialist elements.[1] Two branches of the just war tradition are usually accepted:

1 *ius ad bellum*: the rightness/justice (*ius*) of waging war or going to war
2 *ius in bello*: the rightness of the manner in which one conducts the war (whom you attack; what weapons are used, and so on).

The following elements of *ius ad bellum* are usually identified.

(a) The war must be declared by a legitimate authority: this is usually taken to be an established government of a nation-state.
(b) The war must be waged for a 'just cause', such as the right of self-defence in warding off an aggressor, rectifying an injustice.
(c) The war must be pursued with a right intention: that is, what one is aiming at is morally acceptable (which may or may not be the same as the just cause).

(d) Waging war must be the last resort, with all other remedies having been tried.
(e) There must be a reasonable prospect of success in achieving the goal, since otherwise it is a futile gesture involving unnecessary suffering.
(f) The principle of proportionality must be observed: that is, the amount of good to be achieved must outweigh the harm that is done in waging the war.
(g) It is possible for the war to be fought according to *ius in bello* principles: that is, the war can be fought by using ways which are not ruled out as immoral in themselves.

The two main principles usually invoked in regard to *ius in bello* are:

(a) discrimination: in warfare soldiers should only aim at enemy soldiers or combatants and not at those who are non-combatants (or the 'innocent' in the sense of 'not harming' (*in-nocens*)), such as at least most civilians; nor should prisoners be attacked or mistreated. (Analogously, discrimination is often advocated in regard to kinds of weapons, ones regarded as unacceptable causing excessive suffering.)
(b) proportionality: in any operation what is done should be judged as likely to do more good than harm (including the unintended but predictable effects on civilians even if not the object of attack).

2 *Ius ad bellum:* more detailed analysis and justifications

Considerable differences in practice will emerge depending on the interpretation of the various clauses of *ius ad bellum*. In particular, (a) and (b) can give rise to serious disagreements. Although *ius ad bellum* is usually discussed in regard to going to war, we should remember that it applies also to the continued prosecution of a war. In contrast to questions about how to fight, the issues here are really about the overall direction of a war, not merely about a particular timing before a war starts.

2.1 Legitimate authority

A standard position in the just war tradition has been that it is only nation-states that are the legitimate authorities. There are various reasons for this. A traditional argument, reflected in the writings of a modern Catholic philosopher, G. E. M. Anscombe, was that, because human beings need to live in organized political communities with coercive powers to maintain

order, such political units were divinely instituted for this purpose
(Anscombe [1961] 1970). While this argument had a more extensive application than only to the nation-state system, the latter, as it has developed
from the seventeenth century onwards, reflects this model of a world
ordered in a certain way by being divided into discrete areas of legitimate
control. The more general argument for restricting legitimacy to political
units such as nation-states is the more pragmatic argument that such a
system, by restricting the 'monopoly of legitimate violence' – to use a
phrase of Weber's – to them limits violence in a world which would be
much more violent without such an ordered system. It is reflected in the
rationale for the view expressed in *An Agenda for Peace*, in which Boutros
Boutros-Ghali, the then UN Secretary-General, argued against the legitimacy of secessionist movements in countries liable to break up for ethnic
reasons, on the ground that such violent unravelling of existing state
boundaries would lead to even greater breaches of peaceful coexistence
than we currently have in the world (Boutros-Ghali 1992).

But this conservative view has always had challenges from those who
argue that other bodies can also have legitimacy. After all, if we took the
view that only established governments had the right to wage war, then
we would be saying that any other group does not, and this would include
any secessionist movement which wanted to become a separate political
community from the wider political unit which is oppressing it (such as
Kosovo in relation to Serbia), any liberation movement in a country occu-
pied by a colonial power (such as in the American War of Independence),
and any civil war in which the party not in power wishes to institute a new
form of government in their own country (such as the African National
Congress (ANC) in South Africa). Many would argue that such bodies
could have legitimacy in the sense that, if other criteria such as just cause
are satisfied, their engaging in armed struggle is not ruled out simply
because they are not established governments. Even someone who is critical of the whole idea of the moral legitimacy of fighting at all may recognize that if violence were legitimate there would be no good reason to
restrict it to the governments of states.

What is striking about the list of alternative units that are said to have
legitimacy is that they are all in a sense 'political' units, in that they have
political goals (such as the establishment of a new regime that is more
just), claim to have wide popular support analogous to that which legiti-
mates government, and are organized as being or at least supporting a
government-in-waiting. Other kinds of organizations, such as the mafia,
criminal gangs, or military-style units supporting multinational companies,
would not count as legitimate authorities. Terrorist organizations such
as al-Qaeda raise special problems, in that they may have both wide

popular support and broadly political objectives, such as the rejection of Western values and the desire to see Muslim values inform politics, but they do not conform to the standard model of a political unit wanting to take over and form a government. If we have serious objections to terrorism, however, it is likely to be over the means that they adopt (see chapter 7).

Much of the discussion about legitimate authority is conducted in the context of interpreting international law, and decisions about whether to allow a group legitimacy have significant implications, for instance on how combatants fighting on their behalf are regarded in international law and thus treated as prisoners. Ethically, however, such legal interpretations may not be decisive over whether to include or exclude bodies as (really) legitimate authorities. Furthermore, much discussion about the criterion of legitimate authority continues as if there had been no significant developments in international law since the founding of the United Nations. The UN Charter, to which all nations have signed up, in certain crucial clauses (UN 1945: Arts 39 & 41) transfers the legitimate authority to the Security Council to wage war, only allowing nation-states an immediate right of self-defence if attacked (ibid.: Art. 51), the idea being that in such a case the matter should be referred to the authority of the Security Council as soon as practicable.

On numerous occasions states have ignored this Charter provision and engaged in military operations without such authorization, and indeed in the face of opposition in the UN. Two examples spring to mind – the NATO invasion of Kosovo and related attack on Serbia in 1999 and the American invasion (with the support of the UK) of Iraq in 2003. On neither occasion was there any immediate attack by another power. However, while doubts about the legal legitimacy of either operation have been the basis – or one of the bases – of much opposition to these actions, many would hold that in both cases these bodies not only had a just cause, they were also from an *ethical* point of view legitimate authorities. Indeed, if one looks at the way states are generally armed and geared for fighting wars, it is clear that leaders and their citizens must either regard their military postures in realist terms as ignoring the ethical issues or regard their states as still retaining the status of being *morally* legitimate authorities, whatever the status of international law.

2.2   Just cause

Many different types of 'justification' have been given for going to war. Here I am considering justifications which are presented as moral arguments addressed to other countries or the world at large. There can be 'justifications' offered by government leaders to their citizens, or by citizens to fellow citizens, that are addressed not to the world but to limited audiences, such as a realist or a militarist might offer. Just war justifications assume some kind of universal moral framework in which certain kinds of consideration are in principle acceptable – even if not actually accepted – by other countries and their populations. Some of these just causes are often expressed in the terminology of international law and, insofar as international law is meant to reflect ethical values which are universally acceptable, get their ethical legitimacy from this – though, as we noted earlier, their being enshrined in international law does not settle whether they really are acceptable ethically one way or the other.

Furthermore, whether the justification of war is couched in traditional just war terminology or in more modern ethical variants, the word 'just' in 'just cause' may or may not be understood in terms of a theory of *justice*, rather than some more general ethical theory about what is morally right. Ceulemans, for instance, couches them in terms of justice (or rather its opposite, injustice): 'having a just cause is essentially about the *correction* and/or the *punishment* of an injustice that has been done, or about the *prevention* of an injustice which is about to happen' (Ceulemans 2002: 26). The first two above are reflected in the following common triad: self-defence, punishment and retaking what has been taken. Teichman summarizes the range of just causes thus:

> The traditional reasons include self-defence, the defence of the homeland, the defence of allies, the bringing about of a return to the *status quo* after the theft of goods or expropriation of territory, the punishment of guilty persons (for example, 'warmongers', generals, war criminals, etc.), and the coercion of wrong-thinking people (as, for instance, heretics, infidels, etc.). (Teichman 1986: 55)

First, there is what has always been regarded as an obvious just cause and is certainly in modern discussion often regarded as the just cause *par excellence*, namely self-defence. That is, a country has a right to defend itself against an attack by another country, just as a person has a right of self-defence against attack. The link with personal self-defence is significant, since the rightness of the latter seems so self-evident to almost all thinkers except strict adherents of the philosophy of nonviolence. National self-defence can be seen either as being analogous to personal self-defence, since the political community under attack is seen as an entity to be preserved like an individual, or as an extension of self-defence, namely self-defence at the collective level. Closely linked to the national defence argument, and with a very similar rationale, is the idea that a country has a right – maybe even a duty – to come to the aid of another country that has been attacked – especially if the two countries are allies or have treaties of mutual support.

These just causes are now enshrined in much international law and are at the heart of the UN Charter conception of the chief 'international sin', namely aggression. Walzer has called this the 'legalist paradigm', in which the defence of sovereignty is the cornerstone of the international society of states (Walzer 1977). Nevertheless this limitation to the scope of what a just cause is has been criticized. Anscombe, in the article already referred to above, is trenchant in her criticism: 'The modern conception of aggression like so many modern influential conceptions is a bad one. The question is not: "who strikes first?" but "who is in the right?"' (Anscombe [1961] 1970: 43–4). Now the question arises: What might make it right for a country to initiate a military action? (What follows is not an exposition of Anscombe's position.)

Two types of reason need to be mentioned first, both because in certain respects they do not depart too radically from the 'defence' model, and because they are commonly accepted as part of our modern approach to justification, which some may argue is compatible with modern international law.

First, there is the idea of pre-emptive strike. That is, a country makes an attack on another country or group of countries because it is clear that it is about to be attacked by that country or group of countries, and to wait for that attack would put the country at a severe disadvantage. The most often quoted case in modern times is that of the so-called six-day war in 1967, when Israel took the initiative in starting a war against the Arab states surrounding her – a war which was about to be launched by them against Israel – and thus achieved a decisive advantage from the swiftness of the operation. This kind of case is in a sense motivated by the same concern for self-defence, and, whether or not it is regarded as really justified, the justification is based on the same moral consideration – the right to defend oneself.

Second, humanitarian intervention is often now regarded as based on a just cause – concern for a group of people within some country whose rights are being violated on a major scale, as in genocide. Again what motivates this is the thought that a group needs defending because they are being attacked, so the idea of defence again plays a crucial role here. This case, though, departs more from the standard UN model precisely because it involves intervention in another county's internal affairs, and therefore from an international law point of view is a form of aggression. What is clear is that, if the idea of self-defence is seen as a legitimate cause in the modern world, the idea of coming to the aid by military intervention of those oppressed or attacked is also one that is regarded by many as a legitimate cause in the modern world (see chapter 7, §4 for more detailed discussion).

So far the idea of a just cause has been premised on the body engaging in it being a nation-state. However, if we accept, as indicated in the previous section, that other non-state bodies could be legitimate authorities, then we need to acknowledge the kinds of just causes that would be relevant to such bodies. Indeed the idea of legitimate authority is conceptually linked to the recognition of possible just causes for such bodies. If there were no just causes available to such bodies, then their 'legitimacy' would be empty. In fact there are three types of just cause that have been recognized by many thinkers, both in the past and in the present. They can all three be seen as variants of 'self-defence' since they all involve a group defending itself against some form of serious injustice or oppression. On the other hand, they may be seen as separate categories. First, there is the case of civil war in which the party not in power takes up arms to get rid of a government or political order. Second, there are wars of secession where the just cause is to liberate a people from control by another people and set up a separate political community. And third, there have been anti-colonial wars in which those taking up arms wish to rid a whole geographical area of a colonial government imposed by a foreign power.

We should also consider more briefly a range of other just causes that have in the past been popular and may still be supported by some – and the fact that a form of justification is out of fashion does not of course render it necessarily unacceptable. Other considerations can be put into four kinds of cluster: punishing, maintaining international order, spreading values and securing national interests.

The idea of punishment, which goes back to the influential thought of Augustine (see quotation in Aquinas [1270] 1953: II-II, qu. 40), is that, if a state or political unit has done something regarded as seriously wrong or unjust, including of course attacking others, then the country going to war against it sees itself as restoring justice, which, apart from stopping what is done through victory, includes punishment either as retribution for the wrong done, as reparation for damage done, or as a deterrent to future such action by others. The punishment resides in the war itself and what is done after the war. This emphasizes the link with the idea of penal or corrective justice.

The maintenance of international order, though partly motivated by national interests (since this order is maintained to their advantage), has also been seen as a duty particularly of powerful nations to intervene in various ways, including military action, to maintain the conditions of international order where they appear to be threatened. Thus we have the rationale of what was called 'balance of power' interventions and was accepted in the nineteenth century by many as justified. It probably played a role in some of the 'proxy wars' during the Cold War in Africa and elsewhere, where local wars were partly supported by Western powers and by the Soviet bloc – though by then such a motivation could not be paraded as a 'just cause', given the UN paradigm. Linked to this have been so-called preventive wars or preventive military interventions on particular occasions, where what justifies the intervention is a country's estimate that another country's military developments mean they are preparing for war in the future. Such interventions are quite unlike pre-emptive action against states which are about to attack. The Israeli bombing of an Iraqi nuclear reactor in 1981 would be a case in point, as would, were it to happen, an American attack on Iran (being contemplated at the time of writing this book in 2008), carried out in order to impede or destroy its facilities for potentially making nuclear weapons. While these two cases would not come under any commonly accepted modern justification – at least in international law – nevertheless many may hold that here ethics departs from law and such action would be ethically justified in making that country, or 'the world', safer by nipping such developments in the bud.

The idea that one might go to war to spread certain values or worldviews – either religious or political – which one believes to be right, and therefore to be accepted by all people, has a long history and has inspired many wars. It is of course linked to the idea of crusading, and indeed, while the start of the Crusades was based, in the public pronouncement of Pope Urban II in 1095, on the restoration of Christian property taken by Muslims in the Middle East (see Coates 1997: 106), it very quickly became a protracted struggle between two ideologies.

In its harsher forms the idea is informed by militarist thinking, as we saw in chapter 2, in which there is a desire simply to destroy the other, and likewise often such wars are inspired by realist considerations insofar as countries trying to get other parts of the world to conform to their beliefs make the world more amenable to their interests. It often goes hand in hand with expansionist goals as well. Consider the duality of the whole expansionist project of the European imperial powers in the nineteenth century in carving up Africa – partly a battle for control over territory for economic and strategic reasons and partly a desire to spread Christianity and Western values to the 'benighted' parts of the world.

But the desire to spread one's values by various means, including military engagement, need not be linked to militarist or realist agendas. In one sense it is a consequence of any beliefs about moral values seen as moral truths (or religious truths) – that there are correct views to be held and that people ought to accept these truths (and may suffer, for instance, in an afterlife if they do not) – and so part of any commitment to firmly held beliefs, either by individuals or by whole communities, is a commitment to *spreading* them. If one thinks that military action to secure control of a territory is an effective way to achieve such spreading of values *and* one thinks that such means are ethically justified – as a strong interpretation of the idea that the end justifies the means – then it is possible to hold – and many have held – that the attempted conversion of others by military means is justified.

We should note that by the time of the eighteenth and nineteenth centuries the general consensus in international politics was to reject such justifications. This was partly because of the practical importance of peaceful coexistence and partly because of the thesis of political pluralism which accepted that, whether or not there were universal values, nations could reasonably disagree over what these were. However, the crusading kind of justification resurfaced in various ways in the twentieth century – in the Allies' opposition to German Nazi values and in the Cold War confrontation between Western values and communism, including hot wars such as Vietnam. It was one consideration that lay behind the American invasion of Iraq in 2003 insofar as the desire to spread democracy and Western values played a part. However, while there is clearly a crusading element in the modern confrontation between Western values – partly Christian, partly secular – and Islamic values, it is less clear whether this is in itself something justifying or generally involving military means. At any rate the so-called war against terror is quite separate and appears to be motivated by something completely different – precisely to destroy or immobilize terrorists (which coincidentally probably reinforces anti-Western perceptions among many Muslims who are not involved in or directly supportive of terrorist methods) (see chapter 7, §3).

Historically many wars in the past have in fact been fought in order to acquire territory – and the resources and labour which such territory would provide – or to further geo-political interests in other ways, such as securing trade routes, and so on. While such motivations are often simply realist, they can be more complex. In earlier eras the idea that a dominant country had a right to secure its power in such ways was accepted – that is, accepted by other countries – and so in a sense was an ethical justification. This was particularly so if at the same time it was pursuing other goals such as spreading 'civilizing values' in other parts of the world.

2.3   Right intention

At least three different ideas can be captured by this idea of 'right intention'. They are all in fact relevant to the complete evaluation of *any* act which we try to assess morally. These are: the motivation or spirit behind the act performed, the presence or absence of further intentions or goals beyond the official reasons for an act which may discredit the act, and the wider framework of intentions within which the act is performed. Consider an uncle giving his niece a special present. If he did it out of avuncular affection, that would be fine, but if he did it because he lusted after her or in order to embarrass her parents, it would not. If he did it because he was trying to persuade her parents to favour him in a possible business venture, this further goal would discredit the act. And if his wider intentions did not include being fair to other members of the family, for example giving presents to the niece's siblings, we might regard it as not properly grounded in wider moral commitments, even if it was a morally acceptable act in itself. Consider the parallels with war.

Augustine particularly focused on the first of these factors. He argued that a war could and should be initiated and fought with the desire for peace and for justice to be done rather than from the motives of lust for power, love of violence, cruelty or hatred in one's heart (Augustine [*c*.397] 1872: bk 22, ch. 74). Taken strictly, given that war almost inevitably involves the demonization or dehumanization of the enemy, certainly by soldiers fighting if not by their leaders, this is actually a very demanding condition.

Second, and more standardly, it needs to be clear that, if a war is being fought for a just cause, this is indeed the motivating reason why it is being fought. The point about a just cause is that it is the publicly *declared* reason, and gets its justifying power from being linked to international laws and/or agreed moral norms. If in an operation a power is actually using this as a pretext for pursuing other objectives that would not be seen as justifiable if publicly declared, then this is not a right intention. Many critics of the US-led 1991 Gulf War and 2003 Iraq War strongly suspect that a powerful motive was in fact the desire to secure Western oil interests.[2]

Third, modern writers often want to go one step further and argue that a just cause is not sufficient without there being a commitment to securing a durable or just peace after a conflict is over. In other words, while the just cause identifies, if you like, the immediate objective – stopping the aggression, toppling a regime or bringing to an end human rights violations -- this objective has to be seen in the context of what is *planned* for the outcome after the war has ceased (assuming it has ended on one's terms!). This goes beyond considerations of proportionality (see below) which, strictly speaking, are about the likely *consequences* of what happens during and after a war, whether planned or not. In recent years there has been increasing interest in what is called 'justice/*ius post bellum*', and while this issue is primarily for those *after* a war who have to find the right way *to combine* the legacy of the war with future reconstruction, part of the right intention of those *embarking* on (and prosecuting) a war means, for those who stress this point, having in mind a view about what should be done in the peace that follows (see, for example, Orend 2002, 2006).

2.4 Last resort

This principle is relatively straightforward and bears a consequentialist character. Given the great cost of war, it is clearly necessary to avoid it, if at all possible, by negotiation, diplomacy, and so on. It reflects a widely held norm of moral life in general: given that on many occasions one may have a duty to do something, it is preferable to carry it out, if there are a range of alternative ways of doing it, in such a way as to avoid or at least minimize negative consequences. Many people who are not utilitarians accept this 'negative utilitarian' concern for minimizing negative outcomes as a kind of side-constraint on how one carries out one's duty – where one's duty itself is determined not by consequences but by other moral considerations. So there is nothing peculiar in itself about justifying war in this regard, only perhaps the terminology of 'last resort' being distinctive.

Although the idea itself is clear enough, there are in practice big questions about whether a situation really is one of last resort. It is not simply an empirical question. It turns partly on what it is the last resort for. Achieving exactly what going to war would achieve? Achieving sufficient of one's objectives that, in order to avoid war, one should settle on a compromise? Furthermore, if the rationale of last resort is that of avoiding intolerable consequences (of war), there may be alternatives to war as instruments of policy that have their own consequences which are also extremely bad. The imposition of general economic sanctions on a country, often seen as a step to be taken well before the resort to war, can have immensely harsh effects on a country's inhabitants – especially the least well-off, who may have little to do with the conflict. Many have commented on the severe effects of general sanctions on Iraq in the years before the war in 2003. Whether the alternative in such a case is to go to war sooner, or rather to pursue other policies including targeted sanctions, is another question.

2.5 Proportionality and reasonable prospect of success

I take these two together, since the rationale for both is quite similar. The principle of proportionality requires that a reasonable check be made on whether the likely costs of a war are greater than the likely gains; if they are, then war should not be embarked on. Likewise, if there were no reasonable prospect of winning a war, then it would be foolhardy to embark on it, since such a war would simply involve a lot of bad consequences for no good outcome. Thus, in the face of overwhelming military might, Belgium quickly capitulated to the German advance at the beginning of the Second World War. The two principles are not, however, the same: one could have a reasonable prospect of success but the costs might still outweigh the benefits.

The effects of going to war are notoriously difficult to predict with any confidence even probabilistically, so this is a difficult matter to determine, certainly in a way that would command agreement. It becomes more complex still once one accepts that one is not merely comparing the costs and benefits of actually fighting but also including the costs and benefits of not fighting, and also, for both – fighting and not fighting – the longer-term effects after a war and without a war at all. Furthermore, if one is a war justifier rather than a realist, one is concerned about the effects not merely for one's own soldiers and citizens but also for the same in the enemy country (and indeed other countries affected by a conflict). Realists might run similar considerations, but only insofar as they affect the citizens and soldiers of their own country. Furthermore, if it is thought that 'reasonable prospect of success' should mean more than a 50 per cent chance of winning, there is a paradox that, since it cannot be the case that both sides have this high a chance, at least one side is deceiving itself.

Suppose a country enters a war with its leaders having sincerely calculated the outcome and believing that such a war satisfied both proportionality and reasonable prospect of success. What happens if during a war it becomes clear that they are no longer satisfied? At the extreme, if towards the end of a conflict it is clear that nothing can be done to avert defeat, leaders have a duty to sue for peace since neither criterion is satisfied. But what about cases in the middle where the probabilities do not end up so dramatically? At a certain point in the Second World War anyone assessing Britain's chances of winning against Hitler might well have concluded that there was little prospect – well certainly less than a 50 per cent chance – of success. Should Britain have sued for peace at that point? Strict application of these just war criteria seems to suggest 'yes', and in fact things turned out rather differently. Once the momentum of war takes over, it is much more difficult than in a cool – or cooler – hour before a conflict starts for the application of such criteria to the question of continuing a war to be taken seriously. This does not settle whether they should or should not be made. However, some may say that, once you are committed to war, you need to see it through to the end (and only impending and inevitable defeat makes a difference).

2.6 *Ius in bello* constraints

This condition is often not explicitly stated but in fact it has to be presumed – that, if you are to engage in a war, there are ethically acceptable ways of fighting. Again there is a corollary in the ordinary logic of moral action. If you wish to pursue a goal which appears to be otherwise ethically permitted or even required, then you must pursue it by means that are ethically satisfactory – and if there are no ways that are ethically satisfactory, then you have to rethink the rightness of the goal. I say the ordinary logic of moral action, because it is possible for someone to argue that, in war, the ethics of the end suppresses any independent ethics of the means. In chapter 2, where I discussed this issue, I suggested that this is really a position adopted by many realists. Insofar as a just war theorist adopts this way out of the difficulty and abandons clause (g) of the *ius ad bellum* criteria (see p. 83), he or she is really advocating a mixed position, which is realist in regard to the manner of fighting.

It may be thought that there are always going to be ethically satisfactory ways of fighting, even if one accepts that certain ways of fighting are ruled out. But this is not self-evident. If there were no legitimate manner anticipated in which a particular war could be waged, that would of course rule out the rightness of *initiating* it as well. Perhaps a war reliant on the use of nuclear weapons would be a case in point. Clearly, an anti-war pacifist may take the view that all forms of fighting are ruled out, and so, even if he or she had some sympathy for some of the *ius ad bellum* criteria, this fact rules out any war being rightly embarked upon. This point is not one that only those calling themselves pacifists might make. There are those in the modern world who would regard themselves as just war theorists but come to a *contingent* pacifist position in regard to *modern* warfare as being ruled out. More specifically, as noted above, there are those who would regard themselves as nuclear pacifists (or weapons of mass destruction/biological or chemical weapons pacifists) and so would conclude that, if any war being contemplated could not be successfully prosecuted without either the intention to use nuclear weapons (or other weapons of mass destruction) or the conditional intention to use them if things do not go one's way, such a war could not be ethically embarked upon.

Before offering some critical evaluation of the various *ius ad bellum* criteria, I will first give an account of the *ius in bello* criteria generally advanced.

3   What are the issues raised by *ius in bello*?

3.1   The traditional approach: the doctrine of double effect

Ius in bello relates to the manner in which war is waged. The principles of the reasonable prospect of success and proportionality also operate here (with regard to particular operations). Perhaps the most significant element (philosophically) is the limitation on who may be a direct object of attack. It has generally been held that only combatants may be aimed at, and that it is wrong to aim to kill civilians or indeed soldiers once they have surrendered, become disarmed or become prisoners.

This was traditionally based on the principle that it is wrong (absolutely) to kill the innocent. Since the innocent, whether in the sense of '*in-nocens*' ('not harming'), or in the sense of 'morally blameless', are often killed in war, this principle also depends on the doctrine of double effect in order to avoid breaching the principle of not killing the innocent. This is that we can make a morally significant distinction between what we aim at in our actions ('first effect') and what may or will come about as a result of what we aim at ('second effect') but is not itself aimed at or wanted. We should note, first, that the means taken are included in the intention and, second, that according to the doctrine what is not aimed at is not strictly part of the action, so it is not part of what one 'does' in the morally relevant sense if non-combatants die as a result. Saturation bombing of cities in the Second World War violated the traditional doctrine, and the policy was a matter of grave moral misgiving for many at the time, as killing civilians in order to demoralize the enemy was an instrument of policy, not a side-effect (Walzer 1971).

Although the doctrine of double effect does pick out a significant distinction, in that we do assess ethically rather differently what people do deliberately from what they bring about reluctantly in doing something else, stated on its own it seems inadequate. Suppose, as happened in Vietnam, a village is sheltering several Vietcong fighters and the American forces decide the only way to kill the Vietcong fighters is in fact to incinerate the whole village, are the deaths of everyone in the village merely a side-effect of what needed to be done to kill the fighters or really a means to that end? One cannot just say in one's heart 'I had rather not kill the villagers so I do not intend that': the deaths of the whole village are too integral to the means taken. Even if one thought that these deaths were side-effects, the case illustrates another principle often applied in such extreme war situations, namely the principle of proportionality: even if certain side-effects are not the object of intention, if the anticipated side-effects are sufficiently negative, then the doctrine of double effect cannot justify such an action. As Walzer has put it, there is a principle of 'due care' assumed, and this must be observed even if it raises the risks for the soldiers themselves (Walzer 1977: 156).

There have also been problems surrounding the definition of innocence and, related to that, what constitutes a combatant. Certainly, if 'innocent' means 'not harming', there may be various categories of people who are not fighting as soldiers but are contributing to the war effort – such as munitions workers; if 'innocent' means 'morally innocent', then again quite a number of people on the enemy side are hardly morally innocent – for instance, citizens actively supporting or voting for the war effort. That said, there are clearly large numbers of people who on either interpretation are clearly innocent, such as children, the infirm or indeed ordinary people not involved in the conduct of the war. There are in fact various other ways of marking the ethical difference between combatants and non-combatants which try to get round these definitional difficulties.

3.2 Various forms of deontology

By deontology I mean forms of argument which try to draw a principled distinction between two categories of person, such that it would be wrong inherently to attack people in one category, but permissible or even obligatory to attack people in the other category. Apart from the traditional account above, several attempts have been made to get round difficulties with defining innocence and combatancy and with the doctrine of double effect. These include Fullinwider's account of the right of self-defence, which cannot include civilians who are not attacking one, even if in all sorts of indirect ways they are supporting the other side (Fullinwider 1975), and Nagel's account of the special relationship of hostility between those who recognize one another as agents fighting each other (Nagel 1972).[3]

3.3 Consequentialism

Other ways of finding some basis for the distinction are considerations of general utility or considerations of prudence and mutual interests. The utilitarian justification is that the general good is promoted if there is strict adherence to certain rules – rules concerning not attacking civilians or disarmed solders, not using particularly nasty weapons such as anti-personnel mines, and so on. Richard Brandt and Richard Hare have argued this case (Brandt 1972; Hare 1972b). Two things are worth noting about utilitarian justification. First, it is the interests of *all* those affected which have to be taken into account – enemy soldiers and enemy civilians as well as soldiers and civilians in one's own country – and, we should add, in principle people in other countries, future generations, and so on, if these are affected (see discussion in chapter 7 on nuclear weapons). Second, utilitarian thinking cannot rule out situations in which exceptions to these rules would be justified.

3.4   Convention

If the reasons for limiting the way war is fought are based on prudence and mutual interests, then at best the rules of war are based on conventional agreement, since there would be no motive for limiting one's behaviour unless the other side did so, and this would not happen unless there was some kind of understanding or agreement. So it is simply convention for mutual benefit that limits warfare, as Mavrodes (1975) has argued. Would such a way of understanding limitations on warfare constitute *moral* restraint rather than merely prudence or enlightened self-interest? This touches on more general issues in ethics as to whether the kind of account of morality given by convention-theorists, such as Hume, really counts as a proper morality (Hume [1742] 1978: bk III, §III; see also Harman 1977). The issue partly turns on whether, once they are up and running, the obligation to observe the conventions overrides the pursuit of interests when they clash. If, in the case of the rules of war, the line is that they do override considerations of interest, or do so as long as the general interests of all are served, as a utilitarian might argue, then it can count as an ethical constraint based on convention. If the line is taken that, once the other side has abandoned a restraint, one no longer has any obligation to stick to it, then this is verging on the non-moral (see Mavrodes 1975). Indeed, it is very similar to the line taken by realists, that there are really no moral restraints, though prudence may dictate certain limitations as long as the other side does the same. An example of the issue here was the commencement of saturation bombing in the Second World War, since this policy did break the traditional ban on directly targeting civilian populations.

4   A note on internationalism and cosmopolitanism

It will now I hope be apparent that there are many bases for grounding the claim that there are moral restraints in warfare, in regard to both decisions about going to war and decisions about how to fight a war. Clearly, from an internationalist point of view, the society of states is grounded in the right to sovereignty and the legitimacy of states using military force both to defend themselves and to defend the society of states itself when challenged by acts which threaten international security. The UN, insofar as it is based on statist assumptions, assumes the legitimacy of actions to preserve the sovereignty of member states and common security. The rules of war are seen as validated because they have come to be agreed and accepted, formally or informally, by members of the society of states. The general position here is fairly clear, whatever account one gives of the basis for the morality of states.

Cosmopolitans other than pacifists will also generally support the middle position but, depending on their values and reading of what is realistic in the world, will give different emphases and interpretations on what a just cause would be, on what rules really are for the good of all, and so on. The point is that the rules and norms accepted by states are, in principle, subject to criticism. This concern for the rules of war relates directly to the relationships between human beings involved in war, rather than being mediated by what happens to be agreed among states. In a parallel way, some cosmopolitans, who need not be pacifists, might argue that there ought to be a right to conscientious refusal to engage in military service – an issue much argued over in the Human Rights Commission in Geneva for many years – even though most states do not recognize this and there are not (yet) any international agreements about it.

What is characteristic, though, of many cosmopolitans, particularly those whom I have called 'non-dogmatic', is a certain conception of the world in which the impulse towards peace is dominant, and there is a tendency to say that, while organized violence may sometimes be justified, in practice such occasions are rare. This is linked to a certain way of looking at peace itself, which I return to in chapter 6. (See also chapter 3, §3 for more extended discussion of how cosmopolitans and internationalists look at war.)

5   Objections

There are various kinds of objection to the justification of war. Some are general objections, others focus on particular criteria, such as just cause or proportionality, the necessarily indiscriminate nature of warfare, and so on.

5.1   Rejection of the whole approach

(a)   The perspective of nonviolence/absolute pacifism

There is a quite general objection to the idea of just war that comes from the view that all deliberate killing of fellow human beings is simply wrong. This is often seen as the pacifist objection, but perhaps it would be more accurately described as the objection from the philosophy of nonviolence (as the principled objection to any use of violence). Many pacifists are also nonviolentists, that is, they object to any taking of human life. However, as we shall see in chapter 5, many pacifists adopt a specifically anti-war position, namely that killing in war is wrong because of the nature of warfare itself (or at least modern warfare). I will say no more at this stage about the general objection to all killing of human beings from which an objection to war simply follows. Such a position does not have anything specific to say about warfare. What, however, about objections to warfare in particular?

(b)   The impossibility of fulfilling all the criteria

First there is a general strategy which does not focus on any one particular aspect of the justificatory framework but takes the whole package of the just war approach and, indeed, any analogous approach which offers a significant number of criteria concerning going to war and fighting wars. The argument is that, if all the criteria were fully applied, no actual wars would ever pass the test of moral legitimacy. A slightly less bold version of this objection would be that, while all the criteria could conceivably be satisfied, given the uncertainties of war and the tendency to make biased judgements in one's favour, the overwhelming presumption must be that any proposed war is unacceptable. Now a matter of general interest is raised here.

In the just war tradition, while the principles of *ius in bello* and *ius ad bellum* can be and often are accepted as being combined, there is, for some thinkers, a certain tension between them. If one stresses the justice of the cause of one side (and thus the injustice of the other side) and conceives the fight as being between 'good and evil', one may be less concerned about the morality of the means to victory, and criterion (g) of the *ius ad bellum* criteria (always fighting according to *ius in bello* criteria) is dropped. Whereas if one does not believe that there can be objective or at least internationally agreed principles of justice to settle which side has a just cause, one will be, as internationalists such as Vattel was (Vattel [1755] 1853), concerned primarily with the limitations of violence via agreed rules of war, and the just cause criterion is not taken too seriously (see, for instance, Bull 1966).

There is also a more general issue, of which the first tension is an instance, as to whether the checklist of conditions is meant to be a set of conditions *all* of which need to be satisfied for a war to be satisfactory, or whether, if a sufficient number of them are satisfied, then a war may be justified. This issue is illustrated by the Gulf War of 1991. It was very apparent at the time that the decision to engage in military action in January 1991 to oust Iraq from Kuwait was being publicly justified in just war terms. Clearly Iraq had flouted international law in invading Kuwait, so there was a palpable just cause to rectify an injustice; there was legitimate authority, especially as the action had been endorsed by the UN Security Council; and there was a reasonable prospect of success. On the other hand, others argued that it was not the last resort, since further attempts at negotiation could have been made; and that behind the just cause lay an unacceptable intention to protect American/Western oil interests in the Middle East and to demonstrate American hegemony in the 'new world order'.[4] If the latter analysis was correct, and if all the conditions on the checklist needed to be satisfied, the action was not justified.[5]

A war justifier may defend some wars either by insisting that, even on the strict application of all the criteria, some wars have met them and could in the future meet them, or by adopting a more relaxed view about what is morally required and thus claim that rather more wars meet sufficient of the criteria to be acceptable. The critic of the whole just war approach, however, may want to pose a dilemma: either all the criteria are meant to be met fully or they are not. If they are, then no war ever meets them in the real world in practice, whatever the theory says. On the hand, if they are not meant to be fully satisfiable, then the justificatory basis is inadequate because it allows various forms of serious moral failing to be acceptable.

There is also in fact a range of more specific objections to particular elements of the just war package (or other war justification packages). Here an objection focuses on one or other element and tries to show that, if this element fails, then, because it is essential to the whole position, the whole position fails. Some of the just war criteria are far more open to criticism than others, and I focus on these as providing the key issues.

5.2   Just causes

First, are any of the just causes currently or historically advanced really sound bases for going to war? Clearly, if there are objections to this element, the whole package is undermined. If there are no defensible just causes, the rest of the criteria have nothing to qualify! To take first the four criteria more commonly invoked in the past (crusading; balance of power intervention; legitimate protection of strategic interests; punishment), various arguments can be given for questioning these, certainly in the modern world.

(a)   Crusading

The idea of crusading is an unacceptable form of imposition of values. While we may accept some form of global ethic in which certain values are presented as acceptable all over the world even if they are not currently accepted, these values should be seen as to be promoted by persuasion and dialogue, not by force, and should be consistent with an ethic which accepts a wide variety of cultural expressions and worldviews. The general argument for this kind of non-dogmatic cosmopolitanism is made in chapter 3 and elsewhere in the book. Such a cosmopolitanism takes seriously the 'ethics of the means' and thus, even if one does wish to spread certain values, for instance about the environment or human rights, one will see that the use of military force is wholly inconsistent with such objectives. Another objection to the imposition of values by force (or the desire to spread them) can come from a postmodernist or relativist rejection of universal values as such and thus of any attempt to spread values, militarily or otherwise. While this of course is a way of rejecting the crusading 'just cause', as indeed much else in just war thinking, I have offered objections to this approach in chapter 2, §4.2, in my discussion of realism.

(b)   Balance of power

Whatever may have been the case in the nineteenth century, balance of power interventions are inconsistent with the kind of international order we have developed through the UN system. Military action would generally be counter-productive and, in the rare cases where it might be necessary, would need authorization by the UN Security Council, whose actions would be seen as those of a global police force rather than acts of war committed by particular states.

(c)   Strategic interests

The idea of the use of force as an instrument of foreign policy to secure strategic interests such as economic power is clearly inconsistent with the cosmopolitan perspective being supported in this book, and I refer the reader to the general thrust of these arguments, namely that, if we take seriously the cosmopolitan perspective, what counts as the legitimate furtherance of a particular body's interests – be they those of states, alliances of states or business corporations – is severely restricted by proper consideration of the interests of other states and bodies and of people worldwide.

(d) Punishment

The trouble with the idea that states could engage in fighting in order to punish other states is that states are their own police agents, judges and executioners. As Teichman argued well, there is a radical disanalogy between how a punishment system works within a settled legal system and what happens internationally (Teichman 1986: 40–5). Within a state, individuals who break the law are apprehended by the police, tried by independent, impartial judges and punished by the imposition by others of fines, imprisonment or other penalties, and generally killing is not what is done. While after a war certain things may be done, such as the imposition of reparations or Nuremberg-style trials of leaders, these are the acts of a winning side, not those of impartial judges.

Furthermore, the fighting of war itself is totally unlike a punishment system, since there is no judicial process involved and the routine method of proceeding is the killing of others. Fighting a war is not *merely* seen as a means towards being in a position after victory of punishing the enemy, and if it were it would look like an exceedingly blunt and unacceptable instrument of judicial justice. There must always be a primary just cause, with punishment being a possible secondary motive for dealing with the wrongs of the enemy which gave rise to the primary just cause, for example repulsing aggression. Only if we had something like a world state would military actions against a state in terms of international law be at all analogous to police action followed by judicial action.

We are left with the three kinds of just cause most commonly regarded as plausible in the modern world: self-defence (including aid to others and pre-emptive action), humanitarian intervention and responses by non-state bodies to oppression/injustice within their borders.

(e) Defence

The idea of national self-defence, despite its extreme plausibility, is actually problematic, whether it is regarded as a collective extension of individual self-defence or as an analogy. Rodin has argued effectively against this (Rodin 2002). Here I summarize what is a very sophisticated argument to which the reader is referred.

Rodin shows, first, that, whatever we mean by justified killing, self-defence for individuals is actually a very limited and circumscribed right that has to do with limited responses to an immediate attack and does not entail, for instance, that an individual may be armed to the teeth, and so on. Thus the move from individual self-defence to the defence of the state by deliberate and sustained action with standing armies in a high level of military preparation begs many questions, and cannot be justified as individual self-defence writ large.

If, on the other hand, the defence of the state is seen as analogous to self-defence (not an extension of it), then what we need to justify is the claim that the existence of a particular entity – a particular political entity with a particular history/culture – needs to be defended by extensive killing force. Characteristically, when an enemy attacks a country, what it wants to do is not kill the enemy as such, but rather to take control of that entity, and would rather that that entity accepted the imposition of changes without resistance in war. The question then is: Is the defence of a particular socio-political entity worth a large number of people being dead, and so on? The termination of an independent political community is in itself not the termination of particular human beings' lives – that it generally does involve this is because people decide to resist the change.

Many will reply that the defence of such an entity's existence is indeed worth a lot of people being killed on both sides. But Rodin's point is that, if there is an argument to defend the political community's existence, it gains nothing of its force from the analogy with self-defence. Rodin is sceptical that such an argument really is morally satisfactory. If either of Rodin's arguments works, then we have disposed of Fullinwider's kind of reasoning considered earlier, since, even if Fullinwider is right that individuals have a right of self-defence, this right does not carry over to the case of national defence.

Even if the reader is not convinced by this questioning of the heartland of just war thinking, there are other arguments about the nature of war considered below which may give rise to other kinds of doubt.

(f) Responses to oppression

The case of humanitarian intervention, however, raises special issues, and it may be felt that, especially if an action is authorized by the Security Council, this is surely a form of military action that has justice on its side and indeed is difficult not to support from a cosmopolitan point of view. The reason why such a case escapes the kinds of worry that Rodin raises in regard to the analogy with the self-defence argument is precisely because what provokes the humanitarian intervention is the fact that a target group of people is directly attacked – it is precisely a large number of individuals who are being killed and the bases of their lives destroyed. The extension of the self-defence of individuals seems appropriate – it is simply that they do not have sufficient means to defend themselves without outside help.

However, there are still issues Rodin raises about how similar the use of organized force is to ordinary self-defence, and it is worth observing in passing that, if this were the only just cause acceptable, there would not be standing armies around to respond accordingly – or, if there was one, it would likely be a UN-controlled force whose role in law-enforcement globally as a 'cosmopolitan military' would be conceptualized in rather different ways – an idea that Rodin's argument leads to anyway. But if there are problems with humanitarian military intervention (which I believe there are), these have less to do with the justness of the cause than with other factors. These will be discussed more fully when we deal with the issue in chapter 7, §4.

Although civil wars, wars of secession and anti-colonial struggles are different from one another, they all share a common characteristic of involving a group that considers that it is suffering from such a degree of oppression/injustice from the government in power (or people supporting it) that the resort to arms is justified. For some the bare fact that a dictator exercises power without democratic mandate or popular consent is sufficient basis for rebellion; the bare fact that a country's ruling group will not allow a group to secede when it wishes to is grounds for war; the bare fact that a colonial power rules is grounds for a liberation war. However, if these powers are not also pursuing or condoning serious injustices of other kinds, including *in extremis* genocide and other kinds of human rights violations that occasion humanitarian intervention, then it is not clear why there is a basis for *armed* struggle as opposed to other forms of resistance. But where there are serious human rights violations going on as well, then it may well be that there are grounds for saying that there is a just cause. If one objects to such wars, it is on the grounds that the use of violence even for these purposes is simply ruled out as such, or that such wars fail the proportionality test.

5.3   Proportionality

A common strategy in trying to undermine the whole idea of a war being justified is to argue that the general costs of war are too great. This is in effect to argue that the criterion of proportionality – namely that more good is in prospect than harm caused by going to war (or continuing a war) – is never satisfied. One famous argument of this kind, quoted by Wasserstrom, is that of the nineteenth-century pacifist Adin Ballou, who claimed that the history of war was the history of levels of human misery far in excess of the gains caused by war (Wasserstrom 1970: 91–2: see part of the longer quotation in chapter 5, §3.3). On the other hand, Rodin, who provides a rather different kind of argument against the justification of war, questions the value of this sort of consequentialist reasoning by stressing, using the example of what might have been reasonably calculated at the outset of the Second World War, that the actual course of war was so unpredictable that reasonably accurate assessments could not be made (Rodin 2002: 10–13). The following considerations about this style of reasoning tend to confirm Rodin's assessment.

First, there may be differences of view as to what is to count as the appropriate *domain* of consequences. Is one comparing, for instance, the expected positive effects of war against the negative effects of the war itself? Or is one considering the overall expected effects of a war with the effects of not fighting a war at all? How far into the future are the effects to be calculated? Certainly the effects of war do not stop with its end – indeed, the positive gains of a war reside mainly in the victorious peace and its consequences afterwards – but they also have to include the longer-term costs, in terms of the kind of 'peace' that is often established at the expense of the vanquished, in terms of the continued suffering after the war, and in terms of the effects that such wars have on the continued resort to war in the future, and so on (as compared with the effects of not going to war and the kinds of effects that has for later peace and tendencies to go to war).

Second, there may be serious disagreements as to what is to count as the relevant types of effects. Ballou's calculation tended to focus on the obvious effects, such as death, injury, and so on, but others may feel that the achievement of justice and the maintenance of liberty are important effects.

Third, different thinkers will bring to their analyses different views about causation. Anti-war analyses are inclined to suppose that any war contributes to the perpetuation of violence, both because generally violence begets violence at a psychological level and because the activity of justifying war perpetuates a normative system of justification which is then invoked on future occasions to justify future wars, and so on. On the other hand, war justifiers can argue that the attempt to regulate war according to justifiable criteria has no such general tendencies but rather a tendency actually to limit war. In the light of these factors, it is very difficult to get any agreement on whether wars all fail by the proportionality test, though for thinkers in each camp their interpretation may be among the decisive reasons for the view they take. The arguments that follow do not depend on such controversial estimates of consequences, but on features of war which are deemed unacceptable in themselves.

5.4 Can a war be fought according to the principles of *ius in bello*?

The following five arguments look at the means of war. The ways wars are fought (at least in the modern world) are ruled out as unethical. The strategy here is to show that the attempt to mark out a difference between ethical ways and unethical ways of fighting war is unsuccessful.

(a) The indiscriminateness of killing soldiers

Soran Reader argues that war is necessarily indiscriminate (Reader 2007). The argument is not that war is indiscriminate in that it kills civilians, but rather that the nature of modern warfare means that generally soldiers do not have any direct relationship with the soldiers whom they fight (see chapter 5 for a longer account of this position). In effect, Reader provides an answer to Nagel's argument, considered earlier, that there is a special relationship of hostility between soldiers fighting each other. Nagel's conception might make sense in relation to hand-to-hand combat, where particular soldiers are engaged in killing particular others, but makes no sense in the large-scale and impersonal operations of modern warfare.

(b) Indiscriminate killing of civilians

Another argument concerning indiscriminateness applies to the effects on civilians. Necessarily (in modern warfare and indeed generally in most warfare in the past), Robert Holmes argues, war kills innocent people in large numbers. It does not matter for this argument whether we can get a clear definition of non-combatant or innocent, since clearly there are cases of innocent human beings such as children and babies being involved. If warfare knowingly involves the killing of innocent people, then it is simply wrong. We should note that this argument does not depend on proportionality. It is not that the number of innocent people killed is disproportionate to the expected gains of the military operation. If warfare is known to kill such people, it cannot be right (Holmes 1989: 179–213). (See chapter 5 for a longer account of this position.)

(c) The dehumanizing of soldiers

Another kind of concern is over the kind of conditioning required of soldiers in an army, in regard both to the kind of understanding of the enemy required and to the command structure of an army or military organization. Clearly, for an army to work, there has to be strict discipline and training of soldiers to accept commands without question and to become desensitized to the killing of the enemy, who have to be in a sense 'dehumanized'. Such features of army training often dehumanize soldiers themselves and certainly undermine their autonomy as moral agents. (See chapter 5 for more detail on this.) Such features of military training are regarded by supporters of just war as justified means to goals that have to be pursued, but for others they make it inherently unacceptable as an instrument of policy.[6]

(d)   Consequentialist reasoning and the rules of war

What about a consequentialist approach to the rules of war that some means of fighting are seen as justified and others ruled out? As both Brandt and Hare argued, surely we can make a case for the rules of war which, for instance, limit who may be objects of attack, what weapons to use, and so on, on the grounds that the adoption of such rules leads to general utility. Are such arguments rendered irrelevant by the considerations (a)–(c) given above?

If the person offering a consequentialist defence of the rules of war does so because they are methodologically a consequentialist in all their ethical thinking, then they will simply reject the above non-consequentialist arguments about indiscriminateness vis-à-vis soldiers or vis-à-vis civilians and about dehumanization as beside the point. But, if that is the case, then the utility of the rules of war has to be seen in the wider context of the utility of war, and so we return to the issue discussed earlier as to whether, overall, wars do more good than harm.

If, however, the utility of the rules of war is seen not as derived from a general utilitarian position but as what should guide decisions *once war has started*, then the earlier arguments cannot be dismissed out of hand. If, for instance, war is necessarily indiscriminate, can one make any sense of the utility of having rules? In considering this question, it is worth noting what such arguments do and do not establish. If we consider the conditional question: What *if* nations are going to fight each other, then what should they do? Suppose they should not be fighting wars in the first place, what does one say? One temptation is to say that, given that they do something that they ought not to do, one cannot advise or assess them on how to do it ethically as opposed to unethically. (If someone is going to burgle a house, is there a right way or wrong way of doing it?) However, in many other areas of ethics it is appropriate to consider the right and wrong ways of doing things by people who pursue goals we think are wrong. It is, for instance, possible for someone who advocates gay rights to say that someone trying to ban gays from an organization should still try to do this by ethical means, for instance by dialogue, not force. Likewise, then, someone who rejects war as immoral can intelligibly regard certain ways of fighting as better than others and accept that, even if all ways of fighting are wrong, some ways of fighting are less so than others and rules concerning this can usefully be specified. But this issue does not merely arise for someone who rejects all war. Since in most scenarios (at least) one side in a war should not be fighting it, the same question arises vis-à-vis how they should be fighting it – and on the whole soldiers on the 'wrong' side are expected to follow the same rules of war as those on the 'right' side.

In fact it is perfectly possible for someone to argue – either for consequentialist or for non-consequentialist reasons – that wars should not be fought at all but still contend that, *if* they are fought, then they ought to be fought according to certain rules. Thus a consequentialist might claim, as we noted earlier, that war fails the proportionality test. Yet he may still think, as Brandt and Hare argue, that it makes sense to have rules of war. Likewise, incidentally, someone who rejects war for deontological reasons can also hold that, *if* wars are fought, it is better that certain limits are in place, for instance concerning the difference between soldiers and civilians. As it so happens, neither Brandt nor Hare endorses war overall. Hare in another article maintains that utilitarian thinking, properly thought through, actually rules out going to war in almost all cases and would, if generally adopted, lead to peace. If, as Hare asserts, the two main causes of war are nationalism – putting the interests of one's own country above that of others – and fanaticism – putting ideals above the interests of people – then utilitarianism, in making the equal interests of all central to ethics, actually leads to anti-war pacifist conclusions (Hare 1972a).

The same can be said of the argument from convention/prudence: if the reasons for limiting the ways war is fought are based on prudence and mutual interests, then at best the rules of war are based on conventional agreement. Such agreement may be the premise for limiting the awfulness of war but says nothing about whether going to war is what one should do in the first place. But this is in any case hardly a satisfactory basis for morality (see earlier, §3.4, and chapter 2, §4.6). If it turned out that such reasoning was operative in a war, then in a sense an essential condition of *ius ad bellum* clause (g) is not satisfied.

(e)   The endemic tendency not to observe the rules

Suppose the defender of the possibility of a proposed just war thinks that all the criteria we have considered survive the criticisms mentioned, and in particular that a war can be fought according to norms that are justified either in some non-consequentialist fashion or in some consequentialist fashion, and claims that a war fought in accordance with these criteria would be ethically satisfactory. Nevertheless there is also a line of criticism that real wars rarely observe these norms, or do so only for a while, and that the actual course of wars is so much worse than initially intended – and thus justified – in terms of civilian deaths, atrocities, and so on, that they cannot be justified. Insofar as any side contemplating war either expects this to happen (as they should if they have any knowledge of human affairs) or, even more significantly, conditionally intends to do such things, for instance if military necessity dictates or if they start to lose, then this also provides reason to refrain from war in the first place.

Questions

1 In regard to a recent war you have been concerned about, did it for either side meet the *ius ad bellum* criteria? Was using these criteria the best way for assessing its rightness or wrongness?
2 What method of reasoning, if any, shows that it is right to target combatants but wrong to target non-combatants?
3 Which just causes are the most plausible?
4 Which, if any, of the objections to going to war are for you most plausible?

5 PACIFISM, NONVIOLENCE AND THE WAY OF PEACE

1 Introduction

In this chapter we look at a cluster of approaches which reject the resort to violence in general, or going to war in particular, in response to overt violence, military or otherwise, or indeed to situations of serious moral failure or injustice, such as human rights violations, oppression or exploitation. This chapter concerns questions about acting peacefully in response to situations in which there is not peace. But I defer to the next chapter the actual discussion of various conceptions of peace, and of answers to some rather different questions: What makes peace (in its various senses) valuable and why, in what ways and to what extent do we have duties to support, sustain or promote peace in its various senses?

Both pacifism and the philosophy of nonviolence have served to indicate ethical positions in which violence is rejected as a way of responding to violence – and both positions, as we will see, can be held in absolutist fashion or as a general commitment to which there may be exceptions in extreme situations. The idea of the 'way of peace' is sometimes used as well to indicate such a general commitment. Although it can mean a number of different things, I shall present a distinct interpretation of the way of peace as a general commitment to nonviolence as a way of living and acting generally, combined with a way of promoting whatever ethical causes one has, including the pacificist commitment to promoting peace.

What is central to pacifism and nonviolence is an ethical response to situations and others' actions which are unpeaceful, unjust, and so on. However, the philosophy of nonviolence is on the face of it broader, in the sense that it is about how one responds to other human beings in all kinds of situations, ranging from overt violence and war, through situations of conflict, to aggressive or irritating behaviour in everyday transactions. Pacifism, either in the form that is against all killing or in the form that is against war specifically, is more precisely about the wrongness of using killing force in response to such situations. Theoretically a pacifist could be quite aggressive in ways that fell short of using killing force, and could have negative and condemnatory assessments of others. That said, most pacifists are in fact committed to the philosophy of nonviolence in human relationships more generally and also to promoting peace, justice, etc. (see section 2). Likewise, most advocates of nonviolence are also dedicated to promoting peace, social justice – including 'fighting' injustice – and generally desirable social change. There has in recent years been a marked move in the direction of people describing themselves as committed to nonviolence rather than pacifism because of its more overt general approach, but on more careful analysis we can see that, while there are significant variations in both ideas, given most people's actual fleshing out of what their respective commitments to nonviolence and pacifism amount to, they come to much the same thing. It is largely a question of terminological preference. I shall, however, look at them separately, since the way they are presented can be somewhat different.

2   Nonviolence

2.1   Violence and nonviolence

Nonviolence is partly clarified by its contrast to violence. Violence in itself is a concept that has many different contested meanings. One can identify first what is often called the paradigm case of violence. For instance, Robert Holmes called it 'the use of physical force to cause harm, death, or destruction' (Holmes 1990: 1). John Harris earlier called it the 'rape, murder, fire, sword paradigm' (Harris 1979: ch. 2), but he was quick to point out that, although these examples are clearly instances in which an act of violence is also a case of 'acting violently', such acts need not involve 'acting violently': someone who poisons a water supply in order to kill the villagers may perform his deed ever so smoothly! So too does a commander who orders his men to shoot others, even though he uses only his voice. What is central to the act of violence is the intention (directly, as in shooting a gun, through a longer causal chain, as in the poisoning case, or via the mediation of other agents, as in giving orders) to cause physical harm, destruction or death. Many would include – as Harris does – acts about which it is reasonably foreseeable that they will have these effects even if not intended, and likewise a threat of violence as a way of controlling others is violence.[1]

As implied by the above, many thinkers would accept an extension of violence to include the 'psychological', where the violence involves certain forms other than physical harm – being intimidated, undermined or made subservient, and other ways of being psychologically damaged. Examples might be a husband who dominates his wife through verbal means or demeans her through the use of sexist language, or a manager who in industrial relations takes a tough line against workers trying to assert their rights. Generally aggressive language, including body language expressive of anger and belittling attitudes, can be thought of as violent in this sense.

The discussion of violence so far is of direct relevance to the idea of nonviolence: the philosophy of nonviolence is the renunciation of acts of violence in these senses. There are, however, two further extensions of the idea of violence which are rather more controversial. They are related to nonviolence in somewhat different ways in that they do not so much feature in what the nonviolentist rejects in their own behaviour as provide part of the context to which the nonviolentist is reacting.

First there is institutional (systemic, structural) violence – an approach that in recent years has been associated particularly with Johann Galtung, the Norwegian peace researcher. In addition to the acts of violence by individuals – whether physical or psychological – there is the kind of harm, damage and indeed loss of life that is associated with the way institutions and systems work, whether or not these effects are intended (see, for instance, Galtung 1969). While the idea originated in Marxist critiques of capitalism as causing the suffering and death of poorly paid and ill-protected workers, there are many other forms of institutional violence, for example racial discrimination or, in former communist regimes in Eastern Europe, suppression of liberties. It is worth noting that the etymological root of violence links it to 'violation' (for instance of rights). Two points are worth making about this extension. It is hotly debated whether such an extension is helpful; first, because, as Teichman observes, we may do better to identify various forms of injustice by a variety of terms, such as oppression, exploitation or discrimination, than to subsume them under a vague and contestable conception of violence (Teichman 1986: 25–8); and, second, because such an extension muddies the waters over the justification of 'active' violence. It appears to provide those advocating active violence with an argument that their violence is only a *response* to violence already present and so a form of 'self-defence', whereas it remains the case that the resort to active violence *is* a resort to something quite new and requires a different kind of justification, if there be such, than one merely based on a response to 'violence'. The second main point is that these are precisely the kinds of injustice on a large scale that the nonviolentist has to find ways of combating.

Second, there is the 'negative violence' thesis as put forward by John Harris: we are engaged in negative violence if we knowingly let harm occur when we could intervene to stop it (Harris 1979). Our omission is part of the causal chain that leads to harm or death, just as the absence of oxygen may be a part of the cause of a death, and we could have intervened. This has obvious application to evils such as world poverty (and as such is associated with the 'moral equivalent of murder' argument sometimes advanced in that connection), but it applies to any harms, local or global. For most thinkers this is an extension too far, quite apart from the moral corollary it entails that what we ought to be doing is reduce evils as much as possible. It is certainly a sense of violence that is not really relevant to our understanding of nonviolence. While nonviolentists are clearly committed to tackling large-scale evils such as world poverty, and to doing so nonviolently, this does not distinguish them from many others who would accept that we do have significant obligation to play our part in reducing the evils we can prevent in the world.

2.2 The philosophy of nonviolence

The philosophy of nonviolence, then, is a commitment to nonviolence in response to violence, oppression or injustice, to oneself or others. The phrase 'to oneself or others' covers two distinct features of the approach. First, there is one's commitment to respond nonviolently in one's immediate interaction with others when they attack or act in an aggressive or threatening way. Holmes calls this non-resistance, which is rather like the position of an anti-war pacifist who refuses to fight but does nothing else. Typically the advocate of nonviolence goes further than this. Second, then, it is a way of actively engaging with the world in order to help others who are subject to various forms of violence, including the injustices of systems. Holmes identified two forms of this: first, passive resistance and, second, direct nonviolent action. The example he gives of the former is the African American Rosa Parks, who in 1955 refused to give up her seat to a white on a bus: she did nothing, but in doing nothing she was making a statement in a nonviolent way. The example given of the latter was of Joseph McNeill and other African American students, who in 1960 deliberately sat at a Woolworth's lunch counter in Greensboro, North Carolina (Holmes 1990: 1–2). Much action which is counted as civil disobedience has this form. But nonviolence is not merely a commitment to *confronting* the powers that be; it is more generally a commitment to the use of nonviolent ways of interacting with people, especially those with whom one disagrees – thus emphasizing the role of dialogue, conflict resolution and real listening as well. It should be noted that, as normally advocated, pacifism is also a commitment not merely to 'not fighting' (passivism) but to taking various forms of action both to combat injustice and to advance peace (see later in §3.4). (See also Gene Sharp's early and influential advocacy, in Sharp 1973.)

The ethical basis of such action can be understood in two ways. First, it can be seen as the right way in which to respond to injustice: here is an injustice and here is my response. Second, such action is engaged in because it is believed to be effective in contributing towards the desired social change. This is not based on the expectation that on any particular occasion the action will definitely produce the result in question, but rather that it will contribute towards such change in the long run. In saying that such action can be understood in two ways, we need to note that there is some difference between a principled commitment to nonviolence and the use of nonviolence *as a tactic*.

It is commonly held these days that one of the most effective ways of combating injustice is to engage in nonviolent action, particularly if this is done in concert with others. Examples of this include, in the 1930s and 1940s, the movement in India led by Gandhi against the British Raj and, in the 1960s, the civil rights movement in the USA. In more recent years an inspiration for this approach has come from the way the civil society movements in Eastern Europe played a significant role in the 1980s – at least as understood by advocates of nonviolence – in undermining the Soviet system. Such uses of nonviolence do not entail that those who practise it would always refuse to employ force in extreme circumstances. Many of those who postulate the power of nonviolence in effecting social change accept that it has such power both because of its use by many as a tactic and because of the principled stance of some. Two books that bring out the power of nonviolence are Mark Kurlansky's *Nonviolence* (2006), which traces its long history, and Jonathan Schell's *The Unconquerable World* (2003), which demonstrates its effectiveness in the modern world.

Another point over which, as Holmes points out, there is a difference among advocates of nonviolence is whether or not the commitment is unqualified by including the advocacy of psychological as well as physical nonviolence. Clearly the former – involving the avoidance of hostility towards the 'enemy'/'opponent', of anger or of negative stereotyping – requires a much higher standard. Again, those who advocate it may see it as what is morally required but also as what actually contributes more effectively towards achieving a more nonviolent and just world.

Generally the philosophy of nonviolence is seen by its advocates as superior to approaches that advocate the use of violence. Holmes notes the following points. In taking on an opponent in a nonviolent way one is showing respect for that opponent: he or she is seen as someone who is potentially willing to engage in dialogue and rational negotiation, not as someone to be killed, destroyed or crushed. By contrast, the use of violence necessarily involves a win–lose structure, and it cannot avoid harm and destruction. However, we should note that, from a one-sided perspective, this may seem all right. It is from a cosmopolitan perspective, or one at least that takes the interests and moral status of people on both sides of a conflict seriously, that the use of violence has serious defects. By acting nonviolently, Holmes continues, one is not adding to violence in the world. Furthermore, if one lives nonviolently, one infuses everyday conduct with a nonviolent spirit. In the case of the use of violence, even for winners the means transform the moral quality of the end. Even if the end is seen as noble or just, the means taken affect the moral quality of the overall outcome (Holmes 1990: x). (This remark is very similar to that of Gandhi, that the 'means are the ends in the making'; see §3.2.)

2.3   Objections to nonviolence

What objections can be raised against the philosophy of nonviolence? I shall reserve the specific issues to do with the wrongness of killing either in general or in war until I examine pacifism. Here I look at several possible objections to the more general approach insofar as it goes beyond the issue of killing. To the extent that nonviolence is seen as a general approach to human relationships, it is certainly difficult to criticize – it simply takes further the principles of civility most people take for granted as the basis of ordered and peaceful living. However, it is when its advocates make stronger empirical claims and when it is presented as a principled stance that objections emerge.

First, insofar as it is presented as a tactic for effecting social change and resisting injustice, the empirical record is mixed. As Holmes notes, sometimes nonviolence works in regard to an external objective, for example stopping a particular violence or injustice, sometimes it does not. But the same is true of violence. It is a complex issue, and it is so in two respects: first, it is not merely about comparing empirical results – always difficult – but about different goals/values involved; second, the real issue is over the longer-term effects of different ways of living and dealing with problems, not whether there is success in regard to some particular concern. Here the opposing sets of beliefs become more articles of faith. For some the adage that 'violence begets violence' has almost a self-evident ring of truth about it; but for others the idea that regulated and focused violence can 'nip violence in the bud' is also plausible.

Second, I would mention one specific point in Holmes's position where he says that the policy of nonviolence does not 'add to violence in the world'. Now in a strict sense this is right if one is thinking of the agent's own acts. On the other hand, there is a sense in which this need not be not strictly true. As Nagel pointed out in connection with the principle of non-combatant immunity (not directly attacking civilians), one can *avoid* deliberately killing civilians or carrying out atrocities but one cannot by so doing necessarily *prevent* civilians being killed or atrocities being done by others (Nagel 1972; see Beitz 1985: 62). One's refusal to use violence may not add to the acts of violence by one's own action, but it may occasionally allow others to add to the sum of violent acts in the world. To some critics this is enough to show that a principled commitment to non-violence without exceptions is unacceptable but, even if this is claimed, it does not show that generally nonviolence is not the preferable position in terms of overall consequences. No doubt for a nonviolentist who is committed both to the principle and to the empirical generalization, such a case would pose a dilemma, and, where the consequences are sufficiently bad, the philosophy of nonviolence may allow rare exceptions to its principle. On the other hand, someone who accepts the principle of nonviolence may simply claim that it is about his acts, and not about what others do as a result of his acts or refusals to act, and that, although he is indeed generally convinced that violence begets violence and is interested in trying to bring about nonviolent change, acting in accordance with his principle always take precedence over consideration of consequences (cf. my discussion of the relationship between promoting a value x and acting x-ly in chapter 6, §2.1).

Third, if the philosophy of nonviolence is advocated as a philosophy that ought to be adopted by everyone, then it runs into a problem similar to that faced by a principled pacifism in regard to all killing, and this is in regard to the role of the state and the enforcement of a legal system. The point here is not that the state is ultimately, as a coercive institution, backed by the threat of killing force if all else fails, but rather that the actual punishment system universally employed is in itself violent, in the sense that violence is done to those who are punished – notably in any punishment regime that locks people up for significant periods of time – since deprivation of liberty is itself a significant harm to an individual. An advocate of nonviolence advances (rightly in my opinion) an approach to punishment which stresses reform, rehabilitation or restorative justice, and is less happy with modes of punishment based on retribution or deterrence (where the harm done to the prisoner is seen as a means to the deterring of others).

But it is hard to see how the deprivation of liberty and/or other forms of harm (either intended as punishment or as by-products of the punishment regime, such as loss of self-esteem or maltreatment by other prisoners) can be avoided altogether in any punishment regime associated with any political community at all like the nation-state. One response is to argue, as did Tolstoy (Tolstoy [1902] 1966; see also Brock and Young 1999: 6), that the state is to be rejected, but it is unclear what realistic alternative could be proposed that would avoid the same problem of how law and order is to be maintained at whatever level is proposed. Meantime one has to take up an ethical position vis-à-vis the institutions we currently have. But we should note that, if we accept the 'violence of the magistrate', as Teichman calls it (Teichman 1986), it does not follow that states may punish other states through war (see chapter 4, §5.2(d)).

3   Pacifism

3.1   Basic distinctions

There are many positions covered by the term 'pacifism' (see Teichman 1986: 1–9; Brock 1981; Mayer 1966; Brock and Young 1999). Much pacifist thinking centres on the thesis that all waging of war is morally wrong (and is sometimes called 'anti-warism'); such a view is consistent with accepting limited violence, such as in self-defence (or defence of loved ones) or the threats of violence involved in an organized state, what as we noted above Teichman calls the 'violence of the magistrate'. Sometimes pacifism is a more general position of being opposed to the use of all killing force against others (certainly humans, maybe other living things too) and if it opposes the use more generally of any kind of violence and other kinds of force, then it is equivalent to the philosophy of nonviolence. Since the latter general position against all use of killing force has implications about the legitimacy of the state (as a coercive institution), it can lead to revolutionary pacifism such as that advocated by Tolstoy: the state is itself institutionalized violence and needs to be challenged. However, pacifists who are opposed to all forms of violence need not take such a revolutionary stance but, as Atack notes, adopt a more reformist approach in trying to create a world in which pacifist principles are more generally acted upon (Atack 2005: 76, 85–6).

Generally those who take up the different positions above are inclined to think that their principle is one which is universally applicable: indeed it is commonly held that, if it is a genuine moral position, then it ought to have this implication, and one must make judgements about others' conduct that they may not accept, for instance that what a soldier does is wrong. However, this universalist implication is consistent with many different ways of responding to others – and this partly turns on what more generally one sees as the implications of holding *any* moral position vis-à-vis others who do not agree. First, making judgements about others need not be voiced (or only voiced reluctantly if one is challenged) – a kind of ethical quietism and, if one *does* nothing as well, a kind of passivism. Second, judgements may be voiced in a condemnatory way, rejecting what others do as simply wrong. Third, they may be voiced in such a way that one wants to enter into dialogue with others who disagree, and with a nuanced approach that, while all fighting is wrong, some forms of fighting are not as bad as others. There may be, that is, a range of views about how one relates to those – currently the majority – who do not accept this position and believe certain forms of fighting to be acceptable, ranging from quietism, through respecting their conscientiously held positions and engaging with them in dialogue, to outright rejection or condemnation.

There are, however, those whose pacifism is seen as a personal commitment without the universalist implications for what others should do. While critics often see this as incoherent as an *ethical* position, there are ways of understanding ethics which make it a possible position to hold. One approach, for instance, is to see the position as coming from a religious *calling* or vocation in which God (or other Supreme Being) calls one to take this stance (without implying that God calls others to do the same). This 'vocational pacifism' may be advocated within a wider moral approach (see, for instance, Ihara 1978). Consider the analogous case of the vocational commitments of monks to lives of simplicity or celibacy, which can be seen as playing a particular role in the wider society by the rest of a religious community who do not accept these norms for themselves. This example is again from a religious background, but there is no reason in principle why someone could not take a pacifist stance for the sake of peace for secular reasons, perhaps believing that peace as a general condition is furthered if some people have a stronger commitment to the 'way of peace'. The point is that, if a person makes a *public commitment* to live according to certain standards as a way of advancing those standards, then he or she has a moral commitment which others do not have. While this kind of pacifism without universalist assumptions is certainly plausible and deserves more serious consideration than it is usually given, I shall in what follows focus more on pacifism as a universalist claim – since this is what it is generally understood to be, certainly by those who are critical of it, as well as raising issues of more interest to most people.

It is helpful to make a distinction at this stage between the core idea in pacifism – whether universalist or individualist – and what is usually included in most pacifists' conceptions of their pacifism. Although one could do or say nothing (as noted above) or merely engage in discussion with others about their differing views, generally pacifists do see their commitment as involving much more by way of active engagement to oppose violence, injustice or other forms of oppression, promoting peace and justice in the world, and engaging with others about the value of peace and the role of pacifist vocation in a world where others are prepared to fight. Pacifism is not usually simply a principle 'it is wrong to fight/kill' but a package of ethical commitments emanating from a world-view in which the principle is central. It is not right to say that they are pacifists and also, independently, people who resist violence and promote peace and justice for other reasons. The cluster of commitments comes from their account of human nature and relationships, of peace and justice, and so on. In this chapter I focus on the primary principle and the arguments against it, not on the larger 'ethical packages' held by most pacifists. However, some of the answers to objections we consider later do depend on appealing to these further commitments typical of most pacifists.

Before looking at the arguments for pacifism, I need to introduce one further distinction. This is the distinction between absolute/deontological/principled pacifism and contingent/consequentialist pacifism. The general contrast is clear enough though the details become more complex.

The latter position, as the word 'consequentialist' indicates, is one based on what the thinker believes are the consequences of fighting in wars (or resorting to violence more generally): the rejection of war is contingent upon what happen to be its effects, which are on this view seriously negative, since far more harm is done than good is achieved. In its strong form it rejects all war, since all wars are believed to have these negative consequences; in a weaker form it rejects almost all wars, but accepts that there could be wars occasionally whose consequences were otherwise (though far more rarely than war justifiers generally suppose).

Now such a position can be adopted by someone who is in his or her *general* approach a consequentialist in his or her ethical thinking. A utilitarian, for instance, interested in maximizing good outcomes and only supporting courses of action which have the best balance of good over bad outcomes, might well be a contingent pacifist (though some utilitarians would do the calculations differently and support some wars). However, contingent pacifism is not merely a position available to a thinker of this general kind. Even someone who thought that morality involved a number of moral considerations other than promoting best outcomes might accept that the enormity of war was such that the duty not to pursue courses of action with seriously bad outcomes simply overrides any other moral arguments about rights or justice one might have that might support going to war. Indeed some just war theorists, though they believe other moral considerations are indeed relevant to war, finish up – at least in regard to modern warfare – adopting contingent pacifist positions (see later discussion of proportionality in §3.3).

By contrast, many pacifists take the view that calculating the consequences of fighting in war is to think about the issue in the wrong way. On this view, there is simply something inherently wrong with fighting in war or using killing force more generally. This is sometimes called 'absolute pacifism', because the view is held is that it is absolutely wrong, in the sense of there being no exceptions, to fight or kill. The term is unduly restrictive, however, since someone could hold that there is something inherently wrong about fighting or killing, or that there is a strong moral presumption against these acts, but that *in extremis* such a moral claim is overridden. The point is that the rationale for the position and the nature of the exceptions do not turn on considerations of overall consequences. The term 'deontological' (or 'duty ethic') captures the idea that there is some kind of moral consideration against fighting and killing that is independent of consequences, but, apart from being a remarkably ugly word, it does not neatly capture the full range of moral arguments, for instance, about rights or virtues which may be relevant to the view advanced. The word 'principled' captures what most people have in mind when they say they have a principled objection to something rather than a pragmatic one based on consequences. However, it does not strictly exclude the consequentialist, who may claim that he too is acting on principle, namely the principle of maximizing well-being! In what follows the reader will see how a number of different kinds of argument are used.

3.2   General arguments against killing

Pacifism has a long history and has featured in all the major religions. It is particularly associated with the first few centuries of the Christian religion and enjoyed a resurgence with the emergence of a variety of the modern peace churches such as Mennonites, Anabaptists and Quakers, which had their origins in the period of religious turmoil several centuries ago. However, adherents to pacifism in the current era draw their inspiration not only from these religious traditions but also from certain forms of secular moral thought.

The early Christian Church was essentially a peace church: the life of Christ was seen as a life based on love, including loving one's enemy and turning the other cheek in the face of aggression. Christ's endorsement of the Old Testament duty 'not to kill' was taken to be quite simply that – an injunction against killing others; 'do unto others what one would have done to one' can also be read as excluding killing others and, if this involves self-sacrifice, the sacrifice of Christ on the cross showed the way. It was only in the fourth century AD, when under Constantine Christianity became the official religion of the Graeco-Roman world, that Christian thought turned away from its pacifist origins – partly because Christians who were now in positions of power had to deal with the problem of maintaining order in the empire.

The religious groups in the sixteenth and seventeenth centuries which turned to pacifism did so in a conscious return to what they saw as the truths of early or primitive Christianity. Quakers, for instance, proclaimed that there was 'that of God' in everyone and that 'answering that of God' was incompatible with trying to kill them; their declaration to Charles II in 1660 rejected all 'outward weapons' in the struggle to create the peaceable kingdom which could only come about through 'living the kingdom' in one's own life (see BYM 1995: §24.04).

Are there secular arguments not based on religious premises? It may seem more difficult to find such arguments. The source of this difficulty needs first to be confronted. A common assumption about the nature of morality (if it is not seen as based on divine creation, command or sanction) is that it is some kind of convention by which human beings seek to regulate their behaviour towards one another. Such a convention may include agreeing not to kill or harm one another. However, what happens if people inside the convention break the convention or others outside the convention ignore it and attack oneself or one's community? The resort to killing force in response is seen as a natural one and not limited by the moral framework. Indeed, it was and is often held that humans have a natural right to self-defence as an aspect of the basic right to life. This line of thought is reinforced given a certain understanding of the nature of political community, which is seen as based on some kind of contract (albeit implicit) for protection by the state in return for which individuals are expected to play their part in that protection, if necessary by being prepared to kill in defence of their political community if called to do so.

This incidentally is why historically most governments have been far less willing to listen sympathetically to claims of conscientious refusal or objection to military service based on secular arguments, since such refusal is seen as a failure to play one's part in a scheme of cooperation. Religiously based conscientious objection has been more commonly (though not universally) accepted precisely because its argument appeals to a different kind of moral claim, namely what the conscientious objector believes to be his religious leading.

But secular arguments do not have to be based on such conventionalist or contractarian reasoning. First, if morality is about respecting other human beings, it is at least plausible to argue that this entails not trying to kill them: the golden rule 'do to others as one would be done to oneself', while a feature of the moral thought of all the major religions, is also a secular principle which can be interpreted to entail a pacifist commitment. The Christian moral principle 'love thy neighbour as thyself', which accords the same moral status to others as to oneself, does not depend on religious premises to be accepted. Although Kant himself was not a pacifist, his categorical imperative 'treat humanity, whether in oneself or any other person, never merely as a means but always as an end as well' can be read as implying a pacifist position.

Furthermore, the Gandhian maxim 'the means are the ends in the making'[2] is perfectly accessible to a secular thinker (and to a religious thinker too of course). I read this as containing two complementary truths, first, normatively, that we *ought* to show the values that we are promoting in the means we take and, second, predictively, that the adoption of certain actions as a means already expresses the real ends we are pursuing and makes them more likely to be fully realized later. Indeed, it seems to be a requirement in a certain sense of ethical consistency internal to the relationship between the particular acts we perform and the courses of action we engage in of which they are part.

Third, in addition to the non-consequentialist arguments above from religious and secular sources, another kind of secular argument based on the overall effects of going to war, or resorting to other forms of violence compared to not doing so, is advanced by those who see a moral case for pacifism in the longer-term effects of actions (as opposed to the immediate nature of the relations we have with fellow human beings, as illustrated in the types of arguments above). An early example of such thinking is that of the nineteenth-century pacifist Adin Ballou (to be discussed below).

Indeed, it is arguments of these kinds – all alternatives to convention/ contract arguments and all independent of religious premises (though to some extent emerging out of the latter) – that lend force to what Hawk has called the 'moral presumption of pacifism' (see Hawk 2006).

All the above arguments are of course against participating in war. If it is wrong to kill fellow human beings generally, then it is wrong to kill them in war, and it is wrong to prepare and train to kill by joining an army. Killing in war may be particularly morally bad because it is widespread and organized, but warfare itself does not provide any new basis for morally condemning killing.

However, there are a number of further arguments which specifically relate to the character of warfare. These are additional arguments for the general pacifist, but for someone who is not a general pacifist they are quite independent.

3.3 Various reasons for anti-war pacifism

What is wrong with fighting in wars (large-scale organized killing, using armies and so on) are factors such as the following.

(a) Dehumanization and impersonality

The dehumanization of war involves two aspects: that of soldiers who do the killing and that by soldiers of enemy soldiers.

First, the very nature of military training involves two elements: soldiers are trained to accept orders without question. This deprives a soldier of his autonomy. Since the exercise of autonomy is part of what makes us fully human, such training make the soldier less than fully human. One aspect of this is that a soldier is expected not to exercise independent moral judgement; and again the exercise of independent moral judgement is part of what makes us fully responsible human beings. Second, although there is a traditional perception of discipline and training making 'Men' out of 'men' and of bringing out military virtues, it is also often recognized that such training actually hardens and maybe sometimes brutalizes soldiers, and certainly those actually involved in combat are often left with various forms of trauma and other psychological problems. An ancillary point to add to this is that, by splitting responsibility, the military command system permits things that would never be done without a chain of command. That is, there are many situations in which A commands B to do x and B does x, but x would not be done if A had to do x himself and B would not have done x but for the fact that he was commanded by someone else to do it. Neither agent takes full responsibility for such acts, and each can say that the other person is really responsible for them.

For the anti-war pacifist the endemic loss of autonomy (for all but the most senior of military officials) and the serious possibility of various forms of desensitization of soldiers both provide moral grounds for rejecting such treatment of human beings.[3]

Second, the training of soldiers involves drilling men to dehumanize other human beings; that is, if an army is to be an effective force, soldiers have to forget or suppress their knowledge of the essential humanity of the enemy soldier. Soldiers have to be turned into efficient 'killing machines'. As Coates remarks, 'in this way behaviour and attitudes that in peacetime would be regarded as beyond the pale become in war the moral and professional norm' (Coates 1997: 29). Even the much praised Second

World War general Field Marshal Montgomery advised that 'the troops must be brought to a state of wild enthusiasm once the operation begins . . . they must enter the fight with the light of battle in their eyes and definitely want to kill the enemy' (Montgomery 1958: 88–9, quoted in Coates 1997: 29). Furthermore, although this is not the case with all warfare, there is a tendency to characterize the enemy in terms that make them less than fully human, and either demonize them, bestialize them or otherwise diminish their status.

Third, there is a related argument drawn from a certain strand within feminist thought called the 'ethics of care', in which the value of caring is seen as ruling out fighting, and rejects war as based on the impersonal nature of international relations and the universal norms of just war theory or realism that inform it. For instance, Ruddick, in arguing for 'maternal thinking', claims that:

> When maternal thinking takes upon itself the critical perspective of a femi-
> nist standpoint, it reveals a contradiction between mothering and war. Moth-
> ering begins in birth and promises life; military thinking justifies organised,
> deliberate deaths. (Ruddick 1990: 135)

(b) Indiscriminateness

The claim that fighting armies in war is necessarily indiscriminate can take two forms.

First, there is a general argument, as advanced by Soran Reader in her article 'Cosmopolitan pacifism' (Reader 2007). She regrets the fact that many cosmopolitans seem still to hold to a just war theory of some kind, wanting for instance to justify humanitarian intervention. She argues that, given a plausible reading of cosmopolitanism which claims that all human beings have equal status and have rights not to be arbitrarily attacked, then what happens in warfare is an undermining of these rights. On this view even enemy soldiers who happen to be part of a large number of different people on the 'enemy side' are, if attacked, attacked in an indiscriminate way. The point here relies precisely on a vast disanalogy from a situation in which a particular person attacks someone and that person responds in self-defence. When, for instance, a military person releases bombs from a gun or aeroplane, he has really absolutely no idea just who he will kill or injure among the enemy soldiers. The relationship a soldier has to his country is too indirect for an enemy soldier to be properly discriminating in whom he is attacking.

A second argument focuses on the collateral damage to civilians in modern warfare. The point here is that, even if military operations are directed towards military targets – the intention may be to discriminate between civilians and military – the effects include and are known in advance to include civilians. In reality the effects of warfare are indiscriminate. The moral premise behind this anti-war argument, as advanced by Robert Holmes (Holmes 1989: 179–203), is that it is always wrong to engage in actions which cause the deaths of innocent human beings. This argument depends on disputing the ethical significance of the doctrine of double effect, which, as we saw in chapter 4, seeks to downgrade the ethical significance of civilian deaths if they are anticipated as side-effects of military action. In effect Holmes's rationale depends on adopting Bentham's adage that 'we intend all that we foresee'. In terms of moral responsibility we are responsible for the deaths of innocent human beings which we knowingly bring about. War – certainly modern warfare – involves such deaths and is therefore wrong. We should note that, even if the combatant/non-combatant distinction is fuzzy – since many civilians are involved in various degrees in a war effort – there are nevertheless many who are clearly on the 'innocence' side, such as children, the infirm and the elderly. We should also note that this argument merely relies on the wrongness (knowingly, even if not as one's goal) of killing innocent civilians, not on the idea of proportionality, discussed in the next section. It is not how many civilians are killed that is at issue, but the fact that warfare involves – and not merely accidentally – the deaths of civilians (perhaps one should add 'on some significant scale').

(c)   Anti-war pacifism and just war theory

Two strategies are available here. The first is to argue, accepting the framework of just war thinking, that, even if in theory some wars might be justified, in practice, if all the just war criteria are applied fully, no war turns out to be justified and no fighting in a war is justified. The second is to reject the framework and argue that one or other of the just war conditions is in itself unacceptable, so the just war approach (along with all other justificatory moves that share the same problematic features) fails.

The first strategy is that, if any given war has to be fought according to all the criteria, then doubts about any one of them being fully met undermine the rightness of a war – for instance about proportionality, last resort, war needing to be fought in accordance with *ius in bello* criteria, the 'just cause' not being compromised by further goals and motives not in accordance with 'right intention', and so on. It is an article of faith to suppose that no war proposed will ever meet all the criteria, but at least there is a *presumption* to that effect. It would take too long to go over a very wide range of scenarios, but the general approach should be clear enough. Two remarks are in order, one to do with a particularly troubling feature of war – the proportionality test – the other to do with an implication of the above presumption.

The proportionality argument is very simply the argument that more good comes out of war than harm. The contingent pacifist simply disputes whether this is ever really the case. If we are truly candid about the horrors of war and we count the harm done to soldiers and civilians on the other side properly, that is, as having equal weight to that of those on our side, then war is not justified. A particularly famous example of such an approach is that of the nineteenth-century pacifist Adin Ballou. In a long passage of rhetorical eloquence, quoted at length in Wasserstrom's survey article, Ballou indicts the historical record of war. Here is just one small part of it:

> If it [self-defence] be the true method, it must on the whole work well. It must preserve human life and secure mankind against injury, more certainly and effectually than any other possible method. Has it done this? I do not admit it. How happens it that, according to the lowest probable estimate, some fourteen thousand millions of human beings have been slain by human means, in war and otherwise? (Ballou [1866] 1995: 31; quoted in Wasserstrom 1970: 91)

As implied by this quotation, the proportionality test should not be merely about whether more good than evil comes out of fighting, but about whether the total balance is better than the balance of the alternatives of not going to war (including nonviolent resistance).

The second point relating to the first strategy is what I call the 'probability and autonomy' argument. Even if general worries about war meeting all the criteria fail to rule out all wars, there is, if their cumulative impact is recognized, a strong presumption against any war being justified. So from the point of view of any ordinary soldier who is meant to obey orders without question, and who is not generally in a position to know all the relevant factors concerning justification and motivation that enter into their calculation by politicians and generals, there must be a strong probability that the war in which he is being expected to participate is actually unjustified. So, he should not as an autonomous agent engage in something which is at risk of being seriously morally flawed, it would be wrong for him to participate in any war, and it would also be wrong to put himself in a position of having to fight in such a war. So he ought not to join an army in the first place. Interestingly Rawls comes close to this position when he says:

If the aims of the conflict are sufficiently dubious and the likelihood of receiving flagrantly unjust commands is sufficiently great, one may have a duty and not only a right to refuse [military service]. Indeed, the conduct and aims of states in waging war, especially large and powerful ones, are in some circumstances so likely to be unjust that one is forced to conclude that in the foreseeable future one must abjure military service altogether. (Rawls 1971: 334–5)[4]

The second general strategy is to question one or two of the just war's key conditions. At the heart of any approach to the justification of war must be two conditions, that the body which carries out war is legitimate and that that body has a good reason, that is, a just cause, for doing so. All the other criteria are in a sense secondary to these and act as limitations.

First, the idea that any political unit large enough and organized enough to be in a position to engage in war (as opposed to other forms of violence) might turn out to be illegitimate may seem a difficult thesis to maintain, but it is a thesis which has some adherents. In a sense Tolstoy's famous indictment of the state as institutional violence was a way of delegitimizing the idea of a state that uses violence over its own citizens as well as other groups of human beings. Augustine had a sense of this when he recognized that justice was not truly realized in human affairs since states were in a sense robbers writ large (Augustine [c.412] 1947: bk IV, ch. 4). States, based on the principle of partiality (which converts egoism into patriotism), are, in practice if not by nature, guilty of systemic bias and therefore, whatever just cause they have, are bound to pursue policies which are biased and unjustified.

Second, in chapter 4 we considered a line of objection to the just war theory according to which none of the various 'just causes' commonly proposed were really on closer inspection plausible. The reader is referred to the more detailed analysis given there. As a general anti-war argument (as opposed to an objection to certain types of war) this does of course depend on showing that *all* the different 'causes' have objections to them. This may not seem plausible to many. However, the full success of this line of argument is not necessary to the anti-war pacifist position. First, even if some just causes, such as self-defence or humanitarian intervention, are thought to be plausible in themselves, such wars may turn out to be unacceptable because of all the other considerations given earlier. Second, if a major type of just cause is shown to be problematic, then, if this is the chief basis in practice for having armies at all, the *de facto* consequence is that armies would lose their legitimacy.

This particularly relates to the criticism that Rodin offers of the argument from national self-defence. If his reasoning against this 'just cause' is indeed effective (see chapter 4), then it would in practice undermine the legitimacy of national defence systems, since this is the key justification of them. If it turned out that the only 'just cause' acceptable was humanitarian intervention, then that would be insufficient reason for countries to have armies anyway (cf. chapter 4, §5.2). What it would mean perhaps is that there would be a case for a cosmopolitan military under, say, UN command whose function was to deal with such issues (cf. chapter 3, §2.1). Not all anti-war pacifists would accept such a special case, since it would still involve the use of coercive killing force to deal with the issue. But even if they did, what is being considered is something that may be conceptualized in a quite different way – namely as some kind of global *police* action, which because it is a form of the 'violence of the magistrate' need not be denied by the anti-war pacifist.

3.4   Assessment of pacifism

Many different kinds of difficulties can be raised concerning these arguments for pacifism. First I consider some of the difficulties with absolute pacifism and replies, and then consider the anti-war pacifist arguments. Such arguments and counter-arguments are necessarily inconclusive, but my intention is to outline a number of moves that can be made. It is up to the reader to determine where the balance lies.

(a)   Incoherence

Jan Narveson, in an article entitled 'Pacifism: a philosophical analysis', claimed that the absolute pacifist position is not merely mistaken, it is incoherent in that it involves some kind of contradiction (Narveson 1970). It is based on the absolute right not to be attacked, but sometimes the condition necessary to realize that right is that one defends it by all necessary means, which include the use of killing force. I give here the gist of a long and complex argument which has been subject to complex replies by others, including an effective analysis by Teichman (Teichman 1986: 29–37). I restrict myself to two general moves in reply. First, his way of representing pacifism is unusual in that what lies at the heart of absolute pacifism is not a claim about rights but a claim about duty, namely that it is my duty (without exception) not to use killing force, even against those who attack me or those close to me. It is true that rights and duties generally go together (the correlativity thesis), so one could say that, if I have an absolute duty not to kill you, you have an absolute right not to be killed by me. But it is the claim about duty that here carries the primary moral significance. Even if we think of pacifism in terms of a right not to be attacked, having a right to something does not entail that I am entitled to do anything to secure that right. Even if we think of a right as absolute – the right not to be tortured is a widely accepted example – it does not follow that I, the right-holder, have a right to do absolutely anything to prevent its being violated, rather the absoluteness relates to the duties others have. Showing that the pacifist position is not incoherent does not show that it is right. So let us now turn to other arguments.

(b) The acts and omissions problem

This objection, raised for instance by Glover, is based on the claim that pacifism depends upon an extreme and unacceptable distinction between acts and omissions (Glover 1977: 257–8). It depends, that is, on saying that we are responsible for what we do but not for what we allow to happen. Supposing that one is in a situation where one could kill one person who is about to detonate a device that will certainly kill many people, and there is no other way of disabling him. Does that not show how implausible the absolute pacifist position is? Incidentally this objection need not be based on the utilitarian principle that we must always produce the best results. We may recognize that we are *more* responsible for what we do than for what we let happen (killing someone is far worse that failing to prevent someone killing someone else), but still acknowledge that, where the consequences are sufficiently bad, we cannot plausibly stick rigidly to the simply duty not to kill people. There are at least three different ways a pacifist may respond to this kind of objection.

Pacifists can stick to their position and argue that, indeed, there is a major difference between what they can avoid (doing an evil thing) and what they can prevent (others doing evil things); this is rather like the line taken by Williams (1973) in his famous discussion of Jim, Pedro and the Indians (see chapter 1, §7.2). Pacifists, it should be noted, are generally keen to stress that we do have significant responsibilities, not merely not do what is wrong but to promote what is good and oppose what is bad; most are engaged in work for peace and social justice. But the duty to respond in various ways to the bad things done by others in the world can be taken quite seriously without one's having to break the rule about not killing people.

Second, they can concede that in extremely unusual situations we may have to make exceptions. The position is no longer absolutist but it is still based on a principled objection to killing. There is still a presumption against killing which would apply in almost all real-life situations. (Just as, in law, hard cases make bad law, one needs to be wary of very unusual scenarios thought up by philosophers. The Jim–Pedro case is at least one that could well happen, unlike those in science fiction, but still it has to be treated with caution.)

Third, it might be conceded that what really underlies the position is a principle such as 'always do what is most life-affirming'. This would turn the pacifist principle into a kind of consequentialist principle, but it could retain both the presumption of pacifism and its character *in practice* as a duty-without-regard-to-consequences. This could be done if, for instance, one employed the split-level analysis that R. M. Hare once introduced between moral thought at the intuitive level and moral thought at the reflective level. That is, the life-affirming principle at the reflective level underlies our commitment in ordinary moral thought to the pacifist principle, and only in extreme situations would we need to go back to the higher-level principle and recognize that rare exceptions need to be made (Hare 1981: chs 1 & 3).

(c)   The unacceptable trade-off issue

Glover also introduces another kind of difficulty with pacifism, and that has to do with the claim that pacifism puts an unacceptably large value on preserving life as compared with the value of certain features of human life such as liberty or justice (Glover 1977: 257–8). Pacifists seem to have to accept that they and others have to live in situations of oppression or face the possibility of the imposition of this state by an invading power, and that this is preferable to taking action to attain or preserve liberty by resistance that will involve the deaths of some people. This is not an acceptable preference. Values such as these are worth fighting for.

There are two kinds of reply that can be given. First, what the acceptable trade-off is is a matter of debate. For those who die in a struggle, liberty and justice are of no account: you have to be alive to enjoy these. As some in the Campaign for Nuclear Disarmament movement during the Cold War used to say: 'better red than dead'. Second, and more to the point, this consequentialist argument hardly undermines the principled objection to killing people: if it is wrong to kill people, it does not matter what values you may want to promote or preserve – life itself, flourishing life, life according to your preferred religious or political vision, life in conditions of justice, civic freedom, enjoyment of rights or national independence. Whatever you do in furtherance of these ends, you should do in accordance with this moral principle – and indeed whatever other moral principles you hold. Pacifists are not generally passivists. There is nothing in pacifism that prevents a pacifist from being involved in the most vigorous promotion of such goals, and indeed most are as active as any other in these ways, as we noted in §3.1.

(d)   Unacceptably high standards

Some have argued that pacifism, by setting such a high ideal standard, leads to more atrocities in war because in fighting soldiers have stepped over the moral line anyway. Anscombe puts it thus: 'absolute pacifism is an ideal; unable to follow that, and committed to "compromise with evil", one must go the whole hog and wage war *à outrance*' (Anscombe [1961] 1970: 48). There are really two issues here. Does the promotion of ideals lead to less observance of less exacting moral standards? Does someone with such ideals lose the ability to make various kinds of moral discrimination which are valid and available to people without such ideals? Generally the answer seems to be 'no' in both cases. The same kind of issue comes up in other areas such as concern for the environment or world poverty. An environmentalist may believe that we really ought radically to change our lifestyles, but they can still welcome whatever smaller steps people are prepared to take. However, if an environmentalist's attitude is one of condemning whatever other people do that falls short of his or her radically simpler lifestyle approach, then indeed others may conclude 'well, I might as well trash the environment anyway since I am not going to live up to that ideal'. And the same would be true of a pacifist who simply condemned the positions of everyone *equally* – from that of a pacificist just war theorist to an out-and-out militarist. But this is not generally the case and is certainly not implied by the pacifist stance, as noted in §3.1. As a matter of fact, most pacifists are in the forefront of particular campaigns against particularly nasty forms of war – nuclear weapons, landmines, the use of child soldiers, and so on. Of course pacifists are against all forms of fighting and preparations for fighting, but they can be *more* against certain forms of war activity and preparation, just as anyone with a normal commitment to social justice can be more against certain forms of injustice than others.

(e)   The violence of the magistrate or state

If pacifism is the view that it is always wrong for anyone to kill, prepare to kill or threaten to kill, then it is in a sense subversive of the state (which is one reason why states have often been hostile to the claims of pacifists). This is because, if a state has the monopoly of the legitimacy of violence (as is often claimed for it), then it is premised on its having the power and the right to use force to maintain both internal order and external independence. The ultimate sanction of the use of killing force by either police or army in respect to internal order and to the maintenance of justice is very much in the background, *but it is there*. The question whether the state has the right to use force in foreign policy is discussed elsewhere and relates to the anti-war arguments. The question here is whether its maintenance of order by coercive means is a problem for pacifists, who are against all killing force. Since for most people the maintenance of a stable political system within which people can live their lives successfully is a clear moral requirement, the consequence is that absolute pacifism cannot be accepted.

Whether this is an acceptable objection to absolute pacifism is a matter for debate. There are at least three options for pacifists on this issue. First, they can indeed, following Tolstoy, reject, in a revolutionary mode, the state and argue for a totally different form of community not premised on the use of force. How realistic this is is a big question. Second, they can argue both for new ways of thinking about the state that do not depend on the possibility of the use of killing force in the background and for a new paradigm of global relations. This is a reformist agenda since, as a matter of fact, all states or at least almost all states do now operate on the non-pacifist assumption. Third, they can accept that, while states are less than perfectly moral institutions (in this and in other ways), this is the reality we have to live with, and that this morally problematic feature is of lesser importance than many of the more specific moral problems, for instance with its specific armaments policies (cf. the point about degrees of moral wrongdoing discussed in §3.4(d)).

(f)   The accusation of cowardice or unfair reliance on others

Pacifists are sometimes accused of being cowards in that they wish to escape from the dangers of fighting in wars, and in that, by trying to avoid fighting in wars, they are relying on others to protect them and not pulling their weight in regard to the common good. I take these two together, though one is about a vice of character and the other about unfairness, because the reply to both of them is similar. If a pacifist were merely to refuse to fight, if his motive were fear and if he was glad to benefit from the dangers others face, these might be fair comments. But in fact a pacifist mode of engagement with those around him may be and usually is quite different. Quite apart from the fact that a pacifist stance, particularly in a society hostile to that stance, is often a courageous one anyway, what a pacifist may do is also oppose the same things that others oppose but do so nonviolently; and he may court or accept dangers in so doing. Many pacifists in the Second World War joined the Friends' Ambulance Unit, which involved non-combatant duties on the front line. NGOs such as Médecins sans Frontières (Doctors without Borders) enter war zones to give medical relief, and many of their operators are personally pacifist.

Hawk gives a very vivid example of a French pastor who opposed Nazi occupation but did so nonviolently (Hawk 2006).

(g) Difficulties with anti-war pacifism

In respect to the more specific anti-war arguments considered earlier, the following general moves may be made. One general move against the argument concerning dehumanization and indiscriminateness would be to say that the goals of war are sufficiently pressing that 'the end justifies the means': all these negative features may be conceded, but simply regarded as the costs of war. Another move is to deny the negative features or at least view them as much less negative than is claimed. Autonomy is not an 'all or nothing' thing, and in many situations in life some people have less autonomy than in others, and often this is the result of their voluntarily (that is, autonomously) undertaking roles and functions that involve restrictions on autonomy. The brutalization of soldiers in military training and the demonization of the enemy are not necessary features of military life and attitudes. Modern warfare does not necessarily involve the indiscriminate killing of civilians on a scale that is unacceptable: if military units are the target and due care is taken to minimize collateral civilian casualties, then this is acceptable; and so on.

The later arguments can similarly be responded to as a group. The argument that all wars fail the test of proportionality can be rejected, if the overall empirical assessment of war is made and comes out with different results. But the main difficulty, as remarked in chapter 4, is that each side may be measuring the results in different ways. One issue relating to Ballou's famous indictment is that he is using too simple a metric of suffering and death, and that such assessments are insufficiently sensitive to other values that are at stake. For instance, is not the argument for collective self-defence in defence of a country's liberty a valid one which overrides any general calculation of consequences? Even if Rodin's argument against reading off the right of national defence from the right of personal self-defence is correct, it may still be the case that a political community has such a collective right, especially if it is clearly the will of the community or is democratically endorsed.

In any case, political communities do have legitimate authority to wage war to maintain their own integrity as limited spheres of order or to maintain the wider order of states in the world. Even if such a way of ordering the world is open to challenge and the world is maybe moving in the direction of a neo-Westphalian order, it is almost inconceivable that what will emerge will not be political institutions which at some level are necessary for good governance both within and between such institutions, and these will need to defend their status by military means. If the argument is that legitimate authority will pass to a world federal body (or, arguably, has already passed to the Security Council of the United Nations), then the right to use military force will exist (or already exists) at that level. Calling such action 'global policing' may in a sense be right but it obscures the real point: a cosmopolitan military would be a military. We should call a spade a spade!

Finally, the argument that the full application of all just war criteria rules out all or almost all wars, even if it is correct (which may be disputed, since it again is an empirical issue), imposes an unrealistic standard. It is not obvious that the just war criteria have to be applied in this way. They provide a framework for moral decision-making in war. Once the assessment has been made, the judgement in particular cases needs to be formulated on the merits of each situation. Furthermore, for many modern war justifiers, the appeal to the just war traditional criteria is neither here nor there. The question is whether a war is justified by the arguments that the thinker regards as valid. The acceptance of the central just cause – self-defence – and a more relaxed view about how wars can be justified means that the presumption against war being justified fails, and so the soldier has no good reason to suppose that it is likely that a war in which he is asked to fight is unjustified.[5]

3.5   The wider implications of pacifism

Before concluding this discussion, it is worth recalling that the conceptions of pacifism nowadays generally go well beyond the core principle of not fighting/killing, and are concerned more with certain perceptions of the dynamics of human nature and with certain ways of making peace (*pacifac*), both in examining the roots of personal and social violence and in looking at the remediable causes of war and conflict. As a contribution to the ethics of international relations it has to be developed into more than a statement about the wrongness of the actions of individuals, since there have to be answers here and now for what nation-states should do. So a whole theory of peace – how to promote, make and keep it – is needed. In other words, pacifism includes a commitment to pacificism, as discussed in the next chapter. Since there are, as we indicated, a variety of ways pacificism may be interpreted, pacifism along with the philosophy of nonviolence will provide fairly distinct analyses of how best to promote peace.

Usually then, as I noted earlier, a pacifist is not merely a person who refuses to fight. A pacifist is someone who sees his or her refusal as part of a wider commitment: the ethical value of 'peace' is such as to draw out a commitment both to live by it and to promote it. That commitment to the wrongness of fighting will lead to: (a) trying to reduce the incidence of people doing what is wrong, by arguing the case with others and creating the conditions which make fighting less likely; (b) avoiding being culpably the beneficiary of or causally contributing to others' violence, by selective forms of withdrawal and/or alternative forms of compensatory positive engagement,[6] such as working for peace and/or being willing to oppose *with risks* by nonviolent means what others oppose by violence, as Hawk stresses.

Put another way, a pacifist will generally have additionally any or all of the following commitments: (a) promoting peace; (b) promoting justice and opposing injustice nonviolently; (c) engaging with others over the ethical issues, including specific issues such as nuclear weapons, child soldiers or landmines (note the issue of degrees or types of wrongness mentioned earlier). In other words, a pacifist usually has a strong cosmopolitan commitment to promoting peace and other values anywhere in the world.

Pacifism, however, does not *strictly entail* such a cosmopolitan approach or any of (a) to (c), for the reasons given in §3.1. But, in practice, most pacifists do include a cosmopolitan commitment to promoting such values, since for them part of the moral force of their pacifism lies in the positive value of peace for everyone.

4 The way of peace

The way of peace, as I am interpreting it, combines the pacifism/nonviolence approach with pacificism. Briefly, as indicated in chapter 1, pacificism is simply the belief that it is possible and desirable that we achieve progressively greater levels and wider extents of peace, and that there is a general obligation towards fellow human beings to work for its progressive realization. There are many things which can be done, ranging from education, institution building, strong formal democracy and informal dialogue mechanisms, to changes in personal lifestyle choices and the availability of mediation services. Such a commitment is, however, consistent with adherents believing that the use of armed force is sometimes necessary and also with their regarding the commitment to nonviolence in personal lifestyles as being a marginally significant part of the picture.

Someone who adopts the 'way of peace' approach to pacificism, however, puts an emphasis on his or her own personal lifestyle and indeed on advocating this to others (mainly by example). He or she is committed to living in a peaceful way, expressing the virtues of peace in his or her own lifestyle, preferring dialogue, listening to others, tolerating difference of views, seeing beyond a person's acts and beliefs to the human being beyond them, and so on. If someone who lives this way does so simply because this is his or her understanding of how one should live, and he or she advocates this to others as a matter of 'truth', then this is expressing a core idea similar to the core idea in pacifism and nonviolence – and I do not deny that this may be for many all that they mean by the 'way of peace'. But I am suggesting that it is helpful to regard the way of peace as including rather more. Someone who lives the way of peace sees his or her own lifestyle and that of others following it as *contributing* to peace more generally. In other words, he or she is a pacificist as well, committed to working for peace. What marks that person out from other pacificists is precisely his or her belief that the way of peace is a central, non-accidental way, and *not merely just one* of a number of other strategies for creating and sustaining effective peace. He or she could even be dismissive of all the other background things that are often advocated and listed above, but generally is not, since he or she sees that all these things are necessary. His or her view is really based on the fact of accepting the two prongs of Gandhi's dictum 'the means are the end in the making'. The means are normatively the end in the making, so we ought to promote peace by the way of peace. But, at the same time, descriptively the end 'peace' will only really come about if it is constituted by acts expressing the way of peace.

Someone committed to the way of peace may, like the pacifist and nonviolentist, do so in a serious but non-absolutist fashion as well as in an absolutist fashion. If, on the conception I am commending, that person is a pacificist, what makes his or her position distinctive within pacificism is his or her view that it is the lifestyle of individuals committed to living peacefully that is central to the pursuit of peace. We now need, in the next chapter, to look in more detail at the more general idea of pacificism and conceptions of peace associated with it.

Questions

1 What are the differences between violence and nonviolence?
2 In what form, if any, would you defend pacifism?
3 Which of the criticisms of pacifism need to be taken most seriously? Are any of them successful?
4 In what ways does the author relate the idea of the way of peace to pacifism and pacificism? Is this a helpful way of thinking about the way of peace?

6 PEACE AND PACIFICISM

The chief purpose of this chapter is to explore the concept of peace, in what forms it is valuable, and whether we have duties not merely to act peacefully but also to support and promote peace, not merely in our own immediate social situations but generally in the world.[1]

1 Peace

As I indicated briefly in the introduction, it is common to introduce the discussion of peace by contrasting a negative conception of peace as the absence of war and a positive conception as wholeness or harmony. I shall first say more about this contrast, and then indicate various positions in the middle. The importance of this lies in clarifying what makes peace a positive value or, rather, since peace in all its main forms has some value, in what forms it is most valuable. This in turn informs how we answer the questions: What are our duties in respect to its value? How significant are these duties?, and Who are the main bearers of these duties?

1.1 The negative conception

Peace is defined negatively in terms of a relationship between countries (or other groups) which are not at war. If war is defined, as it is by Hedley Bull in his seminal work *The Anarchical Society* (Bull 1977: 185), as 'organised violence carried out by political units against each other', then two countries are at peace if they are not at war. This definition fits one common way of thinking of peace which is that, as Grotius put it, 'there is nothing in between (nihil medium) war and peace' (Grotius [1625] 1925: proleg., §29): countries are either at war or they are in a state of peace. This account is slightly more plausible than a wholly legalistic conception according to which countries are at war only if there has been a declaration of war. On this formal account the Falklands/Malvinas conflict between Argentina and Britain in 1982 was not a war, since there was no such declaration. Now this negative conception of peace is certainly not negative in an evaluative sense. It may be very valuable to be in this state. It is only negative in the sense of being a negation of 'war' or as an absence of a positive characteristic, namely war.

1.2 The positive conception

What about the positive conception of peace? Some writers have wanted to argue against the negative conception (seen as the mere absence conception) for one that conceives of peace as consisting of harmonious relationships between individuals and groups. John Macquarrie, whose book *The Concept of Peace* (1973) contributed significantly to this way of thinking, links the idea to that of 'shalom' in Middle Eastern thought and the notion of wholeness in social relationships, and he characterizes peace as 'love socially transposed'. One can argue that this level of peace in social relationships can only really come from people who are either at peace with themselves, achieve inner peace, or are committed to a life of nonviolence (and they could combine all three aspects, though they need not). In many ways the linkage between outer peace in social relations and inner peace is a distinct feature of Buddhist thinking (see, for instance, Kraft 1992).

1.3 Middle ways

There are various ways of getting at the idea of peace as something that lies somewhere in between the extremes.

One way is to ask of the negative conception, What makes it a valuable state to be in? But once we ask what it is that makes this state of being at peace valuable, we realize that more needs to be said than simply a negative claim that it is an absence of war. The trouble with thinking of it as an absence is that it seems simply to be a state we are in, something that happens rather than something which is itself the object of activity. Our interest in peace, however, is as something which we actively maintain if we have it, we promote if there could be more or better forms of it, or we pursue if we do not have it. It is an object of endeavour and is so because we have reasons of enlightened self-interest to make it such. The question of ethical obligation I come on to later.

There are two aspects of peace which make it valuable and something we have good reason to maintain, improve or achieve: first, the fact that it has qualities which are not necessarily present if we are simply not fighting; second, the fact that it is not merely short-term but durable or, we might say these days, sustained or sustainable. Linking peace to sustainability is significant because in fact, if we take sustainability seriously, it is – or ought to be regarded as – one of the key things to be sustained. Since sustainability is generally regarded as a focus of ethical commitment, this will help to make the case that promoting peace is a duty.

We can get a handle on the first idea from what may seem a curious quarter, namely Hobbes. For all his being associated with the realist school of international relations, Hobbes actually had some extremely perceptive things to say about peace. He defined war thus: 'War is not battle but a period of time in which there is a known disposition to battle; all other time is peace' (Hobbes [1651] 1991: bk I, ch. xiii). In other words, real peace depends on the lack of threats or on a known disposition not to hurl massive armaments at others, on mutual confidence, and so on. On Hobbes's analysis the 'Cold War' was rightly so called, since the quality of the peace that prevailed was hardly one that would fit his definition of peace. Although it is supposedly over, the fact that the major powers still have their weapons (if not pointing at each other) 'in the posture of gladiators', to use Hobbes's graphic phrase, and many other countries are working hard to join them, should remind us that the conditions of the Cold War really still exist, though in a less extreme form.

Peace as an absence of war is really only valuable too if it is sustained and has within it the dynamics that make it capable of being sustained. Iain Atack links what he calls the negative conception of peace with security (Atack 2005: 144) and argues that security requires a whole range of measures to be in place: real security does not depend on defensive postures which are based on the threat of win–lose scenarios, but on win–win measures of common security. This is still a negative account of peace – security is what we have when we are not insecure – but it is less extreme because it is understood in terms of various cooperative conditions that have to be in place, and generally cannot be without significant active measures.

We should recall that in past centuries a number of thinkers, notably Kant, saw themselves as trying to work out what would be needed for us to have perpetual peace. Whether or not we can be that optimistic – namely that we could eliminate war altogether from human affairs – we can at least acknowledge the impetus behind such projects, namely seeking ways in which peace can become more durable and war can be made less likely. What is required among other things is arguably the presence of justice – both procedural and distributive – in relations between groups (and individuals) – what Iain Atack calls a version of the positive conception of peace. This has been the approach of the Quaker writer Adam Curle, in his small but intriguing book *True Justice* (1981). Also needed is a general commitment to developing nonviolent ways of responding to conflict. We should note, however, that this positive conception is again put in a less idealistic fashion: it is positive in the sense that it highlights the presence of certain characteristics such as justice and the habits and skills of conflict resolution, and so on, but it does not go so far as to talk about social harmony or inner peace. Given the way Atack presents them, the elements of security and justice are not so much elements of rival conceptions of peace – negative and positive – as two aspects of a dynamic state of peace maintained and sustained by a variety of features.

What emerges so far from this analysis is that peace – if it is to be really valuable and sustained – is not merely an absence but requires the active engagement of people, with most individuals simply observing basic moral norms such as justice, along with others actively promoting the conditions of peace. This is an important result to have established: like development, peace is something that only occurs if people *do* certain things and do them because they are committed to certain values. No doubt peace as temporary respite from actual war, but still under conditions of threat and hostility, is better than its absence. But if we ask what is really valuable about peace, it is a state of affairs which is durable, not based on threats of war, and informed by core ethical values such as justice which are part of what makes it durable.

Two further points need to be made about the linkage between peace and justice. First the importance of justice is not merely that, if peace is just, it is likely to be more durable. Its being just makes it more valuable in its own right. Indeed part of Curle's point was that, if a peace is not just, then it may not be worth much or worth settling for – and thus there are dilemmas about how to respond – whether violently or nonviolently – to a peace that is unjust. In saying that the linkage is conceptual, I am not saying that there is agreement on what the linkage is. Different conceptions of both peace and justice – whether religiously based or secular – are possible. This leads to the second point. Since different groups will have different views about what is just, the real challenge for achieving durable peace is finding ways forward which are *perceived* to be just by all parties – which may not be the same – or at least not so unjust as not to be acceptable in practical terms. Often the key challenge for 'justice *post bellum*' is finding a peace that meets the various conceptions and demands of justice to an acceptable extent, including those of the vanquished as well as the victors. (See also chapter 4, §2.3; for extensive treatment, see Orend 2006.)

1.4   Jenkins's account

In an article entitled 'The conditions of peace', Iredell Jenkins comes to much the same conclusion (Jenkins 1973), but he conceptualizes the field in a rather different way. He argues that we tend to focus a lot of attention on the wrong topic, namely war, and ignore peace, which he characterizes as a 'force, quality, mode of existence that is a real feature of the human world' rather than a mere absence (ibid.: 512), and gives the analogy of health and sickness. If we spend all our time analysing sickness rather than health we would be focusing on the pathological states, not the normal states. Implicit in the approach Jenkins discusses is the assumption that peace is an important subject for research. Although the causes of war are of course crucial areas to investigate and are examined in war studies, peace itself is a complex concept requiring analysis in peace studies.

We all too often, then, have the wrong focus on war: this is like studying illness or a pathological state, not health. In studying war we seek the avoidance of war: measures such as insulating states, reducing armaments, and encouraging the use of international law and international diplomacy. These are in themselves all right, but, Jenkins argues, they are not enough. In a sense the avoidance of war is the wrong goal. Our goal should be to understand peace and its own dynamics. We need to study peace as it is really experienced in the world. The reality, Jenkins says, is that peace exists in the presence of conflict and divisiveness. In all human relationships there is a continuum, from those with more peace and less war or conflict to those with the reverse. In practice we use the word 'peace' where unity and community are appreciably stronger in relationships than the forces of divisiveness, and 'war' otherwise, but the reality is always a mixture; what we need to do is move things on the continuum towards the 'peace' end. So peace is neither the negative conception as an 'absence of war' nor the positive conception of perfect harmony.

One of the impediments to doing this in international relations is a sharp distinction drawn between the greater degrees of peace that exist within national borders and the significantly lesser degrees outside them, and a false assumption why this is so. Commonly it is assumed that peace occurs within borders because of patriotism and legal obedience. But Jenkins suggests there are many other kinds of reason why primarily peaceful relations are possible, and there is no reason in principle why these should not apply to international relations as well. For Jenkins the two main factors are the 'habits of peace' and the existence of divided loyalties. Once people get into the habit of acting peacefully in relation to each other, it becomes hard to break it. More striking is his second reason, namely that, if we have divided loyalties, we are less likely to go to war or engage in serious conflict in the name of one loyalty or sense of identity against other people to whom we also feel some loyalty.[2] What then we need is to encourage far greater international contacts and cooperation – for which, Jenkins notes, there are plenty of challenges in the form of shared global problems. In this connection he notes the usefulness of United Nations institutions such as the specialized agencies *other than* the Security Council and General Assembly, since the latter tend to be forums for national competition.

Does Jenkins provide the right middle way? I have focused on this because I believe it to be a very useful analysis. It helps us to see both that peace needs to be analysed in its own right, and that we are really dealing with a continuum in which the degree or kind of peace which is realistic falls short of some ideal conception, and it also gives some suggestions about how we can move towards the 'peace' end of the continuum. Nevertheless, we need to recognize that there are a number of other factors that are crucial to achieving a degree of peace that is both realistic and desirable, and that these include the kinds of factor we have already considered, for example creating new forms of security and embedding moral norms such as justice into relationships. Furthermore, if we can achieve certain kinds of stable and sustainable relationships in which 'hot' violence is absent and conflict is contained within the framework of negotiation and respect for law, we can be more positive than Jenkins in seeing this as real peace, not merely something on a continuum.

1.5 Peace and violence

Another way we can recognize that peace has to be conceived in a much richer way than merely the absence of war – even sustained absence of war – is to view peace in contrast not merely to war but to violence. We saw in the last chapter (chapter 5, §2.1) that violence can take many forms – physical (where war is organized physical violence on a large scale), psychological (involving often the threat of physical violence, including war, as way of controlling and intimidating others) and also institutional (the violence of oppressive legal systems, economic systems and even cultural norms). It is clear that, if any of these forms of violence are present to a significant degree either within societies or in relationships between countries, then, even without manifestations of civil or international war, what we have are situations and relationships which do not really constitute peace. This is why, as we noted earlier, there really needs to be security as freedom from fear of possible attacks, military or otherwise, and forms of justice in place which are acknowledged by all parties to be reasonable and not merely the 'justice' of the dominant group or winning party, which others only accept with a sense of grievance because they are weak.

1.6 The value of peace

What I am arguing for is the practical importance of a conception of peace that falls somewhere in between the negative and positive conceptions:

- (A) peace as (mere) absence of war (either temporary or over a longer period)
- (B) peace as durable, justice-based, with the absence of the threat of non-peace (war, violence)
- (C) peace as social harmony/wholeness.

Why is peace valuable? First we need to note that peace (A) is something that is valuable, particularly if it is more than very short-term. After a war is over the tangible benefits of peace are felt by most people immediately. Like the pleasure that comes from the relief of pain, the fact that one is no longer in danger from attack is very significant. Life can return to normal. Such an absence of overt conflict is a precondition for the pursuit of most human activities, or at least their more effective pursuit. Nevertheless, if such a peace is characterized by continued insecurity such as the threat of war being resumed, or if it is consistent with serious ongoing or unresolved injustices, then its value is severely diminished – both because living with a sense of security and living with a sense that justice prevails (and that one is free from injustice) are each in themselves positive human goods, and also because the consequences of insecurity and injustice are generally detrimental to many other goods that people want to achieve. This is why peace (B) is really the condition which is of primary value. From the point of view of the person who is the beneficiary of others around him or her acting peacefully and maintaining peace, such sustained absence of war/violence and absence of the threat of war/violence, along with a sense of a just social order, is the basis on which human flourishing can occur.

  We should note here that what I am arguing for is the value of peace in sense (B), not in sense (C). But is not the idealistic sense important as well? Is such a rich conception of positive peace (which goes far beyond what Atack had in mind in calling positive peace 'peace with justice') to be commended as preferable to negative peace, even as amended by our considerations earlier in conception (B)? After all, if there were total harmony, would not that be even better for the prospects of human flourishing? (For more extensive treatment of what peace means, see Richmond 2005.)

There is no straightforward answer. The following three observations may help to clarify my approach. First, it is undoubtedly true that, if all human beings could achieve such a quality of personal peace in their lives, then the resultant character of social peace would be on a higher plane, as it were, than what is needed for durable peace. Second, since it is unrealistic, however, to suppose that such a scenario could be achieved, in practical terms the main focus of endeavour by policy-makers and by ordinary citizens is to focus on durable peace – that would be a real achievement in itself. What really matters to most people, as people who benefit from others being at peace with them, is that we have a just durable peace not based on threat. Third, nevertheless, the role of people who can achieve inner peace and the way of peace should not be underestimated. This role includes but is not limited to those who take a personal pacifist stance. My point is that a society is generally more likely to be peace-sustaining (in the middle sense I have advanced) if there are those in their midst who live to a more idealist standard. They point to a better way and their lives provide a reminder of what is possible.

Having said that, my own view is that there are many things we need to do to sustain, strengthen or achieve peace in the form that I think is practically most valuable. There is no single-track solution to the question 'What should we do to achieve peace?' such as 'if only everyone achieves inner peace'; 'if only everyone becomes a pacifist'; 'if only everyone becomes a Christian (or Muslim)'; 'if only everyone becomes a Marxist'; 'if only everyone becomes a libertarian'; and so on. This leads into the discussion of pacifism.

2   Pacificism

Pacificism may be characterized thus: a belief in the possibility of making peace a more durable and robust feature in human relationships, both locally and globally, and in its ethical desirability as something that ought – morally – to be the object of human endeavour. A number of other features are generally associated with the approach, as we shall see. One important division of opinion should be noted at the start. Pacificism is not the same as pacifism. Most pacifists are pacificists. Likewise, many war justifiers can also be pacificists; like Coates, they do believe that some wars are justified, but nevertheless they strive to make it less likely that wars, whether justified or not, will actually occur, and commend such striving as a duty (Coates 1997: 117 & ch. 11).

2.1   Pacificism and pacifism

Since pacificism and pacifism sound so similar – and indeed their etymology is identical – I need to clarify the distinction. I shall do this by using a semi-technical device.[3] We need to distinguish between two types of activity vis-à-vis any basic moral value 'x':

acting x-ly)(promoting x

For instance, we can talk of someone acting justly and we can talk of someone promoting justice (or fighting injustice, which is part of the latter). We can talk of someone respecting rights in his or her own behaviour and someone doing various things to protect human rights (or their observance) and opposing their violation by others. We can talk of someone committed to acting truthfully in his or her dealings with others, and someone who wishes to campaign for truthfulness and integrity in business or public affairs. Likewise, we can talk of someone acting peacefully or nonviolently in terms of his or her own behaviour and someone promoting peace and nonviolence. Now it will be apparent from a quick survey of human behaviour that most people fall into three main categories.

Some people focus their moral lives on the first (acting x-ly in various ways), maybe with little or no interest in the wider promotion of such virtues: they might be called ethical quietists. What is important to them is that they keep their own moral house in order. Then there are those who devote a lot of their moral energy to promoting one or other kinds of value, but they may not be particularly attentive to making sure their behaviour fully or always expresses the values they advocate. They may just accept the familiar ethical doctrine of the end justifying the means: that is, we may have to promote peace sometimes by non-peaceful means; sometimes we have cut corners concerning justice and human rights in order to promote these grand goals more effectively. Those who defend ruthlessness in public life are taking sides on an issue such as this. And then there are those who take seriously both acting x-ly and promoting x, and try to live the values that they wish to see widely accepted. On this approach the end does not justify the means. The means has to be ethically assessed not just in terms of its efficacy in achieving an end. It is in this connection that the idea of Gandhi's comes to mind: the means are the ends in the making (see chapter 5, §3.2).

While I believe the third approach is the right one to take, my main purpose here is to distinguish two relationships one can have to a given value, reflected in the following two questions: 'Should we (always) act in accordance with the value?', and 'Should we promote that value in various ways?' We are now in a position to see that pacifism is an answer to one kind of question, Should one act peacefully in responding to violence?, and pacificism is an answer to another question, Should we promote peace and, if so, in what ways and to what extent?

We should note that not all pacifists are pacificists. It is perfectly possible, as we noted in the last chapter, that someone's pacifism in respect to his or her belief in the wrongness of killing (by him or her, or indeed by others) goes along with a pessimism about peace becoming more likely, and with no interest in or even with scepticism about there being a general obligation to create the conditions of peace. But generally pacifists also work for peace as well and believe it can become a greater reality in human affairs.

2.2   General account of pacificism

A. J. P. Taylor used the term 'pacificism' to recapture an earlier set of concerns in previous centuries with a focus on trying to establish the conditions of peace (Taylor 1957: 51n.).[4] These were the agendas behind 'perpetual peace' projects, such as that of Kant. Pacifism had had this connotation, but it became restricted to a more specific ethical position about the wrongness of fighting. Martin Ceadel did much to promote the general approach without endorsing it himself (Ceadel 1987: ch. 6). His strategy was to say that pacificism was premised on the non-inevitability of war and on the emergence of political institutions that had the capacity to make peace an enduring reality. His chapter focuses on the causal questions 'What are the causes of war?' and 'What changes would cause the sustaining of peace?' Many different competing theories are discussed. Three are regarded as 'marginal pacificisms': religious pacificism, disarmament pacificism and conflict resolution pacificism. Ceadel then gives a number of major theoretical analyses, major because they are embedded in wider political programmes: liberalism, radicalism, socialism, feminism and ecologism. He considers the first three major pacificisms mainly in the context of the period between the First World War and the Second World War. Historically in this period in fact many people were desperate to find a way of preventing a repetition of 'the war to end all wars' and looked to the new League of Nations, the development of international law, and general disarmament agreements such as the Kellogg–Briand Pact of 1928 to achieve this. Many claimed that the latter pact provided the basis, as it proclaimed, for the 'renunciation of war as an instrument of policy'. When the rise of Hitler led to war, many gave up their pacificist stance.

It is instructive to consider why Ceadel regards the first three as marginal pacificisms. His criticism of religious pacificism is that it assumes the position 'if everyone came to accept our religion, peace would ensue'. This actually highlights a general issue here with any assumption 'if everyone came to accept theory or worldview x, then we would have peace'. The same would apply to all the major pacificisms he mentions too. There are in fact two general problems with any such strategy. First, is it realistic or reasonable to expect everyone do so? Is it reasonable to expect everyone to accept Christianity, Islam, pacifism, just war values, liberalism . . . ? It is rather more likely that people will remain convinced of their various different theories and values, so there is a challenge of finding shared values and related institutions that are realistic and reasonable. Küng may have been over-optimistic when he said 'there will be no peace in the world without peace amongst the religions; no peace amongst the religions without dialogue between the religions' (Küng 1991: cover), but surely the prospects for greater peace in the world are better through convergence over shared values than mass conversion to any one worldview (see my discussion in chapter 3, §§2.3 & 2.4, on a global ethic). Second, even if everyone adopted one worldview, such as Christianity, still there could be extensive conflict, since there are many interpretations, as history has shown.[5]

Ceadel says that disarmament and conflict resolution may be dismissed as not full-blown pacificist programmes because they do not get to the root causes of the problems of war: they address symptoms, not causes. This may be true, but if they contribute to reducing the incidence of war, then they are part of a broadly conceived pacificist agenda. The same in fact goes for all the other versions of pacificist analysis of the causes of war: each may contribute something of the solution – but not necessarily a complete solution. But my interpretation here relates to a deeper difference between our positions.

Ceadel also presents pacificism as an alternative both to what he calls defencism – the form of just war theory that focuses on the right to defence as a just cause – and to pacifism. However, it is not at all clear that this is the right way to conceptualize it. It would be right if the commitment to the non-inevitability of war were taken as a very strong thesis that the pacificist knows exactly what needs to be done to end all wars just like that. As noted earlier, pacificism is historically relevant to the inter-war period, and it is certainly true that many who adopted a pacificist approach did believe that war could be made a thing of the past, and only gave up the position with the rise of Hitler. But the pacificist approach need not be premised on such a strong thesis. All that is required is a belief that war can be made less likely and peace made stronger and more durable by various kinds of measures. This approach is in fact compatible with both pacifism and just war theory (including defencism).

Ceadel also notes that pacifism is often used to mean 'anti-militarist' (Ceadel 1987: 101), and here I believe lies the clue to what is significant about pacifism. The two features we saw of militarism were that war is in a sense inevitable and part of human nature and the human condition, and that in any case it is not undesirable because it expresses certain human virtues. Pacificism rejects both these features. War is not inevitable and war is undesirable compared with peace. The strong thesis is that eventually we could eliminate war, the weak thesis is that we can reduce its incidence. Thus, as I understand it and indicated in chapter 1, militarism and pacificism represent two alternative approaches to war and peace in a kind of spectrum of attitudes (with mixtures of attitudes in the middle), and as such this contrast cuts across the usual triple division into realism, just war and pacifism.

Ceadel does not explicitly discuss an ethical dimension to all these approaches, but there is an implicit ethical perspective in that a serious interest in peace is premised on regarding it as desirable and as something which, at least collectively, we have a duty to promote. Let us now consider this normative aspect.

2.3   Pacificism as an ethical obligation

Ethically, why should we work for the reduction of the incidence of war and more positively the strengthening of peace? The quick answer is that peace is, compared with war, decidedly desirable and preferable, and in two senses.

1 Peace is a precondition of human well-being and good generally. That is, peace is a condition we enjoy because of what others do as regards us – they do not fight us, threaten us or oppress us. This is centrally true of peace in sense (B) above, and to some extent true of peace in sense (A) above. In that condition we can pursue our goals successfully.
2 Peace is desirable in respect to various pacific virtues and duties which people show in their lives, both in living/acting peacefully (which maybe contributes to peace in sense (C) above) and in accepting responsibility to promote peace. Pacificist virtues, unlike the so-called military 'virtues', are generally win–win in their consequences, not win–lose.

As I have analysed it, pacificism contains two main elements: a view that the incidence of war can be reduced and the ethical desirability of its reduction. The common – one might say default – interpretation of the latter element includes two further claims: first, that there is an obligation on the part of any human beings in any society to promote and maintain the conditions of peace *in their society*; and, second, there is an obligation, in principle, on the part of individuals and groups to promote, maintain and not undermine peace for others *in other parts of the world*.

We can locate these two further claims and their contested character in relation to four main ethical positions concerning global relations: relativism, which rejects the first claim (and by implication the second claim); realism, which rejects the second claim; internationalism, which usually accepts the first claim and gives limited support to the second; and cosmopolitanism, which endorses both claims fully. As I hope to show in what follows, pacifism in its full-blown version is really a cosmopolitan thesis.

Those who were ethical relativists and rejected the possibility of making universal judgements might not accept either thesis. They might, for instance, believe that at least they and members of their own society should promote peace – if that was a value of interest to the society in question – but in other societies this might or might not be a central value – they might after all be warlike or militarist societies. Given this theoretical approach, ethical relativists cannot either make universal claims about what is of value or advocate transboundary responsibility to promote it.

Realists, as we noted in chapter 2, unlike militarists (unless they are also militarist in approach), do regard order in the world as on the whole important: general order in the world is good for commerce, war anywhere can be disruptive of foreign policy, and wars near to hand can impact negatively on one's own country's direct interests. Realists are likely to have a serious interest in the promotion of peace – durable peace – in the world and indeed, when it suits them, employ the language of ethics to this purpose, but they do so for reasons of national interest. For realists, the obligations of leaders are to their citizens, not to others, and they reserve the right to break the peace when it suits their country's geopolitical interests.

There remain two approaches, both of which can be said to adopt an ethical approach to the promotion of peace as a value anywhere in the world – namely internationalism and cosmopolitanism.

Internationalism, as we saw in chapter 3, is based on a morality of states in which states have obligations to respect one another's sovereignty, to maintain peace and order among themselves, to observe the restrictions in war based on *ius in bello* and *ius ad bellum*, and to honour agreements and treaties. As such it is clearly part of the internationalist approach to be concerned about peace and order in the world and not merely as it affects each state. However, someone who is an internationalist need not be a pacificist in the sense I have outlined, any more than a just war theorist (who may also be an internationalist) needs to be. He or she may regard war as an inevitable if somewhat controllable feature of the human condition and not share the optimism of the pacificist, and may not accept a robust duty actually to promote the conditions of peace.

Or, if the internationalist does accept such a duty, then, while still maintaining the central role of states and the society of states in global affairs, his or her position may move towards that of an ethical (rather than institutional) cosmopolitanism. He or she may indeed accept that states should play their part in maintaining international order and respond to activities that threaten or undermine international order, and may support international laws and institutions such as the United Nations to this end. After all the United Nations was set up with the primary goal of preventing war, and in this regard can be seen as a product of the internationalist way of thinking. But the degree of commitment to promoting the conditions of peace anywhere as opposed to observing peaceful norms may be very variable. Furthermore from an internationalist point of view the duty resides primarily with states themselves, not their citizens, and the range of measures seen as pertinent to their promotion of peace is also focused on what states can do, unilaterally or via international institutions and laws. The duty of states is primarily in regard to maintaining and promoting peace in the sense (A) discussed above.

The distinctive features of the cosmopolitan approach (at least in the non-dogmatic form I am advocating) are by comparison four things: first, there is a robust commitment to promote the conditions of peace; second, the kind of peace we are interested in is peace in sense (B); third, it is not merely states or their international institutions that are important but individuals and organizations outside the formal state sector; fourth, a much wider range of measures are generally to be advocated. The first two features relate to the crucial 'nature and extent of obligation' question, the second two to the 'who?' and 'how?' questions.

Given the central importance of peace in sense (B) for almost all human goods and virtues (excepting the military virtues admired by militarists, which are not really to be reckoned as unqualified virtues anyway), including the pursuit of genuine development, we have duties not merely to maintain peace in *our* relationships with other countries and groups, but also to promote peace *anywhere* in the world.

If wars, conflicts, threats of war and of conflict, and forms of injustice undermine the flourishing of human beings anywhere in the world, seeing how to help others maintain peace elsewhere where they have it, and, where there is war, to help to stop it and build a durable just peace is part of our cosmopolitan responsibility – in much the same way that we should accept a responsibility to give or support aid to relieve poverty and oppose economic practices that contribute to poverty elsewhere. Put another way, the key point here is that if, as many do, we accept a duty to alleviate poverty as undermining well-being, then, *by virtue of the same reasoning*, we should accept a similar duty to oppose other factors which undermine well-being – namely war and violence. Whether people call either duty 'cosmopolitan' is a secondary matter, though on my analysis this is how they should be understood.

The link with development is actually central to the analysis. Genuine development as a process of enlarging people's capabilities to lead full lives (see Sen 1999) is partly strengthened by the conditions of peace, and conversely development contributes to peace. There is generally a two-way 'virtuous' causal circle here. The cosmopolitan implication of this argument is that richer nations and individuals ought to support both peace and development and that this should be done on a significant scale – generally at a much higher level than is actually the case.

This also has an important implication for priorities in national expenditure in regard to armaments. Many thinkers have noted the negative impacts of arms spending on the levels of aid that richer countries are prepared to spend. It has been remarked in respect of nuclear weapons (but it applies to arms spending generally) that 'the arms race is killing'.[6] Eisenhower once famously said 'every gun that is made, every warship launched . . . signifies in a final sense a theft from those who hunger . . .' (Eisenhower 1953). Many observed after 9/11 that increased spending on security measures would mean less aid, and this appears to have been confirmed. Of course no one will make these kinds of remarks unless they intend the ethical corollary: we are unjustified in having such priorities. The cosmopolitan standpoint simply makes this kind of ethical implication quite explicit.

Cosmopolitanism (unless it is pacifist) does not imply that no spending on armaments is justified. What it does do is require that any spending which is justified from a legitimate national interest point of view is set in the context of our cosmopolitan obligations – to aid generally and to peace promotion in particular – with the implication that our priorities should be changed. Any such claim also has a secondary benefit, namely that such reductions in arms spending are likely to render the world more secure and peaceful anyway. A related thesis is that war and preparing for war is no longer in the twenty-first century an effective instrument of policy, from either a national or a global perspective (Westmorland General Meeting 2005).

We can illustrate the cosmopolitan approach by using the analysis which Henry Shue once introduced in talking about basic rights. He identified the basic rights as preconditions for the enjoyment of other rights and goods – the right to subsistence, the right to security and the right to liberty (Shue 1996). Corresponding to all three rights are three kinds of duty: a duty not to deprive anyone of that to which they have a right, which is a duty of anyone to refrain from various types of action; the duty to protect from standard deprivations of rights, which is a duty fulfilled significantly by relevant social institutions supported by individuals; and the duty to come to the aid of those who are deprived of their rights, which again is a duty shared by individuals and institutions. Since the right to security – security of the person not to be attacked and of that person's possessions – is essentially the right to live in a peaceful environment, we can see how this links to peace as a basic value. The cosmopolitan nature of this is brought out by the recognition that the obligations corresponding to such rights are in principle held by anyone anywhere. Basic rights or, as Luban interpreting Shue says, basic human rights are 'the minimum demands of all humanity on all humanity' (Luban [1980] 1985: 211–16). How this works out in practice in terms of how much individuals should do and how international institutions should function to further such rights is a matter for debate, but the approach is clear enough (see §3 for criticisms at the end of the chapter and, for a more cautious account of human rights, see Bull 1979).

There is a further question, 'Who has the ethical commitment to promote peace?' A range of answers may be given. The duty rests with different groups of agents according to different theories. To start with the analyses mentioned by Ceadel, according to liberalism, leaders and institution builders need to create the laws and institutions that are necessary; according to socialism and radicalism, ordinary people need to overturn capitalism and the establishment; according to feminist analysis, women need to lead the way in challenging masculine practices and attitudes which underlie aggression; according to ecological or environmental approaches, people need generally to oppose the materialist growth-based ways of life that cause conflict. Other possibilities more recently discussed include modern peace advocacy, based on peace research; the training of experts in the skills of peacebuilding and conflict management; modern peace education, in which people educate children about the world, about respecting diversity and about the obligations of global citizenship; and so on (see, for instance, Boulding 1990).

From a cosmopolitan point of view the role of individuals as global citizens is central. This can be indicated briefly (see Dower 1997 or 2007; Dower 2003; Heater 2002; Dower and Williams 2002). First, an individual can do a lot to contribute towards global goals such as peace, development, environmental protection and human rights concerns through his or her own actions, especially through various kinds of NGO. Second, there is a specific role for individuals as citizens to engage in bringing about political change; this can be done through international NGOs, but more commonly what is needed is 'globally oriented' political action within nation-states (see Parekh 2002). After all, the governments of countries are unlikely to make major changes in what they do vis-à-vis other countries unless sufficiently large numbers of citizens indicate in various ways that that is what they want their governments to do.

There are also many different answers – some complementary, some competing – to the question 'How should we promote the conditions of peace in the world?' Some of these have already been mentioned in passing: the importance of justice; the role of pacifism and inner peace, at least in some in a society; and the development of international law/the global rule of law and of international institutions such as the United Nations (see, for instance, Dower 1998: ch. 10 or 2007: ch. 9; Dower 2003: ch. 7). Others stress the role of peace education among people in general, as well as the wider programme of cosmopolitan education of which it is a part (cf. Nussbaum 1996); the acquisition of mediation skills in some and the techniques of peacebuilding; and the philosophy of nonviolence as a way of tackling social issues. Jonathan Schell, for instance, in *The Unconquerable World* (2003), documents what he sees as the upsurge in the modern world of interest in the techniques of nonviolence as a way of effecting social change.

These proposals are to some extent rival proposals based on competing analyses of what really will conduce to peace, and are to some extent complementary to each other, with each likely to contribute something – especially given that each will have their supporters who *believe* in their own approach.

2.4   Peacebuilding

One aspect of the 'how?' question which has received attention in recent years is the idea of peacebuilding. This can be discussed as a more limited and separate issue, without linking it to the wider pacificist agenda, but it seems reasonable to see it as part of the wider approach, particularly if the idea of peacebuilding is given a broader definition.

As Atack indicates, there is first a narrow conception: 'the central aim of peacebuilding is to provide those countries emerging out of armed conflict with the skills and resources they require not only to rebuild but also to prevent the recurrence of political violence' (Atack 2005: 141).

Peacebuilding is seen as a third stage to peacemaking and peacekeeping. Peacemaking is what is done through mediation, negotiation and diplomacy to bring conflicts to an end,[7] and peacekeeping is the interposition of neutral forces in an area where there has been a conflict and where the presence of such a force – generally lightly armed – helps to maintain peace, at least in sense (A). Ever since the formation of the United Nations, UN peacekeeping forces have played a role in this way: their function is strictly limited and they can be asked to withdraw from an area by the host government(s) involved. Peacebuilding has a more ambitious role in that the aim here is actually to address the root causes of the historical conflict and is more concerned with peace in sense (B). Nevertheless its function is still to *respond* to a situation where there has been a conflict. It contributes to the goals of greater peace in the world, but its goal is strictly localized and limited.

Atack notes a possible wider conception, based on the thesis that armed conflict is 'preventable and conflict management can somehow replace or displace war and armed force as responses to political and social conflict' (Atack 2005: 143). It is still based on the premise of a response to actual conflicts of other kinds – political and economic – but seeks proactively to prevent escalation to military conflict. It makes a wider contribution to the general goals of pacifism – though the latter obviously involves an even wider range of activities designed to strengthen peace in sense (B) which can minimize or avoid the other non-military forms of conflict as well.

'Peace' in peacebuilding is seen as an amalgam of positive and negative peace as defined by Atack and noted earlier – positive peace as linked to justice (not idealistic harmony) and negative peace linked to security (in fact not merely an absence but involving appropriate measures to ensure sustained security). Boutros-Ghali's *An Agenda for Peace* (1992) made much of the idea of peacebuilding and provided a set of prescriptions (noted in Atack 2005: 145) relevant to both narrow and wide conceptions. (For an extensive treatment of peacebuilding, see Murithi 2009.)[8]

2.5 Summary of pacifism

I offer a summary of pacifism, as I have developed it, by marking various contrasts to militarism discussed earlier (though there is really a continuum of views between the two).

(a) Peace is intrinsically good and war is always a failure in some sense. The pacific virtues are important. The exercise of pacific virtues is generally win–win in outcome, whereas the exercise of military 'virtues' is generally win–lose in outcome.

(b) Generally states which are not at war should seek the conditions of peace, that is, the conditions of a sustainable peace. This will involve various types of measures, including disarmament, international agreements, the use of international bodies such as the United Nations and peace education, all of which are designed to promote trust and reduce the occasions of war, if not to eliminate them. The goal of international relations and relations within other groups should be accommodation of mutual interests and the acceptance of diversity within a common framework.

(c) Generally individuals who are in a position to do so should promote the conditions of peace, both in their own societies and in the world as a whole.

(d) It is possible that the incidence of war and violent conflict can be significantly reduced over time, if not eliminated, if the kinds of measures under (a)–(c) are carried out.

The following further features can be identified which apply to situations where war occurs or is contemplated. Here the proposals may be divided between pacifists and war justifiers. Endorsement of these can be made by war justifiers as unconditionally acceptable, but it can be made conditionally by pacifists who do not approve of any war but can still regard wars with the relevant constraint as less ethically objectionable than wars fought without it. Nevertheless between them they provide a distinctive approach not shared by other thinkers about war such as militarists or realists (or indeed war justifiers who do not insist on all the just war criteria).

(e) *If* war is to be engaged in, limits must be taken seriously to limit its barbarity. For instance, there must be a real prospect of success, proportionality must be strategically and tactically seriously observed, there must be limits on types of weapons, civilians should not be made the object of attack, and danger to civilians in military attacks must be minimized.

(f) All ways of resolving conflicts need to be explored to the fullest extent possible: *if* there is recourse to war it must *really* be the last resort (not a move that can be plausibly *presented* as one).

(g) Violence generally begets violence and war generally generates the conditions of future war; therefore, *if* a war is fought, the key goal in a just war should be the mitigation of this effect by achieving a just peace, that is, a peace which is not likely to generate the occasions of future wars.

(h) *If* war is being considered or undertaken, leaders of a country proposing to go to war need to provide transparent justification to *others*, such as self-defence, helping allies, or humanitarian intervention, in contrast to a Realpolitik or a militarist's disregard of a universalism.

3 Criticisms of pacifism

3.1 The inevitability of war issue

The first main claim, that war is not inevitable, is primarily about a factual issue, but one in which there can be radically different interpretations of human nature and of how much or little change can be realistically expected. The issue has already been discussed in connection with the assumptions behind militarism (see chapter 2, §3). Whether or not we could devise institutions and develop practices which could lead to the complete elimination of war (in the material sense, not merely the legal sense defined by internationalist lawyers) is indeed an arguable point. What I have suggested is that pacifism need not be understood in this strong form. If the significant reduction of war is a realistic prospect, then that is enough to form the basis of the ethical project, namely that we ought to take measures to do just that.

Scepticism about the non-inevitability of war usually focuses on the record of international relations, but we need to remember that, in many societies and areas in the world where war had been in the past endemic, there now exist political and social structures which are so well established that war is almost unthinkable. Many well-established and well-ordered societies have these features. The European Union is a good and often quoted example of a political community in which the 'habits of peace' (to use Jenkins's phrase) are so entrenched that war in an area of the world which had for centuries been the theatre for many bloody conflicts seems hard to imagine. War in other parts of the world may seem endemic, but, given the right conditions, change to more pacific relations is possible. Likewise, the progressive strengthening of international institutions and of the reach of diplomacy can reduce, and arguably has already reduced, the incidence of *inter-national* wars anywhere.

Most wars, however, have in recent years been intra-national or have involved interactions between non-state actors and state actors, as in terrorism. Such conflicts centre on issues of serious injustice or perceived injustice (over oppression, failure to recognize claims to autonomy or domination of inappropriate value systems). Since, as I have suggested, durable peace (in sense (B)) depends on the presence of justice as perceived by all parties involved (see, for instance, Curle 1981), the persistence of rival conceptions of what is just or unjust is an impediment to peace, and may in some cases be an intractable impediment. Pacificism does not have to be premised on a naive view that we can simply rectify such injustice and thus peace will prevail. Progress will be slow and involve much hard work, not least from skilled experts in conflict resolution and peacebuilding.

Behind such efforts of skilled experts lie, however, the general attitudes of people anywhere, and there is some evidence that, despite the hawkish or militarist postures of some governments, there is an increasing adoption of pacificist attitudes (and indeed, though less so, pacifist attitudes), and that change in the moral climate is itself a source of hope that the resort to war can become reduced (see, for instance, Schell 2003).

3.2   The ethical desirability issue

It is not usually a matter of dispute that people have general duties within societies to play their part in maintaining order and peace. Primarily this is a matter of acting peacefully in one's overall dealings and also observing the basic norms of morality, which are seen as valuable partly because their collective observance leads to generally peaceful relations. How serious the duty is to *promote* peace and proactively to aim to prevent events that disturb peace may be a matter of dispute. The duties of teachers and parents to inculcate the relevant norms in children are clear enough, but arguably other forms of intervention, such as the exercise of mediation skills, conflict resolution techniques, alternatives to violence programmes (AVP), and so on, have an important role, both reactively and proactively, even in a society which is already largely peaceful.

The real area for dispute is over the cosmopolitan implications of the approach. The debate between cosmopolitanism and communitarianism and internationalism has already been aired earlier in the book (see chapters 2 and 3), but here I should mention several specific points. Cosmopolitan arguments for significant efforts to promote peace elsewhere in the world and in international relations may be criticized for being idealistic, inappropriate or dangerous. It may be idealistic to expect individuals to accept obligations to promote peace in the world or to expect governments to make this a major commitment: morality is no doubt demanding, but not that demanding. It is inappropriate since the extent to which other countries are at peace is largely a function of what they do themselves to promote peace: peace cannot be imposed from outside. It is also inappropriate to expect governments to pursue peace in their foreign policy beyond what is necessary for their legitimate national interests. It is dangerous in the sense that too much attention to the promotion of goals in other countries takes away from legitimate purposes within one's own society, not least adequate attention to legitimate defence.

(a) Idealistic?

If it is idealistic in the sense of unrealistic to expect people to have some concern for distant poverty, for environmental impacts on other parts of the world or for abuses of human rights elsewhere, then maybe it is unrealistic to expect people to be concerned about peace elsewhere in the world. But these other concerns are not generally so regarded. How demanding cosmopolitanism should be on individuals is a general issue discussed in the literature on cosmopolitanism. But there is nothing peculiar about the duty to promote peace that makes it more demanding than other cosmopolitan duties.

The pacificist concern for peace is not merely about peace internal to other countries in the world but about peace between nations, and part of what a pacificist cosmopolitan may feel he or she needs to do is to play a political part in getting his or her own government to adopt more appropriate stances in foreign policy. This is analogous to someone who does not merely give aid to charities to help with distant poverty but engages in political action to change the government's aid or international trade policies.

Whether it is unrealistic to expect a government to pursue a pacificist agenda in foreign policy is mainly a function of where the general public are on the issue. If only a few citizens themselves accept the pacificist obligation, then their governments are unlikely to do the same. What governments can do – both in the sense of what is possible and in the sense of what is legitimate – is indeed a function of sufficient of their citizens adopting the agenda based on such cosmopolitan considerations.

(b) Inappropriate?

Is the pacificist agenda inappropriate? Even if we accept that the prospects for peace in any country are largely a function of what local people think and feel, it still remains the case that outsiders can help create the appropriate pacificist attitudes and skills. Much of what is called peacebuilding, which was discussed earlier, involves the intervention of outsiders with appropriate skills and mindsets. Teachers going to other countries may, even if their primary subject is not peace, by what they do contribute to peace nevertheless. In any case there is increasing interest in peace education as an explicit goal. Such interventions by outsiders would not occur unless they, and indeed many others in supporting organizations, actually accepted the pacificist obligation. Again, since the pacificist agenda is as much to do with promoting the general conditions of peace *between* countries in various parts of the world, there is plenty to be done in terms of the political agenda of one's own government, as noted in the previous paragraph.

But the challenge is: Is it appropriate to get governments to act beyond legitimate national interests? While, on the internationalist model, clearly the pursuit of national interests does need to be constrained by some ethical rules and, indeed, by the consequences of international agreements, the *promotion* of peace is surely something that lies beyond this. Here the cosmopolitan simply has to insist that, in principle, governments may indeed ethically need to do more than the traditional model expects. Those who argue, for instance, for robust aid policies or reforms of the international economic rules do so in the clear knowledge that this goes beyond the consensus in international relations circles. The same can apply to the advocacy of pacificism. But the cosmopolitan can also say that, in practice, it simply is not true that governments should only pursue what is narrowly in a country's interest. If sufficient of a country's citizens think that their government ought to do something, even if it is not to be done for reasons of national interest, then that is what a government ought to do in terms of democratic theory. If someone prefers to think of the national interest as the national *moral* interest, that is, the interest incorporating the moral views of citizens, then substantively we get the same result – policies informed by cosmopolitan considerations.

(c)   Dangerous?

Is cosmopolitanism dangerous? Does acceptance of cosmopolitan obligations undermine what is valuable in one's own society? Does it undermine defence? Perhaps an extreme and uncompromising cosmopolitanism could have these effects, but there is nothing in the general idea that has these implications. Significantly higher expenditure on foreign aid, whether directed to poverty reduction, to peace education, or whatever, would not undermine what is valuable in a country. If such commitments (taking to heart the moral force of 'the arms race is killing') lead to inroads into the kinds and levels of expenses in national defence, would that be dangerous? It might be risky if taken rapidly to a dramatically reduced level (as the pacifist might argue) and the risk might be worth taking. But a pacificist war justifier need not argue for things to be taken that far, though he or she might argue for significant reduction in arms spending, both for the sake of what could be done with the resources released and because such reductions would actually contribute to greater security for that country and a more peaceful world (for further consideration of security, see chapter 7, §5).

We should note that, whatever levels of reduction were advocated, they would not be implemented unless there was general consensus that they should. What happened in Costa Rica is interesting in this regard: after a very brief civil war in 1948, Costa Rica decided to disband its army because of a general desire to do so. More generally it is likely that, were there a move based on consensus in a country in the direction of a significant reduction in arms spending for the sake of freeing up more resources for cosmopolitan purposes, including the strengthening of peace globally, this would lead to a more secure environment for that country itself. No doubt, if there were a general acceptance of cosmopolitan arguments, including commitment to the pacificist agenda, there would be a small revolution in general attitudes and policy orientations. But arguably it would not be dangerous.

Questions

1 Is it useful to distinguish different senses of 'peace'? If so, why? If not, why not?
2 Is there an obligation to promote peace anywhere? Does one have to be an optimist to accept this?
3 What is peacebuilding? How important is it in the range of things we can do to further peace?
4 Is cosmopolitan pacificism unrealistic, dangerous, both or neither?

7 MODERN ISSUES

In this chapter we look at a number of issues relating to war and peace in the modern world that were identified in the first chapter but have not been considered elsewhere in more than passing fashion. These are: nuclear weapons, modern wars, terrorism, humanitarian intervention, and security in relation to human security.

1 Nuclear war and deterrence

It may be thought that twenty years after the end of the Cold War the issue of nuclear weapons has become relatively unimportant: some recent books on the ethics of war do not even consider it. However, the ethical issues surrounding nuclear weapons do remain important. The major nuclear powers still possess massive stockpiles of these (even if substantially reduced), other countries have joined the 'club', and many more wish to do so. It is not inconceivable that a nuclear war could start, either by accident or by design. The question whether it could be right to use such weapons remains critical, as does the ethical legitimacy of countries possessing nuclear weapons with a conditional intention to use them. There is also an issue in the ethics of international relations as to whether countries with nuclear weapons have a right to try to stop other countries acquiring them (as is currently happening vis-à-vis Iran), however much they may dislike the idea or believe the world is becoming more dangerous. The latter consideration should remind us that the possession of nuclear weapons by any country constitutes a danger for the world. Furthermore, a discussion of nuclear weapons rather neatly raises a number of more general issues in the ethics of war (see also Stein 1961 and Fisher 1985).

1.1   The background

On 6 August 1945, on the order of US President Harry Truman, an atom bomb was dropped on the Japanese city of Hiroshima, and three days later a second bomb was dropped on Nagasaki. Six days after that the Japanese surrendered, bringing the Second World War in the East to an end. It is estimated that as many as 140,000 people in Hiroshima and 80,000 in Nagasaki died by the end of 1945, roughly half on the days of the bombings. Many more died later from radiation-induced illnesses. Whatever one makes ethically of these events – I discuss this briefly below – it was generally recognized that they ushered in a new era in warfare. Although attempts were made to forestall what actually happened in the ensuing years, the development of nuclear weapons by the USA, followed by the USSR, the UK and France, proceeded apace and by the beginning of the 1950s there was a nuclear arms race. By the mid-1950s smaller fission bombs were being supplemented with much more powerful fusion bombs (so-called hydrogen or thermo-nuclear bombs). If we compare the TNT equivalent of fission bombs (13 kilotons for Hiroshima; 21 for Nagasaki) with the typical hydrogen bombs in the megaton (millions of tons) range (the largest ever detonated in a test being 50 million tons), we can get a limited understanding of just how destructive such weapons would be – hundreds of times more devastating than the bombs used in Japan in 1945. From then on, until 1989 with the collapse of Soviet Union, the world lived under conditions called the Cold War. Both sides had massive arsenals of such weapons, capable of being delivered through various types of systems such as planes, submarines or land-based rockets. Both sides realized that, however a nuclear war might start, the other side would retaliate with such weapons, and that one's own side had no way of preventing such retaliations being sufficiently successful to inflict massive and unacceptable damage.

The system that developed was one of mutual nuclear deterrence. A vast amount of intellectual energy was poured into formulating and refining systems of deterrence, much based on game theory and calculations of psychological probability (see Lackey [1982] 1985, 1989: ch. 5). But in essence (oversimplified but sufficient for the purposes of the ethical discussion to follow) deterrence depends upon one's having a nuclear weapons system capable of causing unacceptably high damage to the side that might attack. There are two elements to this system actually having the desired effect: (i) a retaliatory strike can be and is known to be capable of being delivered, that is, the other side cannot either wipe out in its first strike one's entire weapons system or adequately defend itself from incoming missiles; (ii) there is a reasonably high probability, known or at least firmly believed by the other side, that the weapons will actually be used if there is an attack. The defence system is therefore meant to work on the basis of MAD, that is, mutually assured destruction. This acronym by the way is not the invention of the critics but used by defenders of the deterrence system because it highlighted the logic of the system: no side would deliberately start such a war from simple considerations of national survival.

We should note that condition (i) requires that neither side is capable of stopping effective retaliation against it. This explains why much effort during most of the Cold War period was put into preventing the development of other weapons which would undermine this. Thus we have the so-called ABM treaties, that is, treaties banning the development of anti-ballistic missiles. It also helps to explain why during the 1980s the deterrence system was threatened and East–West relations became more tense because of Reagan's 'star wars' initiative, in which the official intention was to develop laser weapons that could destroy all incoming missiles or planes before they reached their targets. This would have undermined condition (i).[1] For condition (ii) to be operative, there must actually be either a firm intention on the part of those in control of the nuclear button, or at least a willingness to see the option as really available. A third possibility is that a leader might not intend to use the weapons but provide a bluff that he would or might. Apart from problems of real credibility involved here, it seems to have been the case anyway that the intention to use nuclear weapons was (and is) firmly embedded in the nuclear deterrence position.

Since 1989, with the end of the Cold War, the sense of a threat of nuclear weapons has receded. On the other hand, the nuclear powers continue to hold large stocks of these weapons and other countries are joining them. Attempts to stop this expansion through the Nuclear Non-Proliferation Treaties have not proved successful. Despite the World Court opinion delivered in July 1996[2] that nuclear weapons were contrary to international law (though a qualification in the opinion has led nuclear powers to regard themselves as justified in continuing their policy) and a quite unequivocal clause that says that the nuclear powers should take steps to engage in nuclear disarmament, the relevant states have not done so (see Mothersson 1992). In 2007, for instance, the UK parliament voted to support the government's proposal to renew the Trident submarine programme, despite considerable opposition within the UK to this. This was a significant missed opportunity for a nuclear power to take the lead in discouraging the tendency towards proliferation.

1.2   Ethical issues

(a)   Hiroshima and Nagasaki

A useful way into the ethical assessment can be via a consideration of Hiroshima and Nagasaki, over which controversy still continues. For those who considered the bombings from a just war perspective, the *ius in bello* principle of discrimination was clearly violated: civilians were the target. Those who supported the action pointed out that it brought the war to an end rapidly – a war which would have dragged on for some time and involved more casualties. It was in any case pointed out that the targeting of civilian centres of population had already been a standard feature of the Second World War, both in Europe, with direct attacks on cities such as Coventry in the UK, Dresden in Germany, and so on, and indeed in Japan, where cities had been fire-bombed in the period leading to these events: there was no difference in principle (see for instance Walzer 1971). Critics replied that prior practice did not make it right: the targeting of cities was already an immoral feature of the war effort on both sides; in any case, the atom bomb was different because of the types of effects it had (though, to be fair to defenders, the effects of radiation were far worse than anticipated). They also said that a demonstration could have persuaded the Japanese government (certainly after Hiroshima it was not clear that Nagasaki had to be attacked as well only three days later); that concern over loss of life was focused more on limiting loss of life on the Allies' side, not overall, since the total of all people killed would not have been as high as all the direct and indirect deaths involved; and that a less public motive was a desire to get a Japanese surrender before the Soviet army achieved it later. Defenders claimed that the breach of non-combatant immunity was something justified by the necessity of such war; that saving one's own soldiers' lives legitimately had priority; that getting a Japanese surrender to the Americans rather than to the Soviets was a justified move for geopolitical reasons; and so on. Many of the general moves in the ethics of war discussed in this book are illustrated here.

(b)   Use of nuclear weapons

Whatever is felt about the bombs used in Hiroshima and Nagasaki – by later standards very small bombs with relatively small general damage beyond the areas in which they were exploded – and likewise about even smaller nuclear devices such as battlefield weapons (where it is assumed – no doubt naively – that their use would be strictly limited and not escalate to full-scale employment), it would generally be accepted that large megaton nuclear weapons would have such devastating consequences that their use would be immoral. Such a judgement is based not merely on the traditional concern for non-discrimination and lack of proportionality (see Kenny 1985), but on properties of nuclear weapons which make them especially immoral. Large-scale megaton nuclear weapons, whether employed as counter-value weapons against cities or as counter-force weapons against enemy weapons centres, would have devastating consequences in at least four different ways, from blast and fire in the vicinity, and from radiation and weather effects much farther afield, on millions of people. The cumulative effect of a number of bombs on weather patterns (because of the massive cloud of dust sent up) could result in major loss of sunlight over large areas (leading *in extremis* to a possible 'nuclear winter').

But the key added dimension to the ethical character of nuclear weapons comes from the categories of beings affected by them. In a conventional war the traditional debate about combatants and non-combatants, and whether there is a clear distinction, is really about different categories of people all currently living within the countries in dispute. Large-scale nuclear war changes all that. The three main categories affected (in addition to people living in the states at war) are: (i) people in countries not parties to the dispute; (ii) future generations of people everywhere (where, for instance, babies will be born with severe genetic defects); and (iii) the biosphere as a whole, where countless plants and animals will be severely modified by radiation effects. While not all critics will adopt the latter ecocentric or biocentric perspective, in many ways such an ecological catastrophe underscores the especially troubling feature of nuclear weapons. To be sure, all war has negative effects on the environment – a factor often overlooked by war's apologists – but the nuclear effects (as indeed the effects of biological and chemical weapons) are of a different order.

These considerations go beyond the traditional 'just war' deontological constraint on how war is fought, but they provide further deontological arguments about the inherent wrongness of harming those not party in any sense to the dispute. We should add that there are a range of other general consequentialist arguments which would also lead one to suppose that no overall good could be achieved, either for an attacker or for a retaliator (see Lackey [1982] 1985, 1989: ch. 5, for extended treatment of this approach).

(c) Deterrence

One of the central issues of philosophical interest that arises for those who believe the actual use of nuclear weapons, whether offensively or in response/retaliation to nuclear attack, would be wrong (for the kinds of reasons given above) is whether it is nevertheless morally acceptable (or even obligatory) to rely on a policy of nuclear deterrence, that is, threatening to use nuclear weapons under certain conditions. We noted above two general conditions for deterrence to 'work': a capacity to deliver an effective retaliatory strike and a willingness to do just that.

The interesting questions arise over the second condition. What makes it the case that it is probable that the weapons would be used in response to an attack? If it is taken that it would be either immoral or irrational, or both, actually to use nuclear weapons, what is the likelihood that they will be used? One side would have to believe that the other will (or might well) do what is immoral and/or irrational. That is not impossible, since people do both: deterrence 'works' precisely because each side fears that the other might very well do what is wrong and/or irrational.

But another question arises vis-à-vis the structure of the threat itself. Can it be right to threaten to do what it would be immoral actually to do? (A parallel question can be raised: Can it be rational to threaten to do what it would be irrational to do?) This ethical problem arises precisely because the most obvious interpretation of a threat is that it embodies a *conditional intention*: I will do x under certain conditions. It is widely recognized in moral thinking that, if doing x (under certain conditions) is wrong, then intending to do x (under the same conditions) is wrong. When we assess an action ethically, what we are primarily interested in is the nature of the 'will', or what an agent intends in his or her action. That carries the weight of assessment. This is quite explicit in deontological approaches to ethics. Kant, for instance, saw the 'good will' as the primary focus of ethical value (Kant [1785] 1949: 1), and it is both clear in the earlier thought of Aquinas and reflected in the doctrine of double effect, which distinguishes between what we aim at, including the means taken, and what lies beyond the intention. Even in utilitarian thought it is generally recognized that what we are assessing are intentional acts, but what is included in these acts are all the foreseen or reasonably foreseeable consequences. (An act which quite accidentally and unforeseeably has good or bad consequences is a quite different matter.) So if, for instance, a parent intends to use corporal punishment on a child if he or she misbehaves, then such an intention carries the same moral weight as would the act if carried out when the child misbehaves. Whatever the law says, a plan to murder someone on an occasion x is morally wrong if murdering that person is morally wrong (and never gets carried out because the occasion x never materializes).

Does it make a moral difference if the conditional intention is subordinate to another intention, namely to prevent the condition occurring in which the conditional intention would be carried out? We need to distinguish this particular way in which an intention can be embedded in a further intention. Normally an intention is embedded in another intention because it is the means towards the end intended and, if the end is achieved, the means intended is actually carried out. Consequentialists and deontologists may differ over how ethically to assess the means, and this has been frequently illustrated in the ethics of war. The case here is somewhat different: the point here is that the embedded intention is there precisely because it is also intended that the condition for its exercise should never occur.

Now this only makes sense on the supposition that the intention is publicly announced and backed by evidence that the agent would carry it out. If a parent really intended to do something terrible to his or her child if the child did something and the child did not even know this, then it is hard to see how the assessment of the intention can be any different from the assessment of the action if carried out. The introduction of the public nature of the conditional intention complicates the issue because we now have *another act* – in the case of nuclear deterrence a very complicated policy involving many people, much hardware, and so on! Does the fact that there is a separate act or policy make a moral difference?

There are three responses to this question. First, if the act threatened is intrinsically wrong (evil), then threatening it is wrong – making one's conditional intention public does not alter its wrongness. Second, while the conditional intention in the act makes it *prima facie* wrong, other goals in the act make it *prima facie* our duty, and on balance it is or may be the right thing to do. Third, as consequentialists would argue, since there is now a separate act – the act of deterring – its foreseen or reasonably foreseeable consequences have to be assessed separately from the consequences of the act threatened if carried out, and so the threat may well turn out to be the right thing to do. (This does not mean that utilitarians will necessarily support nuclear deterrence; they may think that there are lots of other costs involved: see below.)

The issues raised here are not incidentally merely relevant to assessing nuclear deterrence. They apply to other aspects of war too. They most obviously apply to the use of biological and chemical weapons: if the use of these is intrinsically wrong, then the same issues arise about developing and stockpiling them and having them in reserve with a view to using them under certain circumstances. What makes these policies even more problematic is that, since these kinds of weapons are officially banned in international law, their possession is actually meant to be secret, so they cannot even be part of an officially stated deterrence policy. But the issues could apply to more conventional forms of warfare too. If a country threatens to use methods which are judged wrong as a way of achieving certain goals by dissuading other countries (or parties) from doing what would elicit the response (for instance, massive use of landmines; targeting cultural artefacts), then similar issues are raised. (This incidentally shows that the ethical issue at root is not merely about the intention to do x to A if A does x to you, but the intention to do x to A if A does not do what you want.)

The first position – that if what is threatened is (absolutely) wrong, then threatening it is (absolutely) wrong – depends as much on a theory of intention (with which the reader may have detected I am sympathetic) as a theory in ethics. Many thinkers feel the force of it (for instance, Kenny 1985). Nevertheless there are those who, while troubled by this 'conditional intention' problem, have still wanted to accept nuclear weapons and have considered such moves as arguing that the threat could be based on bluff or on the possibility, and thus danger, of a response but with no intention either way. The existence of a weapons system up and running is itself an 'existential deterrent' (consider Ramsey 1968). But then deception is involved which is itself ethically problematic (along with the problem that most of the population would have to be engaged in a moral error); and, while a 'willingness that the system may operate' may fall short of a current conditional intention, intention is still there in that one does not intend a policy which rules out the possibility of intending or doing what is horrendously wrong. In any case, neither bluff nor keeping options open would really act as an effective deterrent, and neither appears to have been the real basis of nuclear policy anyway.

Second, the idea that the wrongness of the conditional intention is overridden by other features of the threat was, for instance, supported by Arthur Hockaday. He employed the approach to ethics provided by W. D. Ross, who argued that certain kinds of act could be *prima facie* right or wrong, and that where duties clash one has to do what is more 'incumbent' (Ross 1930: ch. 1). Hockaday reasoned that the goals of deterrence were of sufficiently vital importance – the maintenance of peace and the protection of the free world from the spread of communism – that deterrence was after all a duty (Hockaday 1982). No doubt from the Soviet point of view the checking of the evils of capitalism and Western freedom was an analogous duty. Indeed, this reflects a common assumption that the Cold War was the major factor in keeping the peace from 1945 to 1989. Major issues of interpretation are raised here. How far did the deterrence system itself contribute to the peace between East and West? What kind of peace was it? It certainly was not peace in the richer sense (peace in sense (B)). What were the costs of such a policy? (We should recall the claim that the 'arms race is killing'; see chapter 6.) If we take a wider global view, did it really prevent wars? It certainly did not prevent many wars in many parts of the world, and some such wars were 'proxy' wars (as in Angola or Mozambique) in which East–West antagonisms in the North were played out in arenas in the South. If the communist approach was to be opposed, were there not other ways of doing so? In the end the internal inefficiencies of the Soviet system, combined with the internal nonviolent opposition from civil society movements, played a big role in the demise of the Soviet Union.

Third, there is, as noted earlier, a quite different way of handling the ethics of deterrence, and that is to do a utilitarian calculation comparing deterrence ('equivalence' in Lackey's discussion) with unilateral disarmament. A consequentialist recognizes that intentions, particularly publicly embodied ones (stated or prepared for), have their own sets of consequences and may therefore be evaluated differently from the acts intended. Lackey argued (he was writing at the time of the Cold War) that a clear-thinking utilitarian would opt for unilateral disarmament and that on the whole even prudential reasoning, that is, looking just at American interests, went the same way. His long and rather complex article 'Missiles and morals', much of which works on complex empirical estimates of probabilities which others can dispute, as Kavka does, does bring out a philosophically interesting problem of how you compare alternative courses of action when there is uncertainty as to the outcomes of each (Lackey 1982; Kavka 1983; see also Kavka 1987; Ferguson 1982).

2   Contemporary wars

Many commentators have noted that most of the wars that have been fought in the latter part of the twentieth century and in the twenty-first century have been rather different from the kinds of wars fought in the previous few centuries, which had on the whole been wars fought between nation-states. We need to note some of the characteristics of these wars and then consider what kinds of ethical issues are raised by them. Perhaps the nature of these wars has changed so much that the way we think ethically about them needs to change as well. I shall use as an introduction to this the discussion in Iain Atack's book, in the chapter under the title 'Post-modern war'.

2.1   Features of contemporary war

Atack gives four characteristics of contemporary wars: first, they are often intra-state wars, that is, wars that are fought by groups within nation-states, sometimes between a government and another group, sometimes between different groups; second, there is the privatization of war, with many non-state actors involved; third, there is the civilianization of casualties, in that civilians are often targeted and atrocities often committed as instruments of policy; fourth, such wars are protracted or endless struggles without clearly defined 'end-points' (Atack 2005: 93–7). There are, as Atack notes, three types of intra-state war: first, wars about state control, that is, getting control of the state, as in Mozambique; second, wars about state formation, that is, wars in which a group is trying to create a new state, as in Chechnya; third, wars in failed states, that is, where there is violence in the absence of effective state control, for instance between warlords in Somalia. The first two kinds of contemporary wars are not that different from some of the wars fought in the past. The first is like traditional civil wars and the second is like earlier wars of secession. It is the third category, of wars that take place in failed states, that is the most distinctive in the recent period. Mary Kaldor's book *New & Old Wars* (1999) did much to draw attention to this phenomenon of new or 'post-modern' wars: failed state wars show most clearly these four characteristics. Some wars, we should note, combine elements of all three types, such as the various wars that followed the break-up of Yugoslavia in the early 1990s.

A characteristic of many contemporary wars has been the phenomenon of asymmetry. Asymmetrical wars occur where vastly unequal military power is being exercised and they cover a number of kinds of cases. First, in the Middle East, the Palestinian Intifada involves an asymmetrical relationship between Israeli military power and the kinds of responses open to Palestinians, in the form of suicide missions, and so on. At another level the NATO action in Serbia in 1999 involved bombing from great heights so that there were no pilot casualties during the raids. At yet another level the so-called war against terror led by the USA in response to 9/11 is asymmetrical in that the kind of power exercised by al-Qaeda is quite unlike that exercised by the USA. Whether the latter conflict should be called a war is a matter of dispute, though it has been described as the 'US and al-Qaeda waging borderless war on a global scale' (Atack 2005: 105). The impact of al-Qaeda at least illustrates 'state failure to retain control over organised violence on a global or international scale' (ibid.: 106).

As Atack notes, many modern wars are called post-modern because 'they are characterised by the marginalisation of the state and its diminished capacity to control the use of armed force or violence in the territory under its jurisdiction' (Atack 2005: 102). This explains (but does not justify) why certain characteristics such as the targeting of civilians, frequent atrocities, and the lack of clear end-points are in evidence. Whatever one makes of traditional wars between states, they were on the whole conducted according to rules laid down in inter-*national* law, in which there were reciprocally agreed norms concerning the rules of war, diplomacy, declarations of war and ceasefires, the treatment and status of soldiers, and so on. Since many wars occur outside this agreed framework, there has not been the same framework for limiting war. Hedley Bull's definition of war in a loose sense as 'organised violence which may be carried out by any political unit' (Bull 1977: 185) seems to fit what is going on in new wars. Further features of such wars are that they are often dominated by identity politics to do with people's ethnicity, though, as Atack notes, sometimes struggles in the name of ethnic identity are to some extent a cover for groups engaging in economically predatory or criminal activities; that is, for them, engaging in warfare in situations where state control is lacking is actually a profitable business, in some ways analogous to an organization such as the Mafia running a protection racket.

Atack considers the responses that might be given to the phenomenon just considered of post-modern war from the three perspectives in international relations: realism, internationalism and cosmopolitanism. The realist stresses the need for state-building where states are weak, the internationalist stresses the need for more robust global governance, and the cosmopolitan stresses the need to strengthen transnational civil society as responses to post-modern armed conflict (Atack 2005: 106–8). The assumption behind these proposals is that, if there are stronger states, if there is more robust global governance, and if there is a more effective global civil society, then these features should significantly reduce the incidence of such wars, if not eliminate them. I would make two observations about these proposals.

First, all three positions have something to offer to reduce the incidence of such wars. But are they really in conflict with each other? Could not a cosmopolitan, for instance, have reason to support all three measures? For all the cosmopolitan's concern about a world dominated by states, especially if they pursue their own interests, the last thing that a cosmopolitan wants in the world as it is now are weak or failed states. Likewise, a cosmopolitan is likely to argue *both* for better institutions of global governance *and* for more effective civil society institutions through which the disputes that occasion modern wars can be handled in nonviolent or less violent ways. But, second, if the goal is to reduce the incidence of such conflicts, there also needs to be more attention paid to their root causes. As we indicated in the previous chapter, and as Atack mentions in another chapter (Atack 2005: ch. 10), there is a significant role for conflict management and peacebuilding. But we get a better handle on the issue if we ask whether such wars are ever justified (or examine what justifications are offered for such wars). Atack seems to assume that they are ethically problematic, and he never considers whether any fighting in such wars might actually be right.

2.2   Ethical issues

If one is against all wars, then one will be against these wars as well, and trying to reduce their incidence will be part and parcel of trying to reduce the incidence of any war. But are there features of these wars that raise particular ethical difficulties or issues? If one is not against all wars, then are wars that are state-based, involve political units that are state-oriented (not militia, warlords, gangs, and so on), involve agreed rules concerning limiting warfare (for instance, in regard to non-combatancy) and have limited duration either, unlike these wars, ethically satisfactory or at least ethically *less* problematic than them?

Certainly the most troubling feature of many of these new wars is the feature of the civilianization of casualties and the fact that there is a far greater incidence of atrocities. While, as I noted earlier, this is partly a function of the fact that these conflicts occur outside the agreed international regulatory framework, does that render the traditional principles irrelevant or inapplicable? Although some may argue that the norms of war are not timelessly valid and that the new forms of war generate new or more relaxed norms, this does not match the reality that most people continue to condemn such behaviour in war, and indeed the development of the idea of international law applying to individuals points in the opposite direction. The International Criminal Court, ratified in 2002, is likely to be used more in the future to try soldiers who commit war crimes and crimes against humanity.

Does the fact that such wars are often engaged in by non-state actors raise difficulties about the idea of legitimate authority? In the cases of secession or civil war, it is not clear that the only side that has legitimate authority is the side that is currently the government of an area. In the case of failed states, while one might say that in such anarchical situations no side has legitimate authority, nevertheless in the political vacuum claims by groups that they have the right to fight for what they are trying to achieve cannot be simply dismissed as automatically out of order.

Do the goals of groups fighting such wars have to be dismissed as inappropriate? While I have offered in chapter 4 general criticisms of all the types of claimed just causes, I cannot see how, if one accepts that there can be just causes for war at all, the claim of those who wish to secede from unjust or oppressive regimes or to contest the legitimacy of a corrupt government in a civil war have to be dismissed just because they are features of the troubling forms of contemporary war. Boutros-Ghali, in *An Agenda for Peace* (1992), offered arguments against the propriety of groups engaging in secessionist war. Although he was still appealing to the UN principle of state sovereignty and to pragmatic considerations of how such wars tend to open a Pandora's box of further complications, it is not clear why such wars can be dismissed simply because of the kinds of causes they involve. What does need to be recognized is that, given that they inform the resort to violence, these same causes have to be the focus of efforts to find peaceful solutions to prevent or stop such conflicts.

3   Terrorism

Ever since the planes crashed into the twin towers in New York on September 11, 2001 (also simply referred to as '9/11'), the world has been accustomed to the idea of a 'war against terror', described as a 'borderless war on a global scale' between the USA, with its allies, and al-Qaeda, a network of Muslim extremists opposed to the Western liberal, secular way of life. There is, however, nothing new about terrorism (see, for instance, Wilkinson 1986). Many terrorist acts, large and small, have been carried out over the centuries. In more recent history one can think of the assassination of the Israeli athletes at the Munich Olympics in 1972 by the Black September group or the assassination in 1978 by the Red Brigades of Aldo Moro, a senior Italian statesman. In this section, I make a few remarks about definition (using an important pair of articles by Walzer and Fullinwider written in 1988), and then address two ethical questions, 'What is wrong with terrorism?' and 'How should those of us opposed to terrorism respond to it?'

3.1   What is terrorism?

Terrorism is a highly contested concept. There are many definitions given of it. B. T. Wilkins starts with a very neutral definition: 'terrorism is the attempt to achieve political, social, economic or religious change by the actual or threatened use of violence against persons or property' (Wilkins 1992: 2). As Wilkins goes on to say, this is rather too broad and allows in forms of action we would not normally think of as terrorism. Two things are generally seen as also necessary: first, the immediate aim, whatever the further goals, is the inducing of 'terror' in the wider population (hence the name 'terror'-ism) from which the target group is chosen; second, the people targeted are regarded by normal standards as ordinary citizens not involved in any kind of violent activity in relation to the attackers. Although we tend to think of terrorists as small groups of non-state actors, there is nothing in these further qualifications to rule out states as perpetrators of terrorism, either against their own citizens or against other states, and this seems right: there is such a thing as state terrorism. However, in what follows I focus on the issue of non-state actors as terrorists.

I put the second clause 'people targeted are regarded by normal standards as ordinary citizens not involved in any kind of violent activity in relation to the attackers' in order to offer an ethically neutral account of what is done. It may be that terrorism is indeed to be condemned, but it is better not to build the condemnation into the definition. This, however, is the move that Walzer makes in his article. On his account, terrorism is wrong in itself because it 'targets innocent bystanders' (Walzer 1988: 238). Since targeting innocent bystanders is inherently wrong, it follows that terrorism is wrong. So, according to Walzer, whatever arguments are used by terrorists for their acts are necessarily 'excuses', rather than justifications, since if they were justifications then their acts would not be wrong. Walzer identified four types of 'excuse'. In Luper-Foy's summary it is put this way: 'it is the *last* resort, everything else having failed; it is the *only* resort against powerful states; it is the only *effective* resort; or it is the *universal* resort, the one adopted in secrecy by all states, so that the terrorist is only fighting fire with fire' (Luper-Foy 1988: 237). In his reply Fullinwider argues that it misrepresents the terrorist to see him as offering excuses, not justifications (Fullinwider 1988). Walzer's four excuses are really justifications, since for the terrorist his methods are satisfactory. Fullinwider does think that Walzer's objections to these justifications are generally successful, but that he does not really capture the terrorist's outlook.

Fullinwider's two main points are as follows. First, the terrorist is often characterized as being 'beyond the moral pale'. But terrorism is rather better understood as taking morality into one's own hands in disregard for settled laws. Locke, he argued, saw the escape from the state of nature (in which ethical disputes were settled privately) as one of subsuming ethics under (settled) law (see Locke [1689] 1960). Many groups break law selectively for higher moral purposes, for instance those engaged in attacks on abortion clinics. Terrorists take this idea further, and what they do is often in terms of 'recognisable moral ideas: creating a just and humane society, ending misery and oppression' (Fullinwider 1988: 254). Second, on the issue of innocence, the disputed question is 'Who is innocent?' Was Aldo Moro innocent? He represented the modern Italian, capitalist, bourgeois state – everything that the Red Brigades detested. The Israeli athletes represented Israel at the Olympic Games and so were not seen as innocent. If someone is part of a 'people' then, for anyone who is against a 'people' and what they stand for, any individual is guilty as a member of that 'people'. If we protest that individuals are not just part of a 'people' and have individual rights, this merely brings out the issue: for them we need to reject individual human rights in favour of a robust communitarian conception of identity (ibid.: 255). In many ways the conflict between al-Qaeda and the USA and other liberal democratic countries can be seen in these terms. None of these interpretations is of course meant to show that Moro, the Israeli athletes or ordinary human beings killed in New York, Madrid or London were not innocent, only that we need at least to acknowledge where the terrorist is coming from.

3.2   What is wrong with terrorism?

If we oppose terrorists, why do we do so? What is it that makes terrorism ethically wrong? We can consider this under three headings: objectives, status and methods.

Are their objectives necessarily unethical? This does not have to be the case, as Fullinwider notes. We cannot simply, for instance, distinguish pursuing good causes as the acts of freedom fighters and pursuing bad causes as those of terrorists. Hobbes once remarked, assuming a subjectivist theory of value, that tyranny is merely monarchy 'misliked' (Hobbes [1651] 1991: ch. xix), and it is tempting to make a similar move about terrorists, thereby building into the goal of the terrorist something unacceptable. But this is actually to confuse two very different things. As Graham notes, freedom fighting is so called because of its objectives, namely the achievement of political freedom; terrorism is defined by its means, namely the inducing of terror by attacks on anyone, whatever its broader goal (Graham 1996: 115–25). They may go together. A freedom fighter could use terror as a means to getting what he wanted, though he need not.[3] Terrorism is about the proximate goals, not about the ultimate goals. Generally terrorists do have further ultimate goals – either political or religious or both – but whether we approve of these (and even pursue them or would pursue them ourselves by other means) or disapprove of them, they are quite separate from the nature of the act of inducing terror itself.

Is it because terrorist groups are illegitimate bodies? This may be one of the reasons for rejecting them for some thinkers – for instance, those with very narrow and traditional views about legitimate authority – but we can only say this confidently if we reject all non-state actors as having legitimate authority. This would include rejection of liberation movements such as the ANC or the Palestine Liberation Organization (PLO), the

American revolutionaries, all parties to civil wars other than established governments, and so on. For most thinkers who are prepared to include these as legitimate authorities, this move is not an easy one to make. Of course, for a pacifist, no bodies have legitimacy, but then the pacifist is not marking a *difference* between terrorist groups and other groups in this respect.

Is it because of their means, namely the indiscriminate targeting of civilians? This is the most likely reason why most of us reject terrorism, but if we accept this, we also have to question what is often done by state actors in war. Saturation bombing is also terrorism and, if we accept Wilkins's suggestion that terrorism includes threats, the policy of nuclear deterrence is also a form of state terrorism (for extended treatment of the issue, see Goodin 2006; Rockmore et al. 2005).

3.3   Responses to terrorism

What should our responses to terrorism be? Walzer, in the article discussed earlier, suggests two responses to terrorism: first, we should engage in repression of and retaliation against terrorists themselves, but not against those for whom they claim to be acting; second, we should address the causes for which terrorists sometimes act. This, Walzer notes, is not caving in to terrorists, but recognizing that terrorists do 'exploit oppression, injustice and human misery generally' (Walzer 1988: 244); if we can tackle these, we take away one their 'excuses' (or, if Fullinwider is right, 'justifications'). Walzer's first point is sound enough in respect to its second half, namely that we should not target those for whom terrorists act. Whether, however, 'repression' and 'retaliation' are the best words to use in respect to terrorists themselves is another matter. That terrorists should be punished if caught and duly convicted in a proper court of law is no doubt sound, but retaliation has other connotations. Furthermore, the general idea of 'stopping' terrorists from being able to carry out further terrorist acts is sound enough, but the word 'repression' carries extra connotations which may be questionable. It is certainly the case that, if we are to thwart terrorists, we had better not do so by acting in ways that are equally as questionable morally, such as the holding of terrorist suspects in Guantánamo Bay. There are a whole range of measures that may be appropriate for stopping or immobilizing terrorists (or at least making their acts less likely, since complete security against them is impossible), but in the post-9/11 world we have to recognize that many of these measures involve erosion of the civil liberties of ordinary citizens as well as the undermining of the rights of those who may be detained without trial under 'prevention of terrorism' legislation.

These issues of addressing the root causes have taken on a larger dimension than perhaps Walzer, writing long before the events of 9/11, had in mind. Given the global scale of the struggle between Western states and al-Qaeda, this issue of addressing the factors that might fuel support for the network takes on a controversial nature. Some of the root causes are arguably the existence of extreme poverty in the world, Western hegemony and the projection of Western values, and inappropriate political positions taken in the Middle East (Dower 2002a). Terrorists are not themselves necessarily extremely poor, but they get some of their support and legitimacy from such misery. There needs arguably to be greater sensitivity to non-Western perspectives and a willingness to recognize that our secular growth-oriented approach has its problems. At the very least we need to avoid treating Islam as 'the other', demonizing Muslims or somehow associating Islam with terrorism. A more politically even-handed approach to the Israel–Palestine question would also help. However, in all these cases, if Western thinkers believe that our current attitudes, for instance the current largely pro-Israeli position, are actually completely right, then they will not make such adjustments and will live with the consequences of 'doing the right thing'. The ironic thing is that, on the whole, so far as the 'war against terror' is concerned, it has been counter-productive, and there is now more support for terrorism than before.[4] (For extended treatments and similar lines, see Honderich 2002; Bobbitt 2008.)[5]

The root causes that help to legitimize terrorism are generally global now – certainly in the context of responses to 9/11. What I have suggested is a cosmopolitan perspective, and this is worth making explicit. Action for tackling the root causes could be a concern for *national* security. One may want things to change in other parts of the world – and these may or may not be improvements for people in other areas – but the 'bottom line', so to speak, consists of the benefits for one's own country. This could apply to policies vis-à-vis the environment and poverty reduction elsewhere, as well as issues of security. But if one reason for such measures is a cosmopolitan concern for the well-being of others – including *their* increased interest in all dimensions of their human security – then one's commitment will be stronger, more consistent and more likely to be effective, given the perception by people in other parts of the world that that is *why* one is pursuing such policies.[6] If, for instance, the American government's policy on terrorism were informed, or rather more fully informed, by cosmopolitan considerations, then that policy would take on a rather different form (for more on this possibility, see chapter 8, §3). But this is not likely to be the case unless sufficient numbers of American citizens come to think in these terms. (See §5 on security for further discussion of the contrast between the narrow security agenda and human security and the implications of the latter for foreign policy.)

4 Humanitarian intervention

4.1 Humanitarian armed intervention

Humanitarian intervention can be thought of in very broad terms as any form of intervention in another country for humanitarian reasons. This would include intervening with the consent of the government with emergency relief or aid projects as well as entering a country (unarmed) without the government's permission to provide assistance in, for instance, a war zone, just as Médecins sans Frontières sometimes do. Or, more usually, it can be defined in more narrow terms to mean *military* intervention without the consent of the government. As Atack puts it: 'humanitarian intervention is usually defined as the forceful infringement of a state's sovereignty in order to protect the fundamental human rights of those within its jurisdiction' (Atack 2005: 126). Furthermore, we should note that forceful intervention by military means without the consent of the government also occurs in a number of other contexts, where the motive, whether good or bad, is something other than humanitarian considerations. There are at least five types of case: entering a civil war on the side other than the government's; aiding a secessionist group; imposing democracy or other values; entering another country that started a war in order to defeat them; and, historically, imperialist acquisition of territory.

Humanitarian interventions have occurred on various occasions over a long period of time. In recent years we have notable examples such as the Indian invasion of East Pakistan in 1971 (partly for humanitarian reasons, partly to aid the Bangladeshi liberation movement's efforts to secede), the Tanzanian invasion of Uganda in 1979 to rid that country of the dictator Idi Amin, and, much later, the NATO attack on Serbia in 1999 in order to stop the human rights violations of Albanian Kosovans in the then province of Kosovo. Although the context of the ongoing atrocities in the region by all parties already included Kosovan liberation aspirations, officially the NATO intervention was not about that but about stopping the atrocities at the time. (Kosovo declared itself independent in 2008.)

There are three main types of objection raised against humanitarian intervention: first, it violates sovereignty and undermines international order; second, it provides a new justification of militarism and fails to meet the proportionality test; third, there is simply a principled objection to the use of force, even for such humanitarian objectives.

4.2   The issue of sovereignty

The first general concern, that such intervention violates sovereignty, has been a basic position in the internationalist tradition for a long time, and it is expressly referred to in the UN Charter: 'Nothing contained in the present Charter shall authorize the United Nations to intervene in matters which are essentially within the domestic jurisdiction of any state' (UN 1945: Art. 2.7). International order depends on respecting sovereignty.

However, defenders of humanitarian intervention argue against this position, claiming that international law and order are not undermined by such action, if it is properly limited and if just war criteria are seriously applied to justify it. Wheeler, for instance, argues that, so long as the four benchmark criteria of just war thinking are met (just cause, last resort, proportionality and probability), the other traditional criteria (legitimate authority and right intention) need not be (Wheeler 2000: 38). Wheeler's point about the legitimate authority is that there may be circumstances in which a country (or group of countries) feels that it needs to act even if formally it does not have authority. This covers the case of Kosovo in 1999, since the UN Security Council did not authorize the action. Nevertheless, even if technically it lacked legitimate authority in terms of the UN Charter, many felt that NATO had *moral* authority for the action. Wheeler's dismissal of the 'right intention' criterion is based on the fact that the evils may be so serious that the main thing is to put a stop to them, whatever further objectives may be behind the intervening power's action. Whether this criterion should be so easily dismissed is a matter for debate. Certainly, as we note below, the dispensing with the 'right intention' criterion does open up the prospect of greater militarism.

Whatever one makes of these moves towards seeing such intervention as justified, it is worth noting a major shift in thinking that has taken place since the founding of the UN. When one compares the serious condemnation by the international community of what India did in 1971 and Tanzania did in 1979 with the widespread acceptance of the NATO action in 1999, one needs to recognize a change in thinking. This is a reflection of a major shift in the way human rights have been conceptualized, which is partly to do with a move from regarding individual human beings as being merely objects in international law to their being subjects. This incidentally illustrates a shift from thinking of human rights as being universal rights to considering them as universal rights *with* correlative significant transnational (cosmopolitan) obligations to do something about them.

The difference between a global ethic as merely about universal values and a global ethic which includes transnational responsibility has been a theme in this book. Here the point is that, when the *Universal Declaration of Human Rights* was formulated in 1948 (UN 1948), it was assumed that the primary responsibility for the protection and promotion of such rights resided within nation-states themselves, with the international community merely offering support towards what a country did. As time has gone on it has become increasingly clear that often states themselves are actually impediments to the realization of human rights, if not active perpetrators of human rights violations. So increasingly it has come to be seen as something with which the international community needs to be concerned. While the UN was founded on the internationalist model, over the sixty plus years since, people have increasingly come to expect it in various ways to realize cosmopolitan responsibilities. In this respect Kosovo was a turning point. Since then much thought has gone into this aspect, and there was finally adopted by the United Nations in 2005 a declaration called the *Responsibility to Protect*, referred to as 'R2P' (UN 2005). The General Assembly declared:

> We are prepared to take collective action, in a timely and decisive manner, through the Security Council, in accordance with the Charter, including Chapter VII, on a case-by-case basis and in cooperation with relevant regional organisations as appropriate, should peaceful means be inadequate and national authorities are manifestly failing to protect their populations from genocide, war crimes, ethnic cleansing and crimes against humanity. (UN 2005: §138)

That the UN has declared this does not settle the ethical question. There are two further difficulties.

4.3 Bad consequences

The second objection to humanitarian intervention is that it perpetuates the ideology of militarism and fails the proportionality test. For instance, Atack says: 'the pacifist or anti-militarist critics of armed humanitarian intervention are concerned that such interventions will perpetuate the ideology of militarism and the institutionalisation of military responses to conflict that permeate our political, social and economic structures through processes of militarisation' (Atack 2005: 137). There are really two sorts of issue here. First, there is a straightforward consequentialist consideration about whether such interventions really do more good than harm. Atack notes that, in the cases of Somalia and Kosovo, various thinkers have argued that this is really in doubt. Second, there is a disagreement about the effects of accepting this form of argument on thinking about war because it reinforces an ethically inappropriate militarist approach where what is really needed is an emphasis on pacificism. This involves, according to the former UN Secretary-General Kofi Annan, the protection of human rights through developing a culture of nonviolent preventative diplomacy (Annan, quoted in Atack 2005: 137).

As with all empirical analyses, it is hard to say that all humanitarian interventions do more harm than good. Maybe, however, there is a presumption to this effect. One consideration is that one needs to take the proportionality criterion as being not merely about a comparison of what is likely to happen in an intervention and what would happen without an intervention. One has also to compare the effect of the intervention with what could have been done in other ways vis-à-vis that situation (not merely doing nothing) and also with what could have been done with the resources in all sorts of other ways. It is worth noting that, if a country's government has so much by way of resources it is willing to use for the realization of human rights elsewhere in the world, it may do better to spend its money on ventures that realize human rights in ways that do not have the win–lose character of war. If every dollar spent on a war to save one life could be spent on another venture to save three lives, would it be obvious that the former is the right thing to do? It may be thought that responding to human rights violations is more morally pressing than helping to realize human rights which are undermined by natural factors or the economic system, but it is not obvious why this is so. Such a claim is incidentally *not* parallel to the claim that we have a stronger duty not to violate people's rights than to help realize them. In both cases (military intervention and other forms of aid) we are responding to failures in rights realization; in neither case are *we* the violators (see Dower 2002b).

Does humanitarian intervention perpetuate an ideology of militarism? Given the distinction I drew in chapter 2 between militarism in a strong sense and an ordinary commitment to war justification, this may seem an overly strong claim to make. To be sure, if one thinks that humanitarian intervention constitutes a just cause, then to that extent one is endorsing a war justification position and potentially adding to the occasions for war, and thus reinforcing the need for military preparations in order to make them possible. Pacifists may not like this, but it is hardly an endorsement of militarism *per se*. On the other hand, as we saw in the previous chapter, insofar as a cosmopolitan is concerned with emphasizing the duty of pacificism, including a commitment to the practice of peace-building and conflict resolution in nonviolent ways, it is certainly true that the resort to humanitarian armed intervention as a way of solving human rights issues conflicts with the responsibility to find other ways of dealing with them.

4.4   The principled objection and the duty to protect human rights

The third response is indeed to adopt a principled objection to the use of force for whatever reasons. Such a deontological pacifism asserts the importance of respecting human rights. But does it have to deny the equal importance of protecting human rights? It certainly does have to reject one way of doing so, namely by military force. There is, some may feel, a tension here between a pacifist rejection of force and a full cosmopolitan commitment to do everything that is necessary to protect human rights. Atack appears in his discussion to accept this tension between pacifism and the cosmopolitan duty to protect, but he then concludes: 'what we require are effective peaceful or nonviolent alternatives to armed intervention that can satisfy our cosmopolitan responsibility to both respect and protect human rights' (Atack 2005: 138). Satisfying our cosmopolitan responsibility can of course, as it does for a war justifier, include resorting to armed intervention. But it need not. A cosmopolitan responsibility to protect may be as serious for the pacifist cosmopolitan as it is for the war-justifying cosmopolitan. It is merely that the former is concerned to find the best ways of doing so *consistent with* ruling out the use of force (or arguing that we can find effective alternatives that are better anyway consequentially). We should consider the parallel of someone who is against gambling and may be as keen to raise money for his charitable concerns as the next person, with the same concerns, who accepts gambling as a way of raising money for charity. Seriousness of moral commitment is not measured by the range of things we are prepared to do, but by the range and extent of things we are prepared to do *consistent with not doing what we think to be wrong.*

5   Security and human security

5.1   Security

One of the most interesting developments in the period since the Second World War, particularly in the last twenty-five years since the publication of the report *Common Security* (ICDSI 1982), is a great deal of new thinking about ideas of security, both in terms of what it is about and in terms of how to achieve it.

Traditionally security was focused in two main areas – the security of the person and the security of states. The security of the person – not to be attacked or to have one's property damaged or taken – was largely maintained by a general moral culture in the society in which the individual lived, backed by the coercive apparatus of the political community which maintained 'law and order'. Indeed, for thinkers such as Hobbes, it is precisely the wish for security in this sense that underlay the rationale of the coercive state, this often being understood as an implicit contract. The security of the state itself was a matter of being free, or as free as possible, from armed attacks by other states, and its rationale resided partly in protecting the security of the individual, which would be undermined by foreign attacks, and partly in the value itself of being an autonomous entity as an independent political community. The security of the state itself on the traditional view was to be maintained by having sufficiently strong military defences either to deter possible aggressors or to ward off actual attacks. Such measures might be supplemented by having alliances with other states to come to one another's aid in the case of attack. It is a well-known and paradoxical feature of such attempts that, as each state sets up military preparations to achieve their security, their efforts have the effects of rendering other states less secure, since the same armaments used for defence could generally be used to attack. If various countries fearing possible attacks from other countries then increase their armaments, then we get into the situation of an arms race. This is what happened with nuclear weapons.

It was partly in response to the dangers of arms races, and the 'win–lose' character of such protection, that thought was given to finding other ways of making states more secure in respect to possible attacks. While similar attempts were made in earlier years to contain arms races and to find ways of encouraging disarmament (such as the Kellogg–Briand Pact of 1928), we can point to several developments in thinking in the more recent period. The Commission on Global Governance noted three modern conceptions of security: common security, collective security and comprehensive security (CGG 1995: 79–80).

First, the Independent Commission on Disarmament and Security Issues, also called the Palme Commission, promoted the idea of 'common security' which would 'not be achieved until it can be shared by all', and 'can only be achieved through cooperation, based on the principles of equity, justice and reciprocity' (CGG 1995: 79). It stated:

> Our alternative is common security. There can be no hope of victory in a nuclear war, the two sides would be united in suffering and destruction. They can survive only together. They must achieve security not against the adversary but together with him. International security must rest on a commitment to joint survival rather than the threat of mutual destruction. (ICDSI 1982: introduction)

Somewhat different is the idea of collective security based on the initial vision of the United Nations but understood in inherently military terms, in which members of a particular group renounce 'the use of force amongst themselves while pledging to defend any member of the group attacked by external forces' (CGG 1995: 80). Third, comprehensive security, while still retaining the key idea of security from military attack, challenged the military-based notion of security by stressing 'co-operation, confidence-building, transparency, gradual disarmament, conversion, demobilisation and demilitarisation' (ibid.).

While all three notions of security still focus on the same central problem – how to make nations more secure from external attack – they all challenge the idea of achieving this by a 'go it alone' policy. The first and the third in particular introduce new elements – the first the idea of global common perspective and the third a whole range of measures other than armaments themselves.

5.2   Human security

The issue of what security is and how to achieve it has, however, been much broadened by the introduction of the idea of 'human security'. Although the idea had been around earlier, it came into prominence with its adoption and promotion by the United Nations Development Programme (UNDP) in its 1994 *Human Development Report*. Put simply, human security is concerned with security in all the dimensions of human well-being that are seen to be undermined or threatened/at risk – such as one's economic status, environmental conditions or health.

But before I go any further with this analysis, let me explain why this discussion forms part of a book on war and peace. It may be thought: 'This idea may be all very well and good, and we ought to be concerned to promote human security so defined, but why is that relevant to the challenges of national security understood as security from external military attack? That still remains an issue. You do not tackle or solve it by changing the subject!' There are, I think, three interrelated reasons why the issues are connected: first, the greater achievement of human security anywhere will reduce the need for military security; second, less spending on military preparations and related research would mean more spending on achieving human security; and, third, from a cosmopolitan perspective, the security interests of all people compared with the narrower security interests of states will lead to different priorities in foreign policy. I return to these interconnections later on.

The UNDP outlined four essential characteristics of human security:

Human security is a *universal* concern. It is relevant to people everywhere, in rich nations and in poor . . . The components of human security are *interdependent*. When the security of people is endangered anywhere in the world, all nations are likely to get involved . . . Human security is *easier to ensure through early prevention* than later intervention. It is less costly to meet these threats upstream than downstream . . . Human Security is *people-centred*. It is how people live and breathe in a society . . . and whether they live in conflict or in peace. (UNDP 1994: ch. 2; emphasis in original)

This broad concern was already implicit in the thinking of the UN's founders via the idea of 'freedom from fear' and 'freedom from want'. But, in practice, emphasis had become freedom from fear *qua* national security. The report continues: 'Human security is not a defensive concept – the way territorial or military security is. Instead, human security is an integrative concept' (UNDP 1994: ch. 2).

The Commission on Global Governance, whose report *Our Global Neighbourhood* came out in 1995 and did much to promote the UNDP message, notes that 'the struggle for national security was a perpetual zero-sum game in which some states won and others lost' (CGG 1995: 78), but goes on to say:

Protection against external aggression remains, of course, an essential objective for national governments and therefore the international community . . . other equally important security challenges arise from threats to the earth's life-support systems, extreme economic deprivation, the proliferation of conventional small arms, the terrorizing of civilian populations by domestic factions and gross violation of human rights. These factors challenge the security of people far more than the threat of external aggression. (CGG 1995: 79)

The UNDP report gives a list of seven basic categories of human security: economic security, food security, health security, environmental security, personal security, community security and political security, and concludes that: 'The concept of security must therefore change urgently in two basic ways: from an exclusive stress on territorial security to a much greater stress on people's security; from security through armaments to security through sustainable human development' (UNDP 1994: ch. 2).

Hampson, as noted by Atack, identifies three understandings of human security, only one of which links up directly with the UNDP account: human security as undermined by threats to fundamental human rights; human security in relation to humanitarian concerns with war and its effects; and the sustainable human development conception, linking the achievement of security in the fullest sense with people achieving the goods of development in a way that is sustainable (Hampson 2002, quoted in Atack 2005: 114). While the second focus is indeed a more narrow one of humanitarian concern to protect people from the effects of war, if one sees human rights as being about the range of human goods that we all have an interest in maintaining (see Dower 1995), the first and third are not – or at least need not be – all that different. Indeed the discourse of security and the discourse of sustainability, though on the face of it they are rather different, are connected: the range of goods we wish to sustain are the same ones in which we have a security interest, if we regard them as possibly under threat in the future or actually threatened or undermined now.

5.3   Cosmopolitan implications

I now turn to the cosmopolitan implications of the human security discourse and then assess the relevance of this to more traditional concerns with military security. Atack sees human security as cosmopolitan in a number of ways: first, he writes, 'the referent object of human security is the individuals who constitute humanity as a whole'; second, there is a universality in this conception in that there are shared values at a basic level; third, he notes its indivisibility: 'when human security is under threat anywhere, it can affect people everywhere' (Atack 2005: 120). Atack also observes that there are two kinds of critiques of human security as a cosmopolitan notion: first, a concern for national interests, which may be seen as taking precedence over cosmopolitan considerations in favour of human security, for instance in refusing to sign anti-landmine conventions (where landmines, by exposing ordinary citizens to the risk of explosion both during and after a conflict, erode their security interests); and, second, worries about the abstractness of the idea and its implicit projection of a Western agenda, whether this is an objection to the general idea of 'individuals as the ultimate source or locus of value' or more specifically to human rights (ibid.: 121). I will say no more about these two objections here, since they are simply particular aspects of the general criticism of cosmopolitanism which we have considered earlier.

What, however, of the claim that these features – universal referent, shared values and indivisibility – all point to a cosmopolitan *conception* of human security? Much depends on how these are understood. To clarify the issue, let me summarize here the four ways in which security issues have been broadened:

(a) the content: from defence against military attack to many other kinds of threats (economic, environmental);
(b) the referent: from states to individual human beings/communities;
(c) the scope: from being of concern to states or more limited communities to becoming global (cosmopolitan feature);
(d) the relationship between dimensions: from being independent to being seen as globally interdependent (indivisibility). For instance, you cannot protect your environment by building defences against other countries; you can only protect it by cooperation.

Now, of these four features, only (b) is strictly central to the core concept of human security (though all may be associated with a particular conception of it). Furthermore, someone could accept the broadening of security in all (or any) of the other three aspects, but still not call it human security. Nevertheless, as a matter of fact, the interest in human security is motivated by a cosmopolitan concern to promote the conditions for the realization of human security anywhere, and it does tend to accept its multi-dimensional character and its indivisibility. The question we need now to ask is why this is relevant to the discussion of war and peace.[7]

The main argument is this: the duty to promote human security is intimately connected to the pacificist commitment to promote the conditions of peace. This is a two-way relationship. Promoting human security in all its dimensions – really a way of saying promoting human well-being – contributes to peace anywhere, and creating the conditions of peace (that is, durable, just peace) contributes to the achievement of security in its various dimensions. The pacificist commitment is to promote peace not merely within other countries but also between countries. This includes both the willingness to reduce armaments through measures of common and comprehensive security and the promotion of human security in international circles as a unifying concept within which traditional security concerns need to be embedded in their proper place. Both these features will help to improve the security of other countries and thus an aspect of ordinary people's sense of their own security.

As I have indicated elsewhere in the book, while some cosmopolitans, as pacifists, may reject armaments altogether, other cosmopolitans may accept some limited cases of just wars and thus, by implication, the need for some level or kind of military defence. But, at the very least, serious attention to the reduction of such armaments seems to be a consequence of the cosmopolitan perspective. Such reductions have two distinct advantages: by 'turning national swords into global ploughshares' and promoting human security everywhere, one both reduces one's threat to the world and reduces the threat of the world to oneself.

Questions

1 Is the use of nuclear weapons absolutely wrong? If so, can it be right to engage in a policy of nuclear deterrence?
2 Do the new intra-state wars require new ethical standards to judge them by?
3 What exactly is wrong with terrorism?
4 Is violence for humanitarian purposes a contradiction in terms?
5 Does concern for human security affect the way we should think of traditional security concerns?

8 CONCLUSION

1 The main goals of the book

What I have tried to do in this book is to analyse fairly and clearly the various positions that can be taken on the ethics of war and peace, and also, as a secondary goal, to advocate a form of cosmopolitanism which I have called cosmopolitan pacificism. The main goal has in fact involved the introduction of several sets of distinctions, two familiar and one less so, and to show both that these are not the same sets of distinctions and that the various ways in which they interrelate are complex. The two familiar sets of distinctions are between realism in regard to war, just war thinking (or war justification) and pacifism, and between realism in international relations, internationalism and cosmopolitanism. What I have sought to bring out – something not always done – is that these two sets of distinctions are neither identical nor parallel.

The third distinction I have made something of is between militarism and pacificism. I regard this as important for four reasons: first, it cuts right across the other sets of distinctions; second, in consequence, militarism is not identical to realism (for instance, some just war thinkers may be militarist in approach and some realists more pacificist) and pacificism is not identical to pacifism (some just war thinkers are pacificist, and it is possible to be a pacifist without being pacificist); third, the distinction between militarism and pacificism is of some interest in its own right; but, fourth, it provides the backcloth to my advocacy of pacificism as a distinct position, combining an optimism – albeit a cautious optimism – that it is possible for war to be made less common with a duty to promote the conditions of peace.

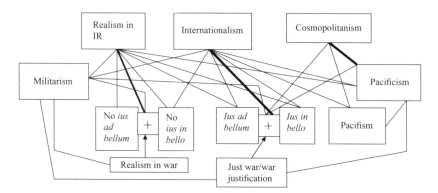

Figure 8.1   Relationships between different positions

For those who like diagrams, I offer in figure 8.1 a schematic represen-
tation of the various positions. The possible combinations are indicated by
connecting lines (the heavy lines being the more common ones).

My advocacy of pacificism is embedded in my advocacy of some form
of cosmopolitanism – an approach I have developed and defended elsewhere in greater detail (Dower 1998 or 2007 and Dower 2003). I say 'some
form of cosmopolitanism' rather than 'cosmopolitanism' *per se*, because
certain forms of cosmopolitanism may well lead to significantly different
ethical conclusions from those I commend. For instance, a proselytizing
zeal to convert the rest of the world to one's religious or political truth
may lead to policies in general, and the resort to war in particular, in ways
which I would not commend, particularly if the use of violent means is
seen as easily justified by the ends. The kind of cosmopolitanism I have
commended may be characterized as (a) non-dogmatic, (b) pacificist and
(c) pacifist. My main concern in this book has been with (a) and (b).
Whether or not a reader is persuaded by a particular position vis-à-vis the
ethics of the means and adopts pacifism, my hope has been that he or she
will accept the non-dogmatic pacificist approach: certainly this stands,
whether or not one is also attracted to pacifism.

The non-dogmatic aspect of cosmopolitanism comes out in the acceptance of a wide variety of ways of living – both of cultural diversity and
of individual lifestyle choices – and also, equally important, the acceptance
of a wide variety of worldviews – religious or philosophical – which may
support a common ethical framework. This does not mean, incidentally,
that one accepts *any* kind of lifestyle or social practice or any kind of
worldview: where the limits are drawn is a matter for debate, and I am
aware that this requires more discussion than I have given in this book

(but see Dower 1998: ch. 6 or Dower 2007: ch. 5). Such an approach is itself a major contribution to the conditions and culture of peace, since mutual acceptance affirms others, and the lack of a desire to change others' ways of living and believing takes away one of the causes of war. It also contributes to peace because the emergence of shared ethical values and norms – indeed at a global level a global ethic – provides a basis for coop-eration, not conflict.

The pacificist element of the kind of cosmopolitanism which I have advocated is really a part of a general feature of a cosmopolitan version of a global ethic. The latter is not merely about universal values – either existing or commended – but about the transboundary responsibility we all have in principle towards anyone else. If we accept that cosmopolitan-ism involves responsibility for helping create the conditions in which human beings can flourish – or at least preventing or removing the circum-stances that undermine well-being – then a dimension of this is helping to create the conditions of peace and combating the situations of conflict and war which generally undermine human well-being. Whatever independent intuitive appeal the idea of a duty to promote peace may have, it is rein-forced by the notion that it is really a corollary of the general idea of a duty to help fellow human beings escape the conditions that undermine well-being.[1]

2   Religion, war and peace

From time to time I have remarked on the contribution of religious thought to issues of war and peace, and it may be thought that, in a book mainly on the ethical issues of war and peace in the modern world, rather more might have been made of this dimension, given that for many people their religious beliefs inform their views on war and peace. There are, however, two related reasons why I have not focused on them.

First, this book has focused on philosophical arguments which do not have as their starting points premises of the kind 'my religion's holy book says w', 'the religious authorities of my religion pronounce x', 'theological reflection on God shows that y' or 'I was told in prayer to do z'. The argu-ments here are intended to make sense or be accessible to a wide range of people, who may have no religious faith or, conversely, who may have a faith that comes from a number of different religious backgrounds. Of course people of religious faith appeal at least partly to considerations of the first kind to do with holy texts, authority, theology or revelation, but that does not mean they do not also accept various other considerations of the kinds discussed in this book.

Second, insofar as they see the importance of trying to get agreement – maybe even global agreement – on certain norms and values, they will, like many secular thinkers, accept the importance of an ethic to which one can 'consent' through agreement with others as well as 'assent' because of their own particular religious worldview (cf. the discussion of Parekh in chapter 3, §2.4). In terms of a distinction I discussed in chapter 3, their interest may be in an ethic or global ethic of norms and values rather than an ethic + or global ethic +, where the ethic they wish to promote is one that includes their own religious or theological justification. A goal of this book has been to commend, as I said above, a kind of non-dogmatic cosmopolitanism to which people – religious or otherwise – can subscribe. To give one example: many people from many different backgrounds have a serious interest in promoting peace – peace that is understood as more than a temporary respite from fighting and one grounded in justice and other values. Now Christians may ground their understanding of peace in biblical insights and the life of Jesus, while Buddhists may ground it in their understanding of inner peace; likewise, many Muslims stress that Islam is a 'religion of peace'. But they are all likely to welcome each other's commitment to peace and, indeed, that of secular thinkers, whose understanding will be differently grounded. They may differ on philosophical and theological issues (and even enjoy disputation at conferences and in print!), but still they are not going to fight, given the practical consensus coming from the range of commitments.

That said, one has also to acknowledge that religious belief has been and continues to be the source of strong motives for going to war. If it is the case that one believes one's religion reveals the 'Truth', and that it is important that others of other religions, in other sects of one's own religion or without faith must be persuaded to accept this 'Truth'– by force if necessary – or must be resisted or crushed if they attempt to convert others to their own 'Truth', then one's religion will lead one to conflict and war – particularly if one thinks that the goal of conversion to one's truth is so important that the end will justify the most extreme or ruthless means. Such religious positions – often characterized as extremist or fundamentalist (though the latter term is misleading, since fundamentalism need not involve the resort to force) – are common enough in the modern world. Examples might be the approach of some of the American religious Right or that of certain Muslim groups (including the al-Qaeda networks), for whom the 'clash of civilizations' is inevitable (cf. Huntington 1996). Such views may involve either realist thinking (including the pessimism of someone such as Niebuhr (1932)) or just war thinking that sees holy wars as providing acceptable just causes.

In terms of the prospect for achieving more peace in the world, the crucial polarity is really between those whose approach is essentially non-dogmatic and pacificist – whether religious or otherwise – and those whose approach is dogmatic and militarist (though there are positions in the middle as well), rather than between those who are religious and those who are non-religious. The Roman atheist Epicurean Lucretius famously inveighed, in his didactic poem *On the Nature of the Universe* (Lucretius [*c*.50 BC] 1994: bk 1), against religion or superstition as the source of so many evils in the world. It cannot be denied that religious motivation has been the source of many wars, but at the same time so has secular motivation, and other kinds of religious understanding and motivation have been among the most powerful forces behind the quest for peace, the commitment to pacifism and the attempt to limit the awfulness and extent of war through the just war principles. And we must not forget that, however secular and legally institutionalized these rules now are, they were essentially grounded historically in religious thought.

3   The future

One can approach the future in two rather different ways, first in predictive mode, second in prescriptive mode. This book has been about the ethical classification and analysis of various positions on war and peace. It has not claimed any particular expertise in analysing empirical data or explaining the phenomena of war, let alone predicting what the future will be. But the general outline of how I see the prospects for war and peace may be helpful if only because, in framing a range of possibilities as I see them, I am also framing the limits for realistic proposals for what ought to be done to limit war and to promote peace.

3.1   Prospects

While is it conceivable that human beings could develop appropriate moral perspectives along with appropriate institutions, laws and cultural norms so that war were to become a thing of the past and so that such use of killing force as was necessary to contain sporadic violent lawlessness by individuals and groups could be seen as global policing action akin to police action within states, it is a prospect that lies a long way in the future. The realistic prospect is that war will continue in various shapes and forms, sometimes between nation-states, more often within nation-states, and that terrorism and violent responses to terrorism – whether on a global scale or in various locations – will remain a significant feature of human interactions. It is also likely that the nuclear powers will continue to keep stockpiles of weapons and that other countries will join them. Although it is rather unlikely (though not inconceivable) that a major nuclear war between superpowers such as the USA, Russia or, flexing its nuclear muscles in the wake of its increasingly powerful role in world affairs, China will occur, it is somewhat more likely that a more limited nuclear war could take place, for instance in the Middle East (with Israel and Iran having nuclear weapons) or between India and Pakistan, partly because the scale would be much smaller – though the devastation in their respective regions would make Hiroshima and Nagasaki look like child's play. (It could be that such an event would be a wake-up call for the rest of the world vis-à-vis these weapons. The same would apply to the significant use of chemical and biological weapons in a future conflict – again not inconceivable.)

While for the foreseeable future the nation-state system will remain the dominant reality in global affairs, there will probably be slow and faltering steps taken towards stronger forms of global governance, in which greater weight will be given to the United Nations and to international law. We will probably have the paradox that, though the international norms governing warfare will be strengthened, the actual conduct of war may continue to show serious disregard for such norms, partly because much conflict will occur outside the institutional framework of relations between states as such.

Progress will probably be made with some more people adopting a pacifist stance and many more people accepting the pacificist approach (including the acknowledgement of the perspective of pacifism as a reasonable one); more countries may accept a right to conscientious objection and even allow a right to have one's taxes used for non-military purposes. Progress will also be made in recognizing that 'justice *post bellum*' is an important dimension of just war thinking. On the brighter side, too, it seems clear that the trend will continue in which significant numbers of people come to see the importance of peace not merely as a condition to be enjoyed but as something that needs to be worked for, whether through education, new forms of governance, new norms and laws, lifestyle changes, the training of appropriate personnel in the skills of peacebuilding and conflict resolution, or, more indirectly, by tackling the root causes of many conflicts, such as global poverty or environmental problems (such as competition for water). Increasingly it will be recognized that major global issues are deeply interconnected, as reflected in the rather ambitious and controversial claim in UN circles concerning the 'indivisibility of human rights'.

3.2   Proposals

If something like the above analysis of prospects is right, it will be clear that, while wars will continue in various forms, there is nothing inevitable about them or the frequency of their incidence. The future is not fixed: if it is a field of possibilities, which ones are realized depends on us – including the moral values which inform our actions.[2] The moral optimism which has run through this book is based not on a blind optimism that the future will be good, but on a cautious optimism that the future could be good, or at least could be better than it would otherwise be, if enough of us adopt the right moral values.

Given the kind of non-dogmatic pacificist cosmopolitanism which I have advocated, what proposals do I set out for making it more likely that these values will be realized? Here I bring together and strengthen some of the ideas I have suggested at various points in the book.

I drew a distinction earlier between ethical cosmopolitanism and institutional cosmopolitanism. Although, as I indicate below, there is a case to be made for the emergence of certain forms of institutional cosmopolitanism, the arguments for and the implications of ethical cosmopolitanism are not affected by what one thinks about the reality or desirability of institutional cosmopolitanism.

If the ethical cosmopolitanism I have advocated involves the serious obligation to further the conditions of human well-being and oppose what undermines it, and this includes promoting peace and countering war and violence in ways consistent with one's basic values, then what does this entail? I shall briefly mention four distinct though related points.

First, what is needed is cosmopolitan education (see, for instance, Nussbaum 1996). It should bring out the importance of pacificism and a richer understanding of peace as just durable peace, and the need for respect for diversity of belief and culture as being valuable in itself and leading to a common set of core values. Explicit education about peace and pacificism should include respect for and acknowledgement of the role of pacifism within it and also – as leaven for outer peace – of the importance of inner peace.[3] It should also, more broadly, get children to understand the idea of one global community and appreciate our obligations vis-à-vis poverty, the environment, and so on.

Second, we need generally to promote in the adult population the idea of global citizenship. Apart from the acknowledgement of our transboundary moral obligations as indicated above, there are several points that need to be stressed. Global citizenship can be expressed either individually or through joining organizations – whether such organizations are locally/nationally based but with global remits or internationally organized. If an aspect of citizenship involves *political* engagement in public affairs, global citizenship can be expressed either via domestic politics (pressure groups; political parties; letters to politicians; use of the media) or via international NGOs. For most people the former – globally oriented engagement within domestic politics – is the more likely option, and its importance cannot be overestimated: the fact is that governments are unlikely to change their policies vis-à-vis war, the environment or anything else unless significant numbers of their electorates signal to them that that is what is wanted.

Third, given that nation-states forming a 'society of states' will remain the dominant reality in global affairs,[4] it is important to press the moral case for them to accept global responsibilities, including the pacificist perspective. This may seem paradoxical, since states are parts of a system which is precisely not cosmopolitan and premised on the right of each one to promote its own interests.[5] However, we need to recall that ethical cosmopolitanism does not entail institutional cosmopolitanism, which in a strong form would indeed propose the abolition of states in favour of a world government or cosmopolitan order of some kind. Some writers have reasonably argued, however, for 'good international citizenship', that is, that states can themselves be good citizens of the society of states by being willing to adopt cosmopolitan goals such as concern for human rights (see, for instance, Williams 2002). The pursuit of state interests can be combined with accepting global obligations, and there is nothing contradictory in the idea of an 'ethical foreign policy'. Although states cannot perhaps fully promote what many cosmopolitans might advocate, they can certainly do so to an extent that is significant and, as noted above, commensurate with what their citizens want. Incidentally, if they did only that, the prospects for peace in the world would be much increased. We should recall that Kant's famous proposal for perpetual peace was premised not on the abolition of states but on states accepting articles of peace in their mutual relations.

Fourth, there are good cosmopolitan ethical arguments for strengthening international institutions and international law. The establishment of the International Criminal Court in 1999 was a step in the right direction, and if the international community were more willing to bring to trial leaders who preside over or authorize war crimes, crimes against humanity or other violations of human rights (or were less willing to grant privileges such as resource privileges to corrupt leaders: see, for instance, Pogge

2003), that would also signal in the future that such activities would not be carried out with impunity.

The last aspect leads to a brief consideration of institutional cosmopolitanism. If this is taken to be the idea of world government, then I am not advocating institutional cosmopolitanism (see Dower 1998: ch. 10 or Dower 2007: ch. 9; Dower 2003: ch. 7). If, however, it is to be comprehended more modestly as the idea of the development of institutions, laws and other forms of global governance which are increasingly understood in terms of promoting goals *justified in cosmopolitan terms*, then we can see the emergence of these in the current world and we can welcome their further development, not merely for promoting peace but for many other reasons too.

For instance, the emergence of what is called global civil society – in which a very large number of international NGOs network with each other and lobby governments and international bodies in respect to various global concerns – can be seen as making informally, if not formally, a significant contribution to global governance. Second, the status of individuals in the international legal system is gradually changing. The protection of human rights is increasingly being seen as the responsibility of the international community, rather than, as understood in 1948, being the primary preserve of nation-states within their own borders. This was witnessed in the declaration *Responsibility to Protect* (R2P) (UN 2005); and the institution of the ICC firmly places the individual human being as a subject, not merely an object, of international law. All this can be seen as demonstrating that international law, though in formal terms the law of nation-states ('inter-national') is becoming in substance 'cosmopolitan law'.

It will be apparent from what I have just outlined that I see the promotion of peace (and other core cosmopolitan values) as taking many forms and occurring at many levels. All too often I have observed over the years that, among those who nobly work for global goals – whether peace, development, the environment, or whatever – there is a tendency to home in on their preferred 'solution to the problem' – '*this* is *the* way' to promote peace, to tackle world hunger, or to save the environment – and to be dismissive or critical of what other individuals and groups are doing or their reasons for doing it. While what others do or think might be wrong, misguided or counter-productive, on the whole we could be a lot more accepting, given what energizes them and the diverse range of things that do contribute to a better world. So I conclude by commending respect for the many ways of promoting peace, just as I have commended respect for the diversity of ways of living and ways of believing.

Questions

1 If you are inclined towards a cosmopolitan approach, would you favour the non-dogmatic and pacificist elements of the position outlined here?

2 How plausible is it to assess the reasonableness of a religious position in terms of its contribution to peace?

3 If you are a moral optimist, what measures for creating a more peaceful and just world would you advocate? If not, why are you not a moral optimist?

NOTES

Chapter 1 The Ethics of War and Peace

1 Likewise, to consider the mixed positions indicated in §3.1, someone could be a realist about foreign policy – that is, about international relations in the strict sense including war – but still accept some universal values relating to how human beings should relate to one another, and thus in war be a realist about going to war but not about how to fight it. Conversely, someone could see international relations as governed by norms agreed on by international custom and convention, but deny any basic universal norms applicable to all human relations, and so in parallel see decisions about going to war as likewise constrained by ethical norms, but the actual manner of fighting not so.

2 The reader may have noticed that the word 'ethics' here is being used, not as the plural of an 'ethic', but to refer, as a grammatically singular expression, to an intellectual *activity*, namely the study of or critical enquiry into ethical issues. As such it is contrasted to an 'ethic' as a set of beliefs about ethical norms and values.

3 For useful discussions of the two approaches, see Frankena (1973) and Smart and Williams (1973).

4 This is an adaptation from an article which I was invited to contribute to the *International Encyclopaedia of Peace* (Oxford University Press, forthcoming).

Chapter 2 Realism and Militarism

1 This has been particularly popular in Western political thought in the contract tradition of Hobbes ([1651] 1991), Locke ([1689] 1960), Rousseau ([1762] 1966) and Kant (1970).

2 It is interesting to note that, in 2007, the UK parliament voted to renew the Trident nuclear submarine programme, though it was apparent that there was

widespread – possibly majority – opposition to renewing it from the public. No referendum was sought, and it was of course constitutionally a democratic decision, but serious questions were raised about the ethical if not the legal situation.

Chapter 3   Internationalism and Cosmopolitanism

1 For more extensive treatment of the general topics, see Dower: 1998 or 2007. Parts of this chapter are adapted from chapters in that work. See also Nardin & Mapel 1992.
2 The reader may like to relate this to Bull's (1977) definition of war as given in chapter 1 in which war, including justified war, is seen as a form of violence. This issue is taken up again in chapter 5.
3 Whether this liberal, democratic, human rights-based cosmopolitanism tends more towards dogmatism or more towards non-dogmatism depends a lot on how precisely or broadly these ideas are interpreted and on how they are seen to be promoted.
4 I am grateful to Jim Boyd for helping me to clarify what I wanted to say in this section.
5 The idea of a cosmopolitan military is pursued in Elliot and Chesterman 2002. It was the subject of a seminar I attended in 2001 organized by Lorraine Elliot and Simon Chesterman, and I am grateful to the seminar for stimulating my interest in this idea.
6 As Vattel notes, 'the law of Nations is the science of the rights which exist between Nations or States and of the obligations corresponding to those rights' (Vattel [1755] 1853: introduction).
7 For fuller accounts of Kant's complex theory, see, for instance, Brown 1992: ch. 2; Thompson 1992: ch. 2; and Donaldson 1992.
8 The implications of this for international relations and the possible justification for armed intervention are further explored by Luban (1980).

Chapter 4   The Justification of War

1 See chapter 1, §7.2, for an explanation of this contrast. For accounts of the just war conditions, see, for instance, Coates (1997); Coppieters and Fotion (2002); Elshtain (1992); Evans (2005); Graham (1996: ch. 3); Johnston (1999).
2 Supposing the just cause or causes are not mere pretexts but are genuine motivating factors alongside such a further intention, what should we say? Here we have mixed cases where different verdicts may be given. Suppose that the just cause would have been sufficient without the further goal, would that be all right? Many would say yes, though the case may be arguable. Suppose that the just cause and the further intention are both necessary but neither separately sufficient to lead to war, is that all right? If one takes just war criteria very seriously as all having to apply fully, this case looks problematic, but if one regards them more flexibly as providing a framework that does not have to be

fully met in all respects, this case may seem all right. Suppose, however, that the war would have taken place even without a just cause (whether genuinely held or a mere pretext), then this intention seems to invalidate the action. Of course, precisely because such intentions are not publicly announced, it is notoriously difficult to establish either their real presence or their being the motivating factors. One move that can often be used by those who suspect the role of further intention in the second and third cases is to invoke the 'counterfactual' argument. If the just cause really were the determining factor, how is it that other military operations have not occurred in similar situations in other parts of the world, such as in Rwanda in 1994, or in the Sudan over Darfur, and so on?

3   Nagel's article is an important contribution which deserves more attention than I have given it. It is reprinted in many places, for instance in Cohen et al. (1974); Nagel 1979; Beitz et al. (1985). It is a wide-ranging article of interest because of its attack on consequentialism and its general distinction between outcome-centred ethics and agent-centred ethics.

4   For a radical analysis of American hegemony, see Zolo (1997: ch. 2).

5   Furthermore, it might be argued that the long-distance bombing of Baghdad and the mass destruction of the retreating soldiers on the 'road to Basra' were serious violations of 'ius in bello' principles.

6   In November 2007 I spoke to a Belgian academic who said he was a conscientious objector on the grounds that being in the army would deprive him of his autonomy.

Chapter 5   Pacifism, Nonviolence and the Way of Peace

1   A grey area would be when the threat is intended to produce a 'good' outcome, such as the prevention of the thing threatened, as in military deterrence policies (see also discussion of nuclear deterrence in chapter 7, §1). Some may be clear that this should be regarded as violence, particularly if the threats themselves create various forms of harms, such as significant fear and insecurity in the process. Others may feel that, since such 'deterrence' postures are sometimes justified, it is misleading to call them violent. However, we should note that there is nothing in the idea of violence so far to imply that violence *per se* is unjustified. As noted in chapter 1, whether going to war is justified or not, it is better to call a 'spade' a 'spade' and recognize it as a form of violence.

2   I originally saw this on a Quaker poster in the 1970s; although there are frequent references to this being what Gandhi said, I have been unable to track down the exact statement, though the view is clearly part of Gandhi's approach to the philosophy of the means: for a brief introduction to Gandhi's thought, see Gruzalski (2001).

3   Paradoxically, the problem of obeying orders without question does not translate to senior command level. If generals did not follow the commands of their political superiors, then an important relationship between the political community and the military would be undermined. However, the case is somewhat

different in that one does hope that senior military do exercise judgement and give advice to political leaders, even if at the end of the day they need to accept whatever the latter decide to do. It is regrettable that the misgivings that some of the senior military apparently had in the spring of 2003 before the invasion of Iraq had not been conveyed more vigorously to their political masters!

4   I am indebted to Jim Martell, who drew this to my attention in his contribution to a student presentation at Colorado State University in May 2006. His whole piece on pacifism (unpublished but available from the current author) is a robust defence of anti-war pacifism.

5   The attentive reader may have observed that, whereas in the criticisms to the general pacifist arguments I have outlined ways in which the pacifist may reply to the criticism, I have not done this in the case of the arguments against the anti-war pacifist positions. This is not because I think that in the latter case the pro-war arguments have the last word. It is rather that in the latter area it is the pacifist who takes the argument into the area where normally war is justified.

6   We should compare this with engagement in fair trade as a compensatory activity for someone who accepts that his or her whole way of life is one of being a beneficiary of unfair global economic relations.

Chapter 6   Peace and Pacificism

1   For recent discussions focusing on peace see, for instance, Salla et al. (1995); Calvocoressi (1987); Kainz (1987).

2   This incidentally has been a theme of a more recent study by Amartya Sen, who argues that we are more likely to engage in violence if we have one sense of identity which overrides all others. If we take more seriously the idea that we have multiple identities, and that we can *choose* how to act in the face of these multiple identities, there are much greater possibilities for peace (Sen 2006).

3   This terminology is not used so far as I know in any standard textbooks on applied ethics.

4   The term was actually used much earlier though in a less precise sense, for instance by William James in his famous essay 'The moral equivalent of war' (James [1910] 1970). He interestingly contrasts pacificism with militarism, as I do later in this section.

5   The universal acceptance of certain values does not in any case entail universal observance. That is, even if everyone came to accept the same moral code (maybe supported from various worldviews) and also in all concrete instances the same applications or judgements, it is still the case that individuals and groups will sometimes not act in accordance with those judgements. This does not undermine the pacificist project, but it does show that peace as perfect harmony is unrealistic.

6   I saw this on a Quaker poster in the 1960s, which gave as its source Noel-Baker, an intrepid campaigner against the arms race (Noel-Baker 1958), and discussed its ethical significance in greater detail in Dower (1983).

7 Peacemaking may, however, have a rather richer analysis, as in Stassen's influential idea of 'just peacemaking' (Stassen 1992, 1998). In many ways Stassen's analysis is similar to peacebuilding and the idea of just durable peace discussed earlier, except that he sees the source of commitment to it in religious – more specifically Christian – terms, whereas I have stressed that the motivational sources for just durable peace are wide-ranging and can be both religious and secular.

8 Atack (2005: 150) raises the question whether 9/11 etc. involving the rejection of multilateralism and the resort to war as an instrument of foreign policy was a challenge to peacebuilding. I would argue that it has not done so really, though it certainly was an impediment to progress in the gradual development of more pacifist attitudes and techniques. But pacifism as a project is hardly undermined by the unpacificist motivations and actions of some political leaders and other actors.

Chapter 7   Modern Issues

1 The project never succeeded, and it has been suggested that the unofficial reason for it was to draw the USSR into trying do the same, thus draining and weakening the Soviet economy.

2 See http://disarm.igc.org/oldwebpages/worldct.html (accessed 16 September 2008).

3 We should note in passing that guerrilla warfare is not the same as terrorism, though the two may overlap. A grey area here is the issue of attacks on property, not people: despite the inclusion of property in Wilkins's initial definition given above, many would say that, for instance, the attacks on *installations* by the ANC (African National Congress) in the struggle against apartheid was not terrorism.

4 The continuing war in Iraq does not help, though technically it was not – and is not – a war about terrorism.

5 We should note too that, in using the term 'war against terror', a concession is made that many would prefer not to admit, that terrorists are 'warriors' fighting us rather than criminals engaged in crime. The distinction between war and crime turns out to be immensely important from various points of view – a distinction not undermined, but in a way confirmed, by the category 'war crime'. Certainly organized crime, for instance by the Mafia or the drug cartels in Colombia, seems to lie beyond the definition of 'war', even though many of the features of war – organized militias, frequent killings – are apparent.

6 For a rather different reading of the global situation, see Scruton (2002).

7 Thus (for those intrigued by the logical possibilities) feature (a) need not refer to *human* security, since states could broaden their concern for their own security to include economic and environmental security but not have a global interest. Although as a matter of fact human security issues are globally interconnected, they need not be, and could still be of interest to people elsewhere to deal with. Conversely, someone could accept the universality of human

security issues, and indeed their mutual interdependence, but actually be interested only in the human security aspects in his or her own country or state. That is, the security of human beings – though seen as a universal value – might be viewed as the responsibility of each state or political community to attend to (thus we might have a global but not a cosmopolitan ethic). The last point shows, then, that, while as a matter of fact the human security agenda has all these features and is cosmopolitan in approach, interest in human multi-dimensional security need not be cosmopolitan. Furthermore, security as defence against attack could become a 'common security' issue and the security of countries become globally oriented (which was the focus of the Palme Commission) without being human-centred in respect to the good of individual human beings. Finally, an acceptance of the causal interdependence of processes such as climate change is consistent with nationalist concerns to get international cooperation for one's own country's benefit, and this does not necessarily reflect a cosmopolitan ethical perspective.

Chapter 8   Conclusion

1 In Dower 1998 and 2007 I called the general approach solidarist pluralism and contrasted it to libertarian minimalism and dogmatic idealism.
2 Even if the thesis of universal causal determinism is true, there is absolutely no way we humans, with our limited intelligence and knowledge, could possibly know the future's course; and, more to the point, there is no reason to suppose that human beliefs and values do not crucially determine that course.
3 Some pacifists might question this as only going half-way, but if ethics is about shades of grey and the need to work within what is realistically possible, we ought to welcome the wider pacificist agenda.
4 Transnational companies play a significant role in shaping world affairs too.
5 I am grateful to the referee whose comment 'I'm not sure how a state government would act in a cosmopolitan way, in that this undermines what it means to be a state' prompted the following clarification.

REFERENCES

Anscombe, G. E. M. ([1961] 1970) 'War and murder', in W. Stein (ed.), *Nuclear Weapons and Christian Conscience*. London: Merlin Press; repr. in R. Wasserstrom (ed.), *War and Morality*. Belmont, CA: Wadsworth.

Aquinas, T. ([*c*.1270] 1953) *Summa Theologiae*, excerpts in D. Bigongiari (ed.), *The Political Ideas of St Thomas Aquinas*. New York: Hafner.

Archibugi, D., and D. Held (eds) (1995) *Cosmopolitan Democracy: An Agenda for a New World Order*. Cambridge: Polity.

Aristotle ([*c*.350 BC] 1988) *The Politics*, ed. S. Everson. Cambridge: Cambridge University Press.

Atack, I. (2005) *The Ethics of Peace and War*. Edinburgh: Edinburgh University Press.

Augustine ([*c*.397] 1872) 'Contra faustum', in *The Works of Aurelius Augustine*, ed. M. Dods, Vol. 6: *Writings in Connection with the Manichean Heresy*, trans. R. Stothert. Edinburgh: T & T. Clark.

Augustine ([*c*.412] 1947) *City of God*, trans. J. Healey. London: Dent.

Ballou, A. ([1866] 1995) 'Christian non-resistance', in S. Lynd and A. Lynd (eds), *Nonviolence in America: A Documentary History*. Maryknoll, NY: Orbis Books.

Beitz, C. R. (1979) *Political Theory and International Relations*. Princeton, NJ: Princeton University Press.

Beitz, C. R., et al. (eds) (1985) *International Ethics*. Princeton, NJ: Princeton University Press.

Benedict, R. (1935) *Patterns of Culture*. London: Routledge.

Bobbitt, P. (2008) *Terror and Consent: The Wars for the Twenty-First Century*. New York: Knopf.

Bohman, J., and M. Lutz-Bachmann (eds) (1997) *Perpetual Peace: Essays on Kant's Cosmopolitan Ideal*. Cambridge, MA: MIT Press.

Borchert D. M., and D. Stewart (1986) *Exploring Ethics*. London: Macmillan.

Boulding, E. (1990) *Building a Global Civic Culture: Education for an Interdependent World*. Syracuse, NY: Syracuse University Press.

Boutros-Ghali, B. (1992) *An Agenda for Peace*. New York: United Nations.

Brandt, R. B. (1967) 'Ethical relativism', in P. Edwards (ed.), *Encyclopaedia of Philosophy*. New York: Macmillan.

Brandt, R. B. (1972) 'Utilitarianism and the rules of war', *Philosophy & Public Affairs*, 1 (2); repr. in M. Cohen et al. (eds), *War and Moral Responsibility*. Princeton, NJ: Princeton University Press, 1974.

Brock, P. (1981) *Varieties of Pacifism*. Syracuse, NY: Syracuse University Press.

Brock, P., and N. Young (1999) *Pacifism in the Twentieth Century*. Syracuse, NY: Syracuse University Press.

Brown, C. (1992) *International Relations Theory: New Normative Approaches*. New York: Harvester Wheatsheaf.

Bull, H. (1966) 'The Grotian conception of international society', in H. Butterfield and M. Wight (eds), *Diplomatic Investigations*. London: Allen & Unwin.

Bull, H. (1977) *The Anarchical Society*. London: Macmillan.

Bull, H. (1979) 'Human rights and world politics', in R. Pettman (ed.), *Moral Claims in World Affairs*. New York: St Martin's Press.

Butterfield, H. (1953) *Christianity, Diplomacy and War*. London: Collins.

BYM (Britain Yearly Meeting) (1995) *Quaker Faith and Practice*. London: Warwick.

Calvocoressi, P. (1987) *A Time for Peace*. London: Hutchinson.

Carr, E. H. (1939) *The Twenty Years' Crisis: 1919–1939*. London: Macmillan.

Castel de Saint-Pierre, C.-I. ([1713] 1927) *Selections from the Second Edition of the Abrégé du Projet de paix perpétuelle*, trans. H. H. Bellot. London: Sweet & Maxwell.

Ceadel, M. (1987) *Thinking about Peace and War*. Oxford: Oxford University Press.

Ceulemans, C. (2002) 'Just cause', in B. Coppieters and N. Fotion (eds), *Moral Constraints on War: Principles and Cases*. Lanham, MD: Lexington Books.

CGG (Commission on Global Governance) (1995) *Our Global Neighbourhood*. Oxford: Oxford University Press.

Clausewitz, C. von ([1832] 1968) *On War*, ed. A. Rapoport. Harmondsworth: Penguin.

Coates, A. J. (1997) *The Ethics of War*. Manchester: Manchester University Press.

Cohen, J. (ed.) (1996) *For Love of Country: Debating the Limits of Patriotism*. Boston: Beacon Press.

Cohen, M., et al. (eds) (1974) *War and Moral Responsibility*. Princeton, NJ: Princeton University Press.

Coppieters, B., and N. Fotion (eds) (2002) *Moral Constraints on War: Principles and Cases*. Lanham, MD: Lexington Books.

Curle, A. (1981) *True Justice*. London: Quaker Home Service.

Donaldson, T. (1992) 'Kant's global rationalism', in T. Nardin and D. Mapel (eds), *Traditions of International Ethics*. Cambridge: Cambridge University Press.

Dower, N. (1983) *World Poverty: Challenge and Response*. York: William Sessions.

Dower, N. (1995) 'Peace and security: some conceptual notes', in M. Salla et al. (eds), *Essays on Peace*. Rockhampton: Central Queensland University Press.

Dower, N. (1998) *World Ethics: The New Agenda*. Edinburgh: Edinburgh University Press.

Dower, N. (2002a) 'Against war as a response to terrorism', *Philosophy and Geography*, 5 (1).

Dower, N. (2002b) 'Violent humanitarianism – an oxymoron?', in A. Moseley and R. Norman (eds), *Human Rights and Military Intervention*. Aldershot: Ashgate.

Dower, N. (2003) *Introduction to Global Citizenship*. Edinburgh: Edinburgh University Press.

Dower, N. (2007) *World Ethics: The New Agenda*. 2nd edn, Edinburgh: Edinburgh University Press.

Dower, N., and J. Williams (eds) (2002) *Global Citizenship: A Critical Reader*. Edinburgh: Edinburgh University Press.

Earth Council (2000) *The Earth Charter*. Costa Rica: Earth Council; accessed at www.earthcharter.org [March 2002].

Eisenhower, D. D. ([1953] 1980) Speech to the American Society of Newspaper Editors, 19 April, quoted in Iona Community, *The Coracle*, no. 2.

Elfstrom, D. (1990) *Ethics in a Shrinking World*. London: Macmillan.

Elliot, L., and G. Chesterman (2002) *Cosmopolitan Theory, Militaries and the Deployment of Force*. Australian National University, Department of International Relations, working paper no. 8.

Elshtain, J. B. (ed.) (1992) *Just War Theory*. Oxford: Blackwell.

Evans, M. (ed.) (2005) *Just War Theory: A Reappraisal*. Edinburgh: Edinburgh University Press.

Feinberg, J. (1973) *Social Philosophy*. Englewood Cliffs, NJ: Prentice-Hall.

Ferguson, J. (1982) *Disarmament: The Unanswerable Case*. London: Heinemann.

Finnis, J. (1990) *Natural Law and Natural Rights*. Oxford: Oxford University Press.

Fisher, D. (ed.) (1985) *Morality and the Bomb*. London: Croom Helm.

Frankena, W. K. (1973) *Ethics*. 2nd edn, Englewood Cliffs, NJ: Prentice-Hall.

Fullinwider, R. K. ([1975] 1985) 'War and innocence', *Philosophy & Public Affairs*, 5 (1); repr. in C. R. Beitz et al. (eds), *International Ethics*. Princeton, NJ: Princeton University Press.

Fullinwider, R. K. (1988) 'Understanding terrorism', in S. Luper-Foy (ed.), *Problems of International Justice*. London: Westview Press.

Galtung, J. (1969) 'Violence, peace and peace research', *Journal of Peace Research*, 6 (3).

Gewirth, A. (1978) *Reason and Morality*. Chicago: University of Chicago Press.

Glover, J. (1977) *Causing Death and Saving Lives*. Harmondsworth: Penguin.

Goodin, R. E. (2006) *What's Wrong with Terrorism?* Cambridge: Polity.

Graham, G. (1996) *Ethics and International Relations*. Oxford: Oxford University Press.

Grotius, H. ([1625] 1925) *De iure belli ac pacis (On the Law of War and Peace)*, trans. F. W. Kelsey. Oxford: Clarendon Press.

Gruzalski, B. (2001) *Gandhi*. Belmont, CA: Wadsworth.

Hampson, F. O. (2002) *Madness in the Multitude: Human Security and World Disorder*. Oxford: Oxford University Press.

Hare, J. E., and C. B. Joynt (1982) *Ethics and International Affairs*. London: Macmillan.

Hare, R. M. (1972a) 'Peace', in *Applications of Moral Philosophy*. London: Macmillan.

Hare, R. M. (1972b) 'The rules of war and moral reasoning', *Philosophy & Public Affairs*, 1 (2); repr. in M. Cohen et al. (eds), *War and Moral Responsibility*. Princeton, NJ: Princeton University Press, 1974.

Hare, R. M. (1981) *Moral Thinking*. Oxford: Oxford University Press.

Harman, G. (1977) *The Nature of Morality*. New York: Oxford University Press.

Harris, J. (1979) *Violence and Responsibility*. London: Routledge.

Hawk, W. J. (2006) 'Pacifism: reclaiming the moral presumption', in H. La Follette (ed.), *Ethics in Practice*. 3rd edn, Oxford: Blackwell.

Heater, D. (2002) *World Citizenship*. London: Continuum.

Hegel, G. ([1821] 1942) *The Philosophy of Right*, trans. T. M. Knox. Oxford: Clarendon Press.

Hobbes, T. ([1651] 1991) *Leviathan*, ed. R. Tuck. Cambridge: Cambridge University Press.

Hockaday, A. (1982) 'In defence of deterrence', in G. Goodwin (ed.), *Ethics and Nuclear Deterrence*. London: Croom Helm.

Holmes, R. L. (1989) *On War and Morality*. Princeton, NJ: Princeton University Press.

Holmes, R. L. (ed.) (1990) *Nonviolence in Theory and Practice*. Belmont, CA: Wadsworth.

Honderich, T. (2002) *After the Terror*. Edinburgh: Edinburgh University Press.

Hume, D. ([1742] 1978) *A Treatise of Human Nature*, ed. L. A. Selby-Bigge. 2nd edn, Oxford: Oxford University Press.

Huntington, S. P. (1996) *The Clash of Civilizations and the Remaking of World Order*. New York: Simon & Schuster.

ICDSI (Independent Commission on Disarmament and Security Issues) (1982) *Common Security: A Programme for Disarmament*. London: Pan Books.

Ihara, C. H. (1978) 'In defence of a version of pacifism', *Ethics*, 88 (4).

James, W. ([1910] 1970) 'The moral equivalent of war', in R. Wasserstrom (ed.), *War and Morality*. Belmont, CA: Wadsworth, pp. 4–14.

Jeffrey, R. (2006) *Hugo Grotius in International Thought*. London: Palgrave.

Jenkins, I. (1973) 'The conditions of peace', *The Monist*, 57 (4).

Johnston, J. T. (1999) *Morality and Contemporary Warfare*. New Haven, CT: Yale University Press.

Kainz, H. P. (1987) *Philosophical Perspectives on Peace*. Basingstoke: Macmillan.

Kaldor, M. (1999) *New & Old Wars*. Cambridge: Polity.

Kant, I. ([1785] 1949) *The Groundwork of the Metaphysics of Morals*, in *The Moral Law*, trans. H. Paton. London: Hutchinson.

Kant, I. ([1795] 1970) 'Perpetual peace', in *Kant's Political Writings*, trans. H. Reiss. Cambridge: Cambridge University Press.

Kant. I. (1970) *Kant's Political Writings*, ed. H. Reiss. Cambridge: Cambridge University Press.

Kavka, G. (1983) 'Doubts about unilateral nuclear disarmament', *Philosophy & Public Affairs*, 12 (3); repr. in C. R. Beitz et al. (eds), *International Ethics*. Princeton, NJ: Princeton University Press, 1985.

Kavka, G. (1987) *Moral Paradoxes of Nuclear Deterrence*. New York: Cambridge University Press.

Kenny, A. (1985) *The Logic of Deterrence*. London: Firethorn Press.

Kim, Y. (1999) *A Common Framework for the Ethics of the 21st Century*. Paris: UNESCO.

Kraft, K. (ed.) (1992) *Inner Peace, World Peace: Essays on Buddhism and Nonviolence*. Albany: State University of New York Press.

Küng, H. (1991) *Global Responsibility: In Search of a New World Ethic*. London: SCM Press.

Kurlansky, M. (2006) *Nonviolence*. New York: Random House.

Lackey, D. P. (1982) 'Missiles and morals', *Philosophy & Public Affairs*, 11 (3); repr. in C. R. Beitz et al. (eds), *International Ethics*. Princeton, NJ: Princeton University Press, 1985.

Lackey, D. P. (1989) *The Ethics of War and Peace*. Englewood Cliffs, NJ: Prentice-Hall.

Locke, J. ([1689] 1960) *Second Treatise of Government*, ed. P. Laslett. Cambridge: Cambridge University Press.

Luard, E. (1981) *Human Rights and Foreign Policy*. London: Pergamon Press.

Luban, D. (1980) 'Just war and human rights', *Philosophy & Public Affairs*, 9 (2); repr. in C. R. Beitz et al. (eds), *International Ethics*. Princeton, NJ: Princeton University Press, 1985.

Lucretius, T. ([c.50 BC] 1994) *De rerum natura*, in *Lucretius: On the Nature of the Universe*, trans. R. E. Latham and J. Godwin. Harmondsworth: Penguin.

Luper-Foy, S. (ed.) (1988) *Problems of International Justice*. London: Westview Press.

McGrew, A. (2000) 'Democracy beyond borders?', in D. Held and A. McGrew (eds), *The Global Transformations Reader*. Cambridge: Polity.

MacIntyre, A. (1967) *A Short History of Ethics*. London: Routledge & Kegan Paul.

Macquarrie, J. (1973) *The Concept of Peace*. New York: Harper & Row.

Mavrodes, G. I. (1975) 'Conventions and the morality of war', *Philosophy & Public Affairs*, 4 (2); repr. in C. R. Beitz et al. (eds), *International Ethics*. Princeton, NJ: Princeton University Press, 1985.

Mayer, P. (ed.) (1966) *The Pacifist Conscience*. Harmondsworth: Penguin.

Midgley, E. B. F. (1975) *The Natural Law Tradition and the Theory of International Relations*. London: Paul Elek.

Mill, J. S. ([1859] 1962) 'On liberty', in *Utilitarianism*, ed. M. Warnock. London: Fontana.

Mill, J. S. ([1861] 1962) 'Utilitarianism', in *Utilitarianism*, ed. M. Warnock. London: Fontana.

Miller, L. H. (1990) *Global Order: Values and Power in International Politics*. London: Westview Press.

Montgomery, B. L. (1958) *Memoirs*. London: Collins.

Morgenthau, H. (1954) *Politics among Nations*. New York: Albert Knopf.

Mothersson, K. (1992) *From Hiroshima to The Hague: A Guide to the World Court Project*. Geneva: International Peace Bureau.

Murithi, T. (2009) *The Ethics of Peacebuilding*. Edinburgh: Edinburgh University Press.

Mussolini, B. (1936) *La Doctrine du fascisme*. Florence: Vallecchi.

Nagel, T. (1972) 'War and massacre', *Philosophy and Public Affairs*, 1 (2); repr. in M. Cohen et al. (eds), *War and Moral Responsibility*. Princeton, NJ: Princeton University Press, 1974; T. Nagel, *Mortal Questions*. Cambridge: Cambridge University Press, 1979; C. R. Beitz et al. (eds), *International Ethics*. Princeton, NJ: Princeton University Press, 1985.

Nagel, T. (1979) *Mortal Questions*. Cambridge: Cambridge University Press.

Nardin, T. (1983) *Law, Morality, and the Relations of States*. Princeton, NJ: Princeton University Press.

Nardin, T., and D. Mapel (eds) (1992) *Traditions of International Ethics*. Cambridge: Cambridge University Press.

Narveson, J. (1970) 'Pacifism: a philosophical analysis', in R. Wasserstrom, *War and Morality*. Belmont, CA: Wadsworth.

Niebuhr, R. (1932) *Moral Man and Immoral Society*. New York: Charles Scribner.

Noel-Baker, P. (1958) *The Arms Race*. London: Atlanta Books.

Norman, R. (1995) *Ethics, Killing, and War*. Cambridge: Cambridge University Press.

Nussbaum, M. (1996) 'Patriotism and cosmopolitanism', in J. Cohen (ed.), *For Love of Country: Debating the Limits of Patriotism*. Boston: Beacon Press.

O'Neill, O. (1986) *Faces of Hunger*. London: Allen & Unwin.

Orend, B. (2002) 'Justice after war', *Ethics & International Affairs*, 16 (1).

Orend, B. (2006) *The Morality of War*. Peterborough: Broadview Press.

Parekh, B. (2002) 'Cosmopolitanism and global citizenship', *Review of International Studies*, 31 (2).

Parekh, B. (2005) 'Principles of a global ethic', in J. Eade and D. O'Byrne (eds), *Global Ethics and Civil Society*. Aldershot: Ashgate.

Parliament of World Religions (1993) 'Declaration toward a global ethic', in H. Küng and K.-J. Kuschel (eds), *A Global Ethic: The Declaration of the Parliament of the World's Religions*. London: SCM Press.

Paskins, B., and M. Dockrill (1979) *The Ethics of War*. London: Duckworth.
Pogge, T. (2003) *World Poverty and Human Rights*. Cambridge: Cambridge University Press.
Ramsey, P. (1968) *The Just War*. New York: Charles Scribner's Sons.
Rawls, J. (1971) *A Theory of Justice*. Oxford: Oxford University Press.
Rawls, J. (1993) *Political Liberalism*. New York: Columbia University Press.
Rawls, J. (1999) *The Law of Peoples*. Cambridge, MA: Harvard University Press.
Reader, S. (2007) 'Cosmopolitan pacifism', *Journal of Global Ethics*, 3 (1).
Richmond, O. (2005) *The Transformation of Peace*. London: Palgrave.
Rockmore, T., J. Margolis and A. T. Marsoobian (eds) (2005) *The Philosophical Challenge of September 11*. Oxford: Blackwell.
Rodin, D. (2002) *War and Self-Defence*. Oxford: Oxford University Press.
Ross, W. D. (1930) *The Right and the Good*. Oxford: Oxford University Press.
Rousseau, J.-J. ([1762] 1966) *The Social Contract*, trans. G. D. Cole. London: Dent.
Ruddick, S. (1990) *Maternal Thinking: Towards a Politics of Peace*. London: Women's Press.
Salla, M. et al. (eds) (1995) *Essays on Peace*. Rockhampton: Central Queensland University Press.
Sandel, M. (1982) *Liberalism and the Limits of Justice*. Cambridge: Cambridge University Press.
Schell, J. (2003) *The Unconquerable World*. New York: Metropolitan Books.
Scruton, R. (2002) *The West and the Rest: Globalisation and the Terrorist Threat*. London: Continuum.
Sen, A. (1999) *Development and Freedom*. Oxford: Oxford University Press.
Sen, A. (2006) *Identity and Violence: The Illusion of Destiny*. London: Allen Lane.
Sharp, G. (1973) *The Politics of Nonviolent Action*. Boston: Porter Sargent.
Shue, H. (1996) *Basic Rights: Subsistence, Affluence and US Foreign Policy*. 2nd edn, Princeton, NJ: Princeton University Press.
Singer, P. (1972) 'Famine, affluence and morality', *Philosophy & Public Affairs*, 1; extended version, 'Rich and poor', in Singer, *Practical Ethics*. Cambridge: Cambridge University Press, 1979.
Singer, P. (2002) *One World: The Ethics of Globalization*. London: Yale University Press.
Smart, J. C. C., and B. A. O. Williams (1973) *Utilitarianism: For and Against*. Cambridge: Cambridge University Press.
Sorabji, R., and D. Rodin (eds) (2006) *The Ethics of War: Shared Problems in Different Traditions*. Aldershot: Ashgate.
Stassen, G. H. (1992) *Just Peacemaking: Transforming Initiatives for Justice and Peace*. Louisville, KY: John Knox Press.
Stassen, G. H. (ed.) (1998) *Just Peacemaking: Ten Practices for Abolishing War*. Cleveland: Pilgrim Press.

Stein, W. (ed.) (1961) *Nuclear Weapons and Christian Conscience*. London: Merlin Press.

Suarez, F. ([1597] 1866) *Disputationes metaphysicae*, in *Opera omnia*, ed. C. Berton, vols 25–6. Paris: Vives.

Taylor, A. J. P. (1957) *The Trouble Makers*. London: Hamish Hamilton.

Taylor, C. (1989) *Sources of the Self: The Making of Modern Identity*. Cambridge, MA: Harvard University Press.

Teichman, J. (1986) *Pacifism and the Just War*. Oxford: Blackwell.

Thompson, J. (1992) *Justice and World Order*. London: Routledge.

Tolstoy, L. ([1902] 1966) 'Letter to a non-commissioned officer', in P. Mayer (ed.), *The Pacifist Conscience*. Harmondsworth: Penguin.

Tuck, R. (1989) *Hobbes*. Oxford: Oxford University Press.

UN (United Nations) (1945) *Charter of the United Nations*. New York: United Nations.

UN (United Nations) (1948) *Universal Declaration of Human Rights*. New York: United Nations.

UN (United Nations) (2005) *Responsibility to Protect*, A/RES/60/1. New York: United Nations.

UNDP (United Nations Development Programme) (1990–2008) *Human Development Report*. New York: United Nations [annual].

van den Anker, C. (ed.) (2004) *The Political Economy of New Slavery*. Basingstoke: Palgrave.

Vattel, E. de ([1755] 1853) *The Law of Nations*, trans. J. Chitty. Philadelphia: T & J. W. Johnson.

Vincent, R. J. (1986) *Human Rights and International Relations*. Cambridge: Cambridge University Press.

Vitoria, F. de ([1532] 1991) 'De jure belli Hispanorum in barbaros', in *Political Writings*, trans. A. Pagden and J. Lawrance. Cambridge: Cambridge University Press.

Waltz, K. N. (2001) *Man, the State and War: A Theoretical Analysis*. New York: Columbia University Press.

Walzer, M. (1971) 'World War II: why was this war different?', *Philosophy & Public Affairs*, 1 (1); repr. in M. Cohen et al. (eds), *War and Moral Responsibility*. Princeton, NJ: Princeton University Press, 1974.

Walzer, M. (1977) *Just and Unjust Wars*. New York: Basic Books.

Walzer, M. (1988) 'Terrorism: a critique of excuses', in S. Luper-Foy (ed.), *Problems of International Justice*. London: Westview Press.

Wasserstrom, R. (ed.) (1970) *War and Morality*. Belmont, CA: Wadsworth.

Weber, M. ([1919] 2000) *Politics as a Vocation*. London: Fortune Press.

Westmorland General Meeting (2005) *Preparing for Peace*. Cumbria: Westmorland General Meeting.

Wheeler, N. J. (2000) *Saving Strangers: Humanitarian Intervention in International Society*. Oxford: Oxford University Press.

Wilkins, B. T. (1992) *Terrorism and Collective Responsibility*. London: Routledge.

Wilkinson, P. (1986) *Terrorism and the Liberal State*. 2nd edn, New York: New York University Press.

Williams, B. A. O. (1973) 'A critique of utilitarianism', in J. C. C. Smart and B. A. O. Williams, *Utilitarianism: For and Against*. Cambridge: Cambridge University Press.

Williams, J. (2002) 'Good international citizenship', in N. Dower and J. Williams (eds), *Global Citizenship: A Critical Reader*. Edinburgh: Edinburgh University Press.

Wong, D. (1984) *Moral Relativity*. Berkeley: University of California Press.

World Court (1996) *Advisory Judgement on the Legality of the Threat or Use of Nuclear Weapons*. General List no. 95, 8 July.

Zolo, D. (1997) *Cosmopolis: Prospects for World Government*. Cambridge: Polity.

INDEX